AF560252

Samuel Beckett

WAITING FOR GODOT

Samuel Beckett

WAITING FOR GODOT

[Edited with Complete Introduction, Biography, Author's Background, Complete Text, Study Questions, Select Criticism and Bibliography]

Mansi Sachdeva
B.A. English (Hons), Delhi University;
M.A., M. Phil. (English), IGNOU

ANMOL PUBLICATIONS PVT. LTD.
NEW DELHI - 110 002 (INDIA)

ANMOL PUBLICATIONS PVT. LTD.

H.O.: 4374/4B, Ansari Road, Darya Ganj,
New Delhi-110 002 (India)
Ph.: 23278000, 23261597

B.O.: No. 1015, Ist Main Road, BSK IIIrd Stage
IIIrd Phase, IIIrd Block
Bangalore - 560 085 (India)
Visit us at: www.anmolpublications.com

Waiting for Godot

First Published, 2009

PRINTED IN INDIA

Printed at Mehra Offset Press, Delhi.

Contents

Preface

On 13th April, 1906 in Dublin, Ireland, a great Writer Samuel Beckett was born in a middle class home. His father was a quantity surveyor and mother was a nurse. He had frequent bouts of depression, as he had commented that, ""I had little talent for happiness." In order to resist the Germans, during the World War II, he also joined the underground movement.

A few of Samuel Beckett's popular works comprise of Waiting for Godot, Eleutheria, Endgame, the novels Malloy, Malone Dies, The Unnamable, and Mercier et Camier, two books of short stories, and a book of criticism. Waiting for Godot is undoubtedly one of the finest works of Samuel Beckett. It was originally written in French in 1948 and later translated into English.

Author

Chapter 1

Introduction

Waiting for Godot qualifies as one of Samuel Beckett's most famous works. Originally written in French in 1948, Beckett personally translated the play into English. The world premiere was held on January 5, 1953, in the Left Bank Theater of Babylon in Paris. The play's reputation spread slowly through word of mouth and it soon became quite famous. Other productions around the world rapidly followed. The play initially failed in the United States, likely as a result of being misbilled as "the laugh of four continents." A subsequent production in New York City was more carefully advertised and garnered some success.

Waiting for Godot incorporates many of the themes and ideas that Beckett had previously discussed in his other writings. The use of the play format allowed Beckett to dramatize his ideas more forcefully than before, and is one of the reasons that the play is so intense.

Beckett often focused on the idea of "the suffering of being." Most of the play deals with the fact that Estragon and Vladimir are waiting for something to alleviate their boredom. Godot can be understood as one of the many things in life that people wait for. The play has often been viewed as fundamentally existentialist in its take on life. The fact that none of the characters retain a clear mental history means that they are constantly struggling to prove their existence. Thus the boy who consistently fails to remember either of the two protagonists casts doubt on their very existence. This is why Vladimir demands to know that the boy will in fact remember them the next day.

Waiting for Godot is part of the Theater of the Absurd. This implies that it is meant to be irrational. Absurd theater does away with the concepts of drama, chronological plot, logical language, themes, and recognizable settings. There is also a split between the intellect and the body within the work. Thus Vladimir represents the intellect and Estragon the body, both of whom cannot exist without the other.

Biography of Samuel Beckett 1906-1989

Samuel Beckett was born near Dublin, Ireland, on April 13, 1906 into a Protestant, middle class home. His father was a quantity surveyor and his mother worked as a nurse. At the age of 14 he was sent to the same school that Oscar Wilde attended.

Beckett is known to have commented, "I had little talent for happiness." This was evidenced by his frequent bouts of depression, even as a young man. He often stayed in bed until late in the afternoon and hated long conversations. As a young poet he apparently rejected the advances of James Joyce's daughter and then commented that he did not have feelings that were human. This sense of depression would show up in much of his writing, especially in Waiting for Godot where it is a struggle to get through life.

Samuel Beckett moved to Paris in 1926 and met James Joyce. He soon respected the older writer so much that at the age of 23 he wrote an essay defending Joyce's magnum opus to the public. In 1927, one year later, he won his first literary prize for his poem entitled "Whoroscope." The essay was about the philosopher Descartes meditating on the subject of time and about the transiency of life. Beckett then completed a study of Proust which eventually led him to believe that habit was the "cancer of time." At this point Beckett left his post at Trinity College and traveled.

Beckett journeyed through Ireland, France, England, and Germany and continued to write poems and stories. It is likely that he met up with many of the tramps and vagabonds who later emerged in his writing, such as the two tramps Estragon and Vladimir in Waiting for Godot. On his travels through

Paris Beckett would always visit with Joyce for long periods. Beckett permanently made Paris his home in 1937. Shortly after moving there, he was stabbed in the street by a man who had begged him for money. He had to recover from a perforated lung in the hospital. Beckett then went to visit his assailant, who remained in prison. When Beckett demanded to know why the man had attacked him, he replied "Je ne sais pas, Monsieur." This attitude about life comes across in several of the author's later writings.

During World War II Beckett joined the underground movement in Paris to resist the Germans. He remained in the resistance until 1942 when several members of his group were arrested. Beckett was forced to flee with his French-born wife to the unoccupied zone. He only returned in 1945 after Paris was liberated from the Germans. He soon reached the pinnacle of his writing career, producing Waiting for Godot, Eleutheria, Endgame, the novels Malloy, Malone Dies, The Unnamable, and Mercier et Camier, two books of short stories, and a book of criticism.

Samuel Beckett's first play was Eleutheria and involved a young man's efforts to cut himself loose from his family and social obligations. This has often been compared to Beckett's own search for freedom. Beckett's great success came on January 5, 1953, when Waiting for Godot premiered at the Theatre de Babylone. Although critics labeled the play "the strange little play in which 'nothing happens,'" it gradually became a success as reports of it spread through word of mouth. It eventually ran for four hundred performances at the Theatre de Babylone and was heralded with critical praise from dramatists such as Tennessee Williams, Jean Anouilh, Thornton Wilder, and William Saroyan. Saroyan even remarked that, "It will make it easier for me and everyone else to write freely in the theatre." An interesting production of Waiting for Godot took place when some actors from the San Francisco Actor's Workshop performed the play at the San Quentin penitentiary for over fourteen hundred convicts in 1957. The prisoners immediately identified with both Vladimir and Estragon about the pains of waiting for life to end, and the struggle of the daily existence. The production was perhaps the most successful ever. Beckett's second masterpiece. Endgame, premiered on April 3, 1957 at the Royal Court Theatre in London.

All of Beckett's major works were written in French. He believed that French forced him to be more disciplined and to use the language more wisely. However, Waiting for Godot was eventually translated into the English by Beckett himself.

Samuel Beckett also became one of the first absurdist playwrites to win international fame. His works have been translated into over twenty languages. In 1969 he received the Nobel Prize for Literature, one of the few times this century that almost everyone agreed the recipient deserved it. He continued to write until his death in 1989, but towards the end he remarked that each word seemed to him "an unnecessary stain on silence and nothingness."

He befriended the famous Irish novelist James Joyce, and his first published work was an essay on Joyce. In 1951 and 1953, Beckett wrote his most famous novels, the trilogy Molloy,Malone Dies, and The Unnameable.

Waiting for Godot, Beckett's first play, was written originally in French in 1948 (Beckett subsequently translated the play into English himself). It premiered at a tiny theater in Paris in 1953. This play began Beckett's association with the Theatre of the Absurd, which influenced later playwrights like Harold Pinter and Tom Stoppard.

The most famous of Beckett's subsequent plays include Endgame (1958) and Krapp's Last Tape (1959). He also wrote several even more experimental plays, like Breath (1969), a thirty-second play. Beckett was awarded the Nobel Prize in 1969 and died in 1989 in Paris.

Chapter 2

Chronology

1906 Born Good Friday, April 13, at Foxrock, near Dublin, second son of William and Mary Beckett, middle class Irish Protestants.

1919-23 Attends Portora Royal School, Enniskillen, a traditional Anglo-Irish boarding school.

1923-27 Attends Trinity College, Dublin Bachelor of Arts in French and Italian.

1928 Begins two-year fellowship at Ecole Normale Supérieure in Paris. Friendship with Joyce begins, as does immersion in the work of Descartes.

1929 Early writings in Transition.

1930 Whoroscope wins competition for best poem on the subject of time.

1931 Proust published. Returns to Dublin as assistant to Professor of Romance Languages at Trinity. Le Kid, parody of Corneille.

1932 Writes unpublished Dream of Fair to Middling Women.

1933 Death of William Beckett. Begins three-year stay in London.

1934 More Pricks than Kicks.

1936 Travels in Germany. Echo's Bones.

1937 Returns to Paris.

1938 Sustains serious stab wound from stranger. Begins relationship with Suzanne Dumesnil. Murphy.

1939 Returns to Paris after Irish sojourn.

1940 Is active in French Resistance movement.

1942 Flees to unoccupied France to escape

	Gestapo.Works as day laborer for two years in farming. Writes Watt.
1945	Goes to Ireland after German surrender. Returns to France for service with Irish Red Cross. Returns to Paris permanently.
1946-50	Productive period of writing in French, including the trilogy Molloy, Malone meurt, and L'Innommable, and the play En attendant Godot.
1947	Murphy published in French.
1950	Visits Ireland at the time of his mother's death. 1951 Molloy published. Malone meurt published.
1952	Godot published.
1953	First performance of Godot in Paris. Watt published. L'Innommable published.
1955	Waiting for Godot opens in London.
1956	Waiting for Godot opens in Miami, Florida, for first American performance.
1957	All That Fall broadcast by BBC. Fin de partie published first performance (in French) in London.
1958	Krapp's Last Tape and Endgame (in English) open in London.
1959	Embers broadcast by BBC. Honorary degree from Trinity College, Dublin.
1961	Comment c'est published. Happy Days opens in New York City. Shares, with Borges, International Publisher's Prize.
1962	Marries Suzanne Dumesnil, March 25. Words and M[illegible] broadcast by BBC.
1963	[illegible]rmed at Ulm. Cascando broadcast in
196[illegible]	Goes to New York City to help produce his Film (with Buster Keaton).
1969	Nobel Prize in literature.
1972	The Lost Ones.
1973	Not I. 1976 Ends and Odds Fizzles All Strange Away.
1977	but the clouds...
1978	Mirlitonnades (35 short poems).

1980 Company One Evening.
1981 Ill Seen Ill Said Rockaby.
1983 Catastrophe.

Setting

There is only one scene throughout both acts. Two men are waiting on a country road by a tree. The script calls for Estragon to sit on a low mound but in practice – as in Beckett's own 1975 German production – this is usually a stone. In the first act the tree is bare. In the second, a few leaves have appeared despite the script specifying that it is the next day. The minimal description calls to mind "the idea of the 'lieu vague', a location which should not be particularised".

Alan Schneider once suggested putting the play on in a round – Pozzo has often been commented on as a ringmaster – but Beckett dissuaded him: "I don't in my ignorance agree with the round and feel Godot needs a very closed box." He once even contemplated at one point have "faint shadow of bars on stage floor" but, in the end, decided against this level of what he called "explicitation". In his 1975 Schiller-Theatre production there are times when Didi and Gogo appear to bounce off something "like birds trapped in the strands of [an invisible] net", to use James Knowlson's description. Didi and Gogo are only trapped because they still cling to the concept that freedom is possible freedom is a state of mind, so is imprisonment.

Interpretations

Throughout the work one can find religious, philosophical, classical, psychoanalytical and biographical – especially wartime – references, there are ritualistic aspects and elements literally lifted from vaudeville and there is a danger in making more of these than what they are, merely structural conveniences, avatars into which the writer places his fictional characters. The play "exploits several archetypal forms and situations, all of which lend themselves to both comedy and pathos." Beckett makes this point emphatically clear in the opening notes to Film: "No truth value attaches to the above, regarded as of merely structural and dramatic convenience." He made another important remark to Lawrence Harvey, saying that his "work does not depend on experience – [it is] not a record of experience. Of course you use it."

Waiting for Godot also illustrates an attitude toward man's experience on earth: the poignancy, oppression, camaraderie, hope, corruption, and bewilderment of human experience that can only be reconciled in mind and art of the absurdist. If Godot is God, then Didi and Gogo's (mankind's) faith in God is not only subject to doubt, but may also have almost entirely disappeared. Yet the illusion of faith—that deeply embedded hope that Godot might come—still flickers in the minds of Vladimir and Estragon. It is almost as if the faith of these two men has been tested to such extremes that they can perfectly well see the logic of renouncing it—but they cannot completely.

Beckett tired quickly of "the endless misunderstanding. Why people," he said – as far back as 1955 – "have to complicate a thing so simple I can't make out." That said, he has not been forthcoming with anything more than cryptic clues. "Peter Woodthrope [who played Estragon] remembered asking him one day in a taxi what the play was really about: 'It's all symbiosis, Peter it's symbiosis,' answered Beckett."

Beckett directed the play for the Schiller-Theatre in 1975. Although he had overseen many productions this was the first time he took complete control Walter Asmus was his conscientious, young assistant director. "The production was not naturalistic. Beckett explained:

It is a game, everything is a game. When all four of them are lying on the ground, that cannot be handled naturalistically. That has got to be done artificially, balletically. Otherwise everything becomes an imitation, an imitation of reality ... It should become clear and transparent, not dry. It is a game in order to survive."

Over the years, Beckett clearly realised that the greater part of Godot's success was down to the fact that it was open to a variety of readings and that this was not necessarily a bad thing. Beckett himself sanctioned "one of the most famous mixed-race productions of Godot to be performed at the Baxter Theatre in the University of Cape Town, directed by Donald Howarth, with ... two black actors, John Kani and Winston Ntshona, playing Didi and Gogo Pozzo, dressed in checked shirt and gumboots reminiscent of an Afrikaaner landlord, and Lucky ('a shanty town piece of white trash') were played by two white actors, Bill Flynn and Peter Piccolo ... The Baxter production has often been portrayed as if it were an explicitly political production, when in fact it received very little emphasis. What such a reaction showed, however, was that, although the play can in no way be taken as a political allegory, there are elements that are relevant to any local situation in which one man is being exploited or oppressed by another."

Other interpretations abound: Political: "It was seen as an allegory of the cold war," or of French resistance to the Germans. Graham Hassell writes, "[T]he intrusion of Pozzo and Lucky ... seems like nothing more than a metaphor for Ireland's view of mainland Britain, where society has ever been blighted by a greedy ruling elite keeping the working classes passive and ignorant by whatever means." The pair are often played with Irish accents, an inevitable consequence, some feel, of Beckett's rhythms and phraseology, but this is not stipulated in the text.

Freudian: "Bernard Dukore develops a triadic theory in Didi, Gogo and the absent Godot, based on Freud's trinitarian description of the psyche in The Ego and the Id (1923) and the usage of onomastic techniques. Dukore defines the characters by what they lack: the rational Go-go embodies the incomplete ego, the missing pleasure principle: (ego-(ego. Di-di (id-id) – who is more instinctual and irrational – is seen as the backward id or subversion of the rational principle. Godot fulfils the function of the superego or moral standards. Pozzo and Lucky are just re-iterations of the main protagonists. Dukore finally sees Beckett's play as a metaphor for the futility of man's existence when salvation is expected from an external entity, and the self is denied introspection."

Jungian: "The four archetypal personalities or the four aspects of the soul are grouped in two pairs: the ego and the shadow, the persona and the soul's image (animus or anima). The shadow is the container of all our despised emotions repressed by the ego. Lucky, the shadow serves as the polar opposite of the egocentric Pozzo, prototype of prosperous mediocrity, who incessantly controls and persecutes his subordinate, thus symbolising the oppression of the unconscious shadow by the despotic ego. Lucky's monologue in Act I appears as a manifestation of a stream of repressed unconsciousness, as he is allowed to "think" for his master. Estragon's name has another connotation, besides that of the aromatic herb, tarragon: "estragon" is a cognate of oestrogen, the female hormone. This prompts us to identify him with the anima, the feminine image of Vladimir's soul. It explains Estragon's propensity for poetry, his sensitivity and dreams, his irrational moods. Vladimir appears as the complementary masculine principle, or perhaps the rational persona of the contemplative type."

Existentialist: Broadly speaking existentialists hold there are certain questions that everyone must deal with (if they are to take human life seriously), questions such as death, the meaning of human existence and the place of God in human existence. By and large they believe that life is very difficult and that it doesn't have an "objective" or universally known value, but that the individual must create value by affirming it and living it, not by talking about it. The play touches upon all of these issues.

Biblical: Much can be read into Beckett's inclusion of the story of the two thieves and the ensuing discussion of repentance and it is easy to see the solitary tree as representative of the cross or indeed the tree of life. Likewise, an obvious conclusion many jump to is that, because Lucky describes God as having a white beard and Godot appears also to have a white beard that he must therefore be God. Vladimir's "Christ have mercy upon us!" could easily be taken as corroboration that that is what he at least believes. There can be no arguing that much of Waiting for Godot deals with the subject of religion, there are simply too many scriptural references. For example, the boy claims to be a goatherd, while his brother is a shepherd. In the Bible, goats represent the damned while sheep represent those who have been saved. "[Beckett] always possessed a Bible, at the end more than one edition, and Bible concordances were always among the reference books on his shelves." "Christianity is a mythology with which I am perfectly familiar so I naturally use it," he admitted, but, as one of his biographers, Anthony Cronin, points out: Beckett's biblical references "may be ironic or even sarcastic".

"In answer to a defence counsel question in 1937 (during a libel action undertaken by his uncle) as to whether he was a Christian, Jew or atheist, Beckett replied: 'None of the three'".This was not though the occasion that put Beckett off religion. In a rare 1961 interview, Beckett said: "I have no religious feeling. Once I had a religious emotion. It was at my first Communion. No more ... My brother and mother got no value from their religion when they died. At the moment of crisis it has no more depth than an old school tie." Looking at Beckett's entire œuvre, Mary Bryden observed that "the hypothesised God who emerges from Beckett's texts is one who is both cursed for his perverse absence and cursed for his surveillant presence. He is by turns dismissed, satirised, or ignored, but he, and his tortured son, are never definitively discarded."

Biographical: It has been called a "metaphor for the long walk into Roussillon, when Beckett and Suzanne slept in haystacks ... during the day and walked by night or of the relationship of Beckett to Joyce." The earliest drafts contained significant personal references but these were later excised.

Homoerotic: That the play calls for only male actors and barely references women at all has caused some to look upon Vladimir and Estragon's relationship as quasi-marital: "they bicker, they embrace each other, they depend upon each other ... they might be thought of as a married couple."

Beckett was not open to every new approach to his work and he famously objected when, in the 1980s several women's acting companies began staging the play. "Women don't have prostates," said Beckett, an allusion to the fact that Vladimir

... frequently has to leave the stage to urinate, on account of his enlarged prostate. In 1988 he took a Dutch theatre company, De Haarlemse Toneelschuur to court over this issue. "Beckett ... lost his case. But the issue of gender seemed to him to be so vital a distinction for a playwright to make that he reacted angrily, instituting a ban on all productions of his plays in The Netherlands."

In 1991 "Judge Huguette Le Foyer de Costil ruled that the production would not cause excessive damage to Beckett's legacy" and the play was performed by the all-female cast of the Brut de Beton Theater Company at the prestigious Avignon Festival.The Italian Pontedera Theatre Foundation won a similar claim in 2006 when they replaced Vladimir and Estragon with two female actors albeit playing the roles as males. A 2001 production at Indiana University staged the play with women playing Pozzo and the Boy.

History

"[It was Beckett's escape from the increasingly despotic interiority of the fictional trilogy in Beckett's own phrasing, 'I began to write Godot as a relaxation, to get away from the awful prose I was writing at the time.'" It was inspired, according to Beckett himself, by a painting by Caspar David Friedrich. Ruby Cohn recalls seeing the painting, Man and Woman Contemplating the Moon of 1824, along with Beckett who "announced unequivocally, 'This was the source of Waiting for Godot, you know.'""He may well have confused two paintings since, at other times, he drew the attention of friends to Two Men Contemplating the Moon from 1819, in which two men dressed in cloaks and viewed from the rear are looking at a full moon framed by the black branches of a large, leafless tree." In either case both paintings are similar enough that what he attested to could apply equally to either. However, some sources point to conversations between Suzanne Deschevaux-Dumesnil and Beckett in Roussillon as the inspiration for the work. Beckett admitted such in a New York Post interview by Jerry Tallmer.

"[On 17th February 1952 ... an abridged version of the

play was performed in the studio of the Club d'Essai de la Radio and was broadcast on [French] radio. Although he sent a polite note that Roger Blin read out, Beckett himself did not turn up." Part of his introduction reads:

I don't know who Godot is. I don't even know (above all don't know) if he exists. And I don't know if they believe in him or not – those two who are waiting for him. The other two who pass by towards the end of each of the two acts, that must be to break up the monotony. All I knew I showed. It's not much, but it's enough for me, by a wide margin. I'll even say that I would have been satisfied with less. As for wanting to find in all that a broader, loftier meaning to carry away from the performance, along with the programme and the Eskimo pie, I cannot see the point of it. But it must be possible ... Estragon, Vladimir, Pozzo, Lucky, their time and their space, I was able to know them a little, but far from the need to understand. Maybe they owe you explanations. Let them supply it. Without me. They and I are through with each other.

The Minuit edition appeared in print on 17th October 1952 in advance of the play's first full theatrical performance. On January 4th 1953, "[thirty reviewers came to the générale of En attendant Godot before the public opening ... Contrary to later legend, the reviewers were kind ... Some dozen reviews in daily newspapers range[d] from tolerant to enthusiastic... Reviews in the weeklies [were] longer and more fervent moreover, they appeared in time to lure spectators to that first thirty-day run" which began on 5th January 1953 at the Théâtre de Babylone, Paris.

Early public performances were not, however, without incident: during one performance "the curtain had to be brought down after Lucky's monologue as twenty, well-dressed, but disgruntled spectators whistled and hooted derisively ... One of the protesters [even] wrote a vituperative letter dated 2nd February 1953 to Le Monde. The cast comprised Pierre Latour (Estragon), Lucien Raimbourg (Vladimir), Jean Martin (Lucky) and Roger Blin (Pozzo). The actor due to play Pozzo found a more remunerative role and so the director – a shy, lean man in real life – had to step in and play the stout bombaster himself with a pillow amplifying his stomach. Both boys were played by Serge Lecointe. The entire production was done on the thinnest of shoestring budgets the large battered valise that Martin carried "was found among the city's refuse by the husband of the theatre dresser on his rounds as he worked clearing the dustbins," for example.

A particularly significant production – from Beckett's perspective – took place in Lüttringhausen Prison near Wuppertal in Germany. An inmate obtained a copy of the French first edition, translated it himself into German and obtained permission to stage the play. The first night had been on 29th November 1953. He wrote to Beckett in October 1954: "You will be surprised to be receiving a letter about your play Waiting for Godot, from a prison where so many thieves, forgers, toughs, homos, crazy men and killers spend this bitch of a life waiting ... and waiting ... and waiting. Waiting for what? Godot? Perhaps." Beckett was intensely moved and intended to visit the prison to see a last performance of the play but it never happened. This marked "the beginning of Beckett's enduring links with prisons and prisoners ... He took a tremendous interest in productions of his plays performed in prisons ... He [even] gave [Rick Cluchey] a former prisoner from San Quentin financial and moral support over a period of many years." Cluchey played Vladimir in two productions in the former Gallows room of the San Quentin California State Prison, which had been converted into a 65-seat theatre and, like the German prisoner before him, went on to work on a variety of Beckett's plays after his release.

The English-language premiere was on 3rd August 1955 at the Arts Theatre, London, directed by the 24-year-old Peter Hall Again, the printed version preceded it (New York: Grove Press, 1954) but Faber's "mutilated" edition did not materialise until 1956. A "corrected" edition was subsequently produced in 1965. "The most accurate text is in Theatrical Notebooks I, (Ed.) Dougald McMillan and James Knowlson (Faber and Grove, 1993). It is based on Beckett's revisions for his Schiller-Theatre production (1975) and the London San Quentin Drama

Workshop, based on the Schiller production but revised further at the Riverside Studios (March 1984)."

Like all of Beckett's translations, Waiting for Godot is not simply a literal translation of En attendant Godot. "Small but significant differences separate the French and English text. Some, like Vladimir's inability to remember the farmer's name (Bonnelly), show how the translation became more indefinite, attrition and loss of memory more pronounced." A number of biographical details were removed, all adding to a general "vaguening" of the text which he continued to trim for the rest of his life.

In the nineteen-fifties, theatre was strictly censored in the UK, to Beckett's amazement since he thought it a bastion of free speech. The Lord Chamberlain insisted that the word "erection" be removed, "'Fartov' became 'Popov' and Mrs Gozzo had 'warts' instead of 'clap'". Indeed, there were attempts to ban the play completely. For example, Lady Dorothy Howitt wrote to the Lord Chamberlain, saying: "One of the many themes running through the play is the desire of two old tramps continually to relieve themselves. Such a dramatisation of lavatory necessities is offensive and against all sense of British decency." "The first unexpurgated version of Godot in England ... opened at the Royal Court on 30th December 1964."

The London run was not without incident. The actor Peter Bull, who played Pozzo, recalls the reaction of that first night audience: "Waves of hostility came whirling over the footlights, and the mass exodus, which was to form such a feature of the run of the piece, started quite soon after the curtain had risen. The audible groans were also fairly disconcerting ... The curtain fell to mild applause, we took a scant three calls (Peter Woodthorpe reports only one curtain call) and a depression and a sense of anti-climax descended on us all."

The critics were less than unkind but "everything changed on Sunday 7th August 1955 with Kenneth Tynan's and Harold Hobson's reviews in The Observer and The Sunday Times. Beckett was always grateful to the two reviewers for their support ... which more or less transformed the play overnight into the rage of London." "At the end of the year, the Evening Standard Drama Awards were held for the first time... Feelings ran high and the opposition, led by Sir Malcolm Sargent, threatened to resign if Godot won [The Best New Play category]. An English compromise was worked out by changing the title of the award. Godot became The Most Controversial Play of the Year. It is a prize that has never been given since."

Beckett resisted offers to film the play, although it was televised in his lifetime. When Keep Films made Beckett an offer to film an adaptation in which Peter O'Toole would feature, Beckett tersely told his French publisher to advise them: "I do not want a film of Godot." The BBC broadcast a production of Waiting for Godot on 26th June 1961, a version for radio having already been transmitted on 25th April 1960. Beckett watched the programme with a few close friends in Peter Woodthorpe's Chelsea flat. He was unhappy with what he saw. "My play," he said, "wasn't written for this box. My play was written for small men locked in a big space. Here you're all too big for the place."

Although not his favourite amongst his plays – perhaps because of the way it came to overshadow everything else he wrote – it was the work which brought Beckett fame and financial stability and as such it always held a special place in his affections. "When the manuscript and rare books dealer, Henry Wenning, asked him if he could sell the original French manuscript for him, Beckett replied: 'Rightly or wrongly have decided not to let Godot go yet. Neither sentimental nor financial, probably peak of market now and never such an offer. Can't explain.'

Theme

We can't fail to miss the theme of uncertainty in Waiting for Godot. Uncertainty is pervasive throughout the play: the uncertainty of purpose, of time, place, emotion, relationships, truth, and hope. Existence is the only certainty the play allows. The Cartesian dictum "I think, therefore I am," is challenged, but essentially hold true. Didi and Gogo are themselves vivid dramatic representations of the Descartes' body/mind split. Didi is all mind, Gogo all body. Thinking and inexhaustible talking may not be the same thing, but in the absence of the one the other will do. Throughout the play thinking is associated with doubt, with uncertainty, weariness, or absurdity. Clearly, the image of our ability to think is challenged in this play.

Related to this critique of our rational capabilities is the play's critique of language as meaningless blather and chatter on the one hand and oppressively authoritarian on the other. At times it is coercive; other times it's rhetorically empty, full of hot air-worse than blather-hypocrisy, or mystification. Only rarely does it serve us well, leading us to truth or beauty, but we can't sustain those functions very well. Pozzo's poetic description of the twilight may be true and even beautiful, but it peters out-"And that's how it is on this bitch of an earth." Or we may run from the truth we've brought it to express, as Didi does near the end of the play-"What have I said?"

The critique here seems to stem from a deep, postmodern distrust of the efficacy or absoluteness of language. We place our trust in it, but should we? Language is the source of all our illusions, the source of all the mythic fictions we've invented to console ourselves from an awareness of our real condition. These fictions have blinded us to the reality, the truth of our existence. The only truth is this present moment, and to waste it by hoping for some future "salvation," by waiting for a Godot that never comes, is tragic and absurd.

The language of the play is stripped bare, scaled down to its naked essence. You won't find a writer more capable than Beckett in this regard. The beauty of Beckett's language is in its absolute economy. It's a tight little fist that punches hard. The language of this play forces us to reflect on how we use language, really. Is it as neat and tidy as we think? Are we really that concerned about being logical or rational? Do we really describe "reality," and how rational or logical is reality? How much of what we say is emotional, illogical, and ambiguous?

In all of its aspects, including its language, Waiting for Godot confronts the absurdity of existence and challenges us to figure out who we are and what we're doing here. In this random universe, where everything who lives and who dies, who's up and who's down, is a matter of pure chance, and the odds aren't necessarily in our favour, what do we do? What's our purpose? The existentialist would say that our purpose is to confront our existence, our being, to be aware of and a part of every passing moment-to make choices, to act-to live authentically, in good faith, aware of our essential freedom and responsibility. This is what Didi can't or won't do, and he persuades Gogo to keep him company while he continues to wait for Godot, while he pins his hopes on a future that may never arrive. His futile waiting is either absurd or heroic, depending on your own interpretation.

Beckett was interested, it seems, in the relationship between hope and despair. Are Didi and Gogo in despair? Or do they have faith?

There's quite a lot more we could observe in terms of theme, though having said so much already, I think meaning in this play is probably best approached subjectively. How do you talk about the meaning of a circle? My observation of the play and everything I've read about it leads me to conclude there is very little objective interpretation which will make this play mean much more than it means quite obviously on the surface. Two tramps are waiting for someone they think will help them, but this person, Godot, never arrives. It seems reasonable to assume that Godot will never arrive, but Didi and Gogo go on waiting, perhaps because they hold out hope that he will, perhaps because they have nothing better to do.

But what is this play really about? What does it all mean? What does it all have to do with us? Some audiences see immediately how they, like Gogo and Didi, are waiting, too. Maybe not for "Godot," but for something. A little help, a little push, a little sunshine, a little windfall. The play takes pains not to be specific, to provide the space to read into it any way we want to. It does not preach a "message." But when you think about it even a little bit, you realize that, just like Gogo and Didi, we're waiting all the time, too. Think about it: aren't we waiting for the war in Iraq to end, waiting to catch Osama bin Laden, waiting to win the war on terror? We're waiting for President Bush to smoke out the evil-doers. If you're a banker or a stockbroker you might be waiting for an end to bankruptcy court or class action suits or social security or taxes. Or an end to racism.....an end to poverty, drug abuse, domestic violence... Many of us are waiting for environmental disaster, the next world war, the next flu epidemic, the next school shooting, the next terror attack... we're waiting for security, good times, that great vacation, that better job, that better wardrobe, that better car, that smaller computer, smaller cellphone; we're waiting for the perfect soul mate, the perfect body, the perfect moment... we're waiting for our hopes to be heard, our prayers to be answered, our wishes to be granted... we're waiting, and meanwhile, we're....here.

Waiting for Godot is a poignant play about such waiting, about the repetition, the meaninglessness, the absurdity of waiting, of feeling (and being) suspended in time instead of moving forward in a meaningful direction. It's not necessarily about the absence of God, or about Christian salvation, or existential despair, or nihilistic meaninglessness, or postmodern critiques of language, though interpretation is a subjective enterprise, and we can interpret literature how we choose. Still, many critics agree that a sensitive understanding of this play includes the awareness that it's really an abstract play about waiting, about waiting for the possibility of a better future that we are not quite fully convinced will never arrive.

How do we arrive in this seemingly absurd state of waiting? Laying an existential interpretation atop the play, we might say that this play confronts an unpleasant truth about the human condition. As human beings we're all clinging to the hope of some kind of salvation, some kind of Godot to come and save us from our intolerable suffering-our poverty, our disease, our boredom, our quiet desperation. This hoping, this waiting, removes us from the potentially liberating awareness that the moment we're actually suspended in, this moment between birth and death that glows so briefly, is ultimately more important than any vague "better future" we might desire. Everything in the play points to suspension: suspension of time, suspension of progress, suspension of reason, suspension of purpose. As drama, every convention has been suspended; the characters and their dialogue dance around in the ether of a nearly empty stage. There's no shortage of void, as Didi declares. It seems the only thing that's not suspended is our disbelief. These absurd characters are, ironically, so believable, so ultimately realistic, that it's barely necessary to remind ourselves we're in an imaginary world.

The Imagery

In Waiting for Godot, Beckett's most celebrated play, Estragon "[aphoristic for once]" says: We are all born mad. Only a few remain so.

I believe I am one of those who remained mad, because for more than forty-five years I have not stopped reading and re-reading the books of Samuel Beckett, and I always imagine that others, too, are as mad as I am and that they, too, never stopped reading and re-reading Beckett.

In any case, it is with this idea in mind — with this assumption that everybody has read everything Beckett has written — that I prepared a lecture for this occasion, an extremely complicated lecture, probably boring and much too long, which explained everything Beckett wrote.

I left that complicated and boring academic lecture — in the form of an explication de texte — in the sun of California, and instead I wrote a few notes which I have before me, and with these notes I want to take you on a little journey, an impromptu journey through the landscapes — the somewhat devastated landscapes — of Samuel Beckett's work. Or rather, I want to take you on a visit to the imagery museum of Samuel Beckett, for you may not know this but Beckett was a great artist, yes, a great painter. No, he did not paint with a brush, he painted tableaux (or tableaus) with words. And so I want to take you through some of Beckett's books, not to explain what they "mean" but to show you what there is to see in these books, to have you look at them somewhat like tourists look at paintings on the walls of a museum or exhibit. What I want to try to show you are the great visual tableaux that Beckett has created for us... using words.

Normally, one explains [at least to those who are in need of explanation] — one explains a work of fiction [a novel, a story, a play] by discussing the characters. That is to say, by looking at the human condition as represented in the characters. By discussing the characters of a literary work one usually arrives at the meaning of that work.

But to discuss or analyze the beings [lesêtres] of a novel or a play as if they were real, as if they were living in our world, is to deal with the work in terms of sociology and psychology. It has nothing to do with the aesthetic quality of the work. That kind of sociological and psychological explanation in the end has nothing to do with literature — literature as art, I mean. Samuel Beckett was, above all, an artist. Perhaps the last of the great artists of the 20th century. The British critic, Colin Wilson, once referred to Beckett as The Last of the Mohicans.

To speak of the unhappy condition of Beckett's creatures, the lonely, miserable condition of Gogo and Didi, Molloy, Malone and all the other human wrecks [les épaves humaines], one encounters dans l'oeuvre de Beckett. [Excuse the French intrusions, but when talking about Beckett one cannot avoid being bilingual since he was certainly one of the greatest bilingual writers of all time]. To see only the unhappy, depressing, morbid condition of the Beckettian milieu is not only indulging in sociological misérabilisme, but it is a way of ignoring the artistry and, especially, the beautiful geometry of his work.

By geometry I mean simply the form of the text, the structure of the narration, the shape of the sentences and, especially, the space, the landscape where Beckett's fictions are inscribed and on which they are played out. In other words, what I am proposing here is that in order to seize the work of Beckett — I did not say "understand", but seize, in the sense of apprehending visually and mentally — one must not only look at the beings in that fiction, one must see where and how these beings are situated physically, geographically, geometrically. And so I would like to take you today on a little journey through Beckettian space and show you some of the unforgettable tableaux he has meticulously created in his works. Along the way you will see how, progressively and chronologically and by mocking realism, Beckett's landscapes de-construct themselves and turn to ruins, or rather, one should say, construct themselves anew on their own ruins to become, first in his early works, surrealistic tableaux, then later on into cubist scenes (abstract expressionism) and finally, in his last texts, minimalist and conceptual, all these reconstructions being perfect geometrical figures — circles, squares, cubes, cylinders.

It is by looking at these tableaux that I would like to seize — again, not understand, but seize the work of Samuel Beckett.

End of the preface. Let us set out on our journey — our visit.

First, though, just a short preface before entering the Beckett museum [which is not quite open yet. It will be in a few minutes], a few words about Beckett the man and the artist are necessary. After all, when we go to a museum to look at the work of an artist, we might first try to find out a bit about his life and his work.

Beckett. The French pronounce that name Béquet — in fact that's exactly how one of the characters in the play Eleutheria [1947] — who is a spectator watching the play itself — pronounces the name of the author of the play, a play which he believes is going nowhere. Disgusted with the non-action, the spectator jumps up on the stage and tries to resolve the situation.

Au fait, he says, qui a fait ce navet? [il regarde son programme]. Samuel Béquet. Béquet! Ça doit être un juif groenlandais mâtiné d'auvergnat.

In spite of what that irritated spectator in Eleutheria says, Beckett was certainly one of the most important and influential writers of our time — at least for my generation. [Beckett died on December 22, 1989.]

Certain people throughout history were privileged to have

been contemporaries of accomplished achievers in the arts such as Homer, Shakespeare, Racine, Goethe, Dostoevsky, Proust, Joyce, Carravagio, Rembrandt, Cézanne, Mozart, Beethoven. I lived at the same time as Samuel Beckett. We — you and I — lived at the same time. We were his contemporaries. And he left with us an amazing oeuvre.

Samuel Beckett is no longer in Paris [where he lived and worked], no longer writing another book for us. There will be no more books by Samuel Beckett. But even though Beckett has now changed tense — as a friend wrote to me upon learning of his death — what remains is this immense oeuvre he has left behind. For this we are all deeply indebted to him.

What he left with us are: novels, stories, Texts for Nothing, [Six] Residua, plays for the stage, radio plays, television plays, mimes, videos — even a film — poetry, art criticism, literary criticism, translations and self-translations, and more. And all of these written in two languages by Beckett himself — French and English. An amazing oeuvre indeed.

As we all know, Beckett was an Irishman who lived in exile in France beginning in the early 1930's and who eventually adopted the French language for most of his writing. He translated into English much of the work he wrote in French, and into English much of his originally French work. These translations from one language to the other are a real a tour de force, and how he undertook them would be worthy of a lecture in itself, but I cannot resist, since most readers of Beckett are bilingual if not multilingual, to give just one illustration here [while we are waiting for the imagery museum to open] of what happens when Beckett translates himself.

The novel Watt [written in English between 1943-1945 during World War II and first published in 1953] ends with this statement: No symbols where none intended, a sentence in which we hear the entire tradition of Anglo-Saxon literature and culture. Beckett's French translation of Watt did not appear until 1968, after which I often attempted, myself, to translate that very sentence back into English. Listen to what it became in Beckett's English to French: Honni soit qui symboles y voit. And here we hear the entire French culture and literature. Born in 1906, Beckett settled, for the first of two times, in Paris in 1932. That is to say, at the age of 26 he finds himself in exile. Displaced. Dépaysé, one might say, living in a foreign landscape — since we are talking about landscapes.

Beginning in 1929 [the year of his first publication] and ending exactly 60 years after that, Beckett did nothing else but write, nothing else but line up words on pieces of paper. Therefore, the story of his life was his writing, his life was nothing but words, or as the voice in Texts for Nothing says of his own life: Words. [My life] was never more than that, than that pell-mell babel of silence and words.

That then, briefly stated, is Beckett's life, his biography. Words, in English and in French. For 60 years Beckett locked himself in a room and he wrote. Hugh Kenner refers to this activity as The Siege in the Room. A few more minutes, now, and the museum will be open. Allow me to situate myself in relation to Beckett's work before we go in.

I started reading Beckett in 1956 after I saw the Broadway production of Waiting for Godot, and like everyone else back then I wanted to know what this work of Beckett meant and I wanted to try and understand the universal truths of his books. And so for some 15 years, until about 1970, I set out in the pursuit of meaning in Beckett's work. Like everyone else, I wanted to know what it all meant. Not only did I write a doctoral dissertation on the fiction of Samuel Beckett (which became my first book, Journey to Chaos), but I also published numerous articles, worked for several years with the British critic John Fletcher on a huge critical bibliography entitled Beckett: His Works and His Critics, edited three volumes of essays and documents on Beckett and, of course, taught the works of Beckett in my seminars at the university.

At the beginning of the 1960's a whole team of critics including myself set out to sort out, to explain, to classify, to interpret and to organize the work of Samuel Beckett in an attempt to extract meaning from it. In the process, some very strange, far-fetched, and preposterous interpretations were offered. But as it is said in the novel Watt: What was the pursuit of meaning in this indifference to meaning? And to what did it tend? These are delicate questions. And in the same novel, as if warning us about the futility of seeking meaning, this: But to elicit something from nothing requires a certain skill, and Watt was not always successful, in his efforts to do so.

Nor was Federman successful. Nonetheless, in spite of the warnings the critics stubbornly insisted on this pursuit of meaning.

First it was a matter of finding the literary sources of Beckett's work. Gradually the critics revealed that his remarkable work was inspired by Joyce, Kafka, Proust, Flaubert, Balzac and, moving back in time, the 18th century novel (Diderot and Laurence Sterne) and before that, Racine, Shakespeare, Rabelais, Cervantes, Dante and Homer. So many possible sources were concocted that, finally, one was reduced to saying that the work of Samuel Beckett was, in fact, all of literature — the entire history [and story] of literature. And so, after all of these efforts to ascribe sources to his work, nothing had been said that explained the work of Samuel Beckett.

Then came the critics who felt absolutely compelled to try and discover the philosophical and theological sources. And so Beckett was read as an Existentialist and a Phenomenologist, influenced by Sartre, Heidegger, Bergson and certainly Nietzsche, and by the pessimism of Schopenhauer; by the dualism of Descartes; by the Occasionalism of Malebranche and Geulincx; and, still further back in time, by Luther and Calvin, St. Augustine, the Sophists, Plato and Aristotle and the Pre-Socratics; and of course by the Ancient and the New Testaments. That is to say, once again, that the entire history of philosophy and theology was allegedly contained in the work of Samuel Beckett.

What was curious about this stubborn pursuit of meaning, this search and research in finding literary, philosophical and theological sources for Beckett's work, is that it always seemed to lead to nothing — to self-evidence and non-sense. I am using the term non-sense here in both of its dual meanings: Without direction, without signification.

But Beckett had been warning us all along about the

meaninglessness—or the "Lessness"—of his work. Or as he put it himself in referring to the language of his novel How It Is, meaning is a "rumor transmissible ad infinitum in either direction". And elsewhere he emphasized that Language is what gets us where we want to go and prevents us from getting there.

And so, in spite of the enormous critical industry around Beckett's work, that very work seemed to defy any sensible explanation, seemed to cancel all critical interpretations however convincing they might sound. It made a mockery of criticism. The more one tried to situate, to pigeon-hole Beckett's work, the more it escaped historical and critical interpretation.

Of course there were also the symbolic explanations of the novels and plays. But even these clever explanations did not clarify anything, did not reveal any meaning [or hidden meaning, if there was one] of his oeuvre.

For ultimately, the meaning was neither secret nor hidden. It was right there on the surface of the texts, at the level of the words and the images these words created, perhaps being even too evident. The meaning of Beckett's work was right before our eyes. It was simply a matter of looking rather than thinking. Let me sum up, in the form of a question, what I believe the meaning of Beckett's work is: What am I doing here... doing what I am doing? That's all. Or to put it even more simply and succinctly and echo the words of the old dying woman in the marvelous play Rockaby who, while rocking herself to sleep or to death in an old rocking chair, suddenly shouts: "Fuck life!"

Yes, all along Beckett warned us that it was useless to try and find meaning in his work, especially symbolic meaning. Remember: No symbols where none intended.

The pursuit of meaning in Beckett's work often leads to an impasse, to non-sense, to platitudes, ready-made ideas. As a comparison, the work of Beckett presents itself to us very much like Baudelaire's forest of symbols. But the symbols in the forest of Beckett's words are undecipherable. Therefore it is useless to ascribe a meaning to these symbols for they merely confound us and lead us into ignorance.

In one of the rare but often quoted interviews Beckett gave, he stated: I am working with impotence and ignorance. I don't think ignorance has ever been exploited in the past.

Self-evidence and ignorance: the keys to Beckett's work. A perfect example is the thirty second play written for television entitled Breath — yes, a thirty second "dramaticule", as Beckett called it: Light comes up on a pile of garbage; one hears the cry of a baby; the light goes out. It's as simple as that. Darkness-light-darkness, which, of course, can be read as birth/life/death. It is so evident that even to say this becomes ridiculous.

The meaning of this dramaticule is too obvious even to bother pointing it out. It baffles us by its "evidence". But as an image, as a tableau, as a picture, it is striking, and once it has been seen on the screen it remains engraved in one's mind. A pile of garbage, light, darkness, and the cry of a baby. What a striking tableau that represents.... well, no need to be any more explicit.

The same can be said of the name "Godot", the word that entered our culture in 1951 and has intrigued so many people ever since. To say that Godot means God becomes absurd. It is so evident, so obvious, that to say it is to say nothing. And in fact, as it is said in Waiting for Godot, Nothing is more real than nothing.

You must be wondering why I have spent so much time rejecting, refusing, avoiding, canceling the meaning of Beckett's work. Why this long detour, when I promised you a tour of Beckett's imagery museum. I am coming to that very shortly. But first allow me to explain why, personally, I abandoned the pursuit of meaning in Beckett. [By now you must have understood that what I am doing here with all these digressions within digressions is to avoid saying anything that may become meaningful about Beckett's work — to say something meaningful would be mere competence, as Beckett would say].

In 1972, I was in Paris and Beckett invited me to go, with him and a few other people, to see the dress rehearsal [not the first performance but only the dress rehearsal] of the revival of En Attendant Godot—exactly twenty years after its première. What was interesting about this revival is that the director, Roger Blin, who had also directed the original production, used the same actors for this performance who had played in the original. But this time Blin decided to stage the play literally in slow motion. It lasted two and a half hours. As a result, the tableaux of this version [in which nothing happens twice, as it was once famously said] became fixed, frozen in place, like stills in a film or like paintings, so that the symbolism exploded and became quite quite obvious, especially those symbols that could be interpreted as religious. But the meaninglessness of the play also became more evident. As, in fact, in this exchange between Gogo and Didi:

Didi: This is becoming really insignificant.

Gogo: Not enough yet.

[Are you still with me? – The museum is about to open].

After the performance the actors, Blin, Beckett and I went for dinner in a rather swanky restaurant. I was sitting next to Beckett and at one point I asked him what he thought of this performance, this slow motion staging. He quietly told me:

C'est pas mal, c'est pas mal, he said (we always spoke French together). But then after a moment of silence—the kind of silence only Beckett could make comfortable—he added:

Si seulement ils pouvaient arrêter de me faire dire plus que j'ai dit?

"When will they stop making me say more than I said." It was as if Beckett was warning his readers and critics not to fall into the trap of symbolism and hermeneutics.

Later that evening—or perhaps the next day—in his apartment, we were talking literature and I asked him why he was so fond of a certain sentence which appears several times in his works, and what it meant to him.

This is the sentence:

Do not despair, one of the thieves was saved,

Do not presume, one of the thieves was damned.

[From St. Augustine of course]

And Beckett said to me: It is not the meaning of this sentence that interests me, it is its shape, its movement. It has perfect symmetry, the way it cancels itself. And suddenly I realized that it was not the meaning of words that really concerned Beckett, but the shape of language. Therefore, one should not seek meaning in his work but look at the form of his narrative, the shape of his sentences, the movement of his language. One should simply look at the images he has created in his novels and in his plays and not try to ascribe a meaning to these images.

And certainly Beckett, who loved painting so much, who wrote such profound essays on painting, who could explain painting so well to us, whose best friends were painters [Jack Yeats, Avigdor Arikha, Bram van Velde, Jasper Johns, and many others with whom he collaborated] and who could have, himself, been a great painter, became that painter in his written work. He painted beautiful tableaux for us with words rather than with paint.

And so, in early 1970 I went back to the work of Samuel Beckett, no longer as a critic, no longer as an interpreter, but as a writer [in early 1970, I was myself in the process of becoming a novelist], and I started to look at those strange books in a totally different fashion. I looked at them with my senses rather than with my mind, somewhat like a tourist in a museum. I was looking at these works with a kind of bewilderment, a renewed attention, and suddenly I saw before me an entire gallery of marvelous, striking, unforgettable tableaux — the kind of tableaux that remain engraved in your head and haunt you for the rest of your life. Tableaux made of words in the novels and visual tableaux in the plays which, by their construction, their composition, their design, their topology and their geometry gave me more pleasure than the symbolic meaning I and others had previously read into them.

Let us look then — mentally, of course — at some of the tableaux that one can see and admire in Beckett's novels and plays. Mentally since these tableaux are made of words and as such can be called conceptual, though in the plays the tableaux become visible. Waiting for Godot: As the lights come up in Act 1 we see, in front of a grey backdrop, a deserted cross-road and a dead tree — nothing more. A new day is beginning. Two derelict figures enter. Unforgettable tableau: the entrance of Gogo and Didi and an attempted embrace by Didi. The entire human drama will be played out here in this space, in this no-man's land. The futility and absurdity of life, the impossibility and the necessity of waiting.

Of course, we now know the origin of that tableau. Yes, the landscape of Godot was inspired by two paintings of Caspar David Friedrich which can be seen in the museum of the Charlottenburg Castle in Berlin. One of these represents two figures seen from the back standing in some deserted landscape next to a tree looking at the moon. The other also represents two vague figures in the distance at the seashore.

But there are other tableaux in Godot:

- The stunning entrance of Pozzo and Lucky — the master pulling the slave tied at the neck by the end of a long rope.
- Gogo and Didi doing their exercises next to the dead tree.
- Gogo/Didi/Pozzo/Lucky fallen on the ground, incapable of getting up.
- Didi with his pants down trying to use the piece of rope that held his pants up to hang himself.

Imagine these tableaux fixed, frozen in time, as in the performance I saw in 1972. Or imagine them as paintings on the wall of a museum, and you suddenly realize what a great painter, what a great metteur-en-scène Beckett was. For certainly, on the stage of a theater the author and director function very much like painters in the way the scenes of a play are staged. The tableaux in Godot have the quality, the texture of German expressionism.

Even more striking and memorable is the tableau we see as the light comes up on Endgame. [I should point out that Beckett's plays are never performed with a curtain. The lights initially going down and then gradually returning to light up the stage mark the beginning of a Beckett play. And the light, very much as in a painting, is an integral part of the tableau that we are watching]. In Endgame, as the light comes on we see a room, a totally enclosed space, a chamber. Perhaps the anti-chamber of Purgatory. In the centre, Hamm's chair [his throne]. Before him, two garbage cans containing Hamm's father and mother. Looked at carefully, this setting suddenly reveals itself to be the interior of a skull — a human skull. [I should mention that the decor for the original French première was designed by Alberto Giacometti, the sculptor of "existential reality".] The two windows on the backdrop represent the empty eyes. And within the chamber other tableaux take shape, when the heads of Nell and Nagg appear out of the trash cans or when Clov is pictured standing on a ladder looking out of the windows with his telescope at the ruins of the world outside, if a world still exists outside this space. The tableaux of Endgame are surrealistic.

The experience of seeing these tableaux for the first time is unforgettable, just as seeing a great painting by Rembrandt or Van Gogh is unforgettable.

[As I speak I assume that all of you are seeing these tableaux mentally, and perhaps remembering the initial reaction or shock you felt when you first saw them].

Here we have Krapp's Last Tape: The image of the old Krapp, disheveled, half drunk, leaning over his tape recorder, eating a banana, surrounded by the spools of recorded tapes that contain his life and his memories. Another striking picture. A concrete visual rendering of what memories must look like inside the human skull. Beckett's tableaux are often the exteriorization of what we see inside our heads.

And Happy Days: The disturbing, grotesque and yet almost funny tableau of Winnie buried up to her waist in a mound of earth and, in the second act, to her neck. If you have never seen this play, imagine the shock you will feel when the light reveals this middle-aged woman already half into her tomb holding a parasol over her head and saying casually: Another heavenly day. Allow me to read you the stage directions Beckett gives for this play in order to demonstrate how he carefully draws his tableaux:

Expanse of scorched grass rising centre to low mound. Gentle slopes down to front and either side of stage. Back with abrupter fall to stage level. Maximum of simplicity and symmetry. Blazing light. Very pompier trompe-l'oeil backcloth to represent unbroken plain and sky receding to meet in far distance. Imbedded up to above her waist in exact centre of mound, Winnie.... [then the text goes on to describe Winnie, the central figure].

Beckett's tableaux become even more fascinating, more disturbing, but also more funny, in some ways, as they proceed from one work to the next. In the play entitled Play [Comédie, in French], three human heads appear out of giant urns when the lights come up. In this play, in fact, it is the light, as it moves from one urn to the next, that creates the movement and the drama of this Magritte-like tableau. The mouth of Not I: Yes, just a mouth in this play that becomes a monstrous creature as the lips and the tongue articulate words. Here one thinks of some of Francis Bacon's paintings. Then there is the old woman with the crooked hat on her head rocking herself literally to death in Rockaby while she listens to her own voice on tape rattling off the same old story.

And what about the frozen actor perched on a pedestal being manipulated by the metteur-en-scène in Catastrophe. One can feel the pain that actors must endure in the hands of a director who manipulates their well being in order for them to become the characters in a Beckett play.

What is fascinating about all these tableaux is that they also reflect the medium they are representing, in these cases the theater, the art of the theater. These tableaux and so many others from the plays are haunting, and remain inscribed in our minds after we have seen them, after we have left them, not because they are frightening but rather because they are so real, so true. And therefore it becomes irrelevant to ask, What do they mean, What are they saying to us, just as one does not ask of a great painting, what does it mean — especially not great abstract paintings by Jackson Pollock, Clyfford Still, Motherwell or Rothco, for instance, in which there is "nothing to see but paint".

But it is not only in the plays of Beckett that one sees these magnificent tableaux. They are also in the novels, and are sometimes even more striking here with their originality and their complexity. In the opening scene of the novel Murphy, we see the protagonist sitting naked and tied with seven scarves to a rocking chair. Here is how Beckett introduces — now famously — this tableau: The sun shone, having no alternative, on the nothing new... [First, as always in a Beckett tableau, the light.] Murphy sat naked in his rocking-chair of undressed teak, guaranteed not to crack, warp, shrink, corrode, or creak at night... Seven scarves held him in position. Two fastened his shins to the rockers, one, his thighs to the seat, two held his breast and belly to the back, one tied his wrists to the strut behind...

Can you see that picture, that absurd canvas? One wonders how or if Murphy managed to tie himself in this fashion. Again a very surrealistic painting. The final disposal of Murphy's ashes [after his body, mind and soul have been reduced to chaos by a gas explosion] is an even more absurd surrealistic picture. Without going into the details of how Murphy's ashes ended up in a paper bag, here is what happened: Some hours later, Cooper took the packet of ash from his pocket where earlier in the evening he had put it for greater security, and threw it angrily at a man who had given him great offence. It bounced and burst off the wall and onto the floor, where at once it became the object of much dribbling, passing, trapping, shooting, punching, heading and even some recognition from the gentleman's code. By closing time the body, mind and soul of Murphy were freely distributed over the floor of the saloon, and before another dayspring greyened the earth, had been swept away with the sand, the beer, the butts, the glass, the matches, the spits, the vomit.

This scene, this comic tableau is so visual, so concrete in its absurdity that I don't think it needs to be further explicated. It's almost cartoon-like. The house of Mr. Knott in Watt, inside of which objects are not what they appear to be and where words no longer coincide with objects, is full of striking tableaux. Watt himself, the protagonist, when he first appears looks like a roll of tarpaulin wrapped in dark paper and tied about the middle with a cord. Later there is Watt in an insane asylum, wearing his jacket backward and speaking backward.

Then Watt lying in a ditch listening to frogs croak. The novel is full of such absurd surrealistic pictures.

Bicycles are standard props in Beckett tableaux. The pseudo-couple Mercier and Camier, as they are referred to in the novel by that name, make a rather curious picture as they walk along with their bicycle, one holding on to the handlebar, the other to the seat.

Or in the story entitled The Calmative, the cyclist who crosses the landscape of the city from East to West, riding his bicycle while reading a newspaper. Here is how the unnamed protagonist of this story describes the scene: I only saw one cyclist! He was going the same way as I was. He was pedaling slowly in the middle of the street, reading a newspaper which he held with both hands spread open before his eyes. Every now and then he rang his bell without interrupting his reading. I watched him recede till he was no more than a dot on the horizon.

This type of scene may not add much meaning to the story, but it is the accumulation of such tableaux that creates the Beckettian landscape. Perhaps the greatest Beckettian tableau is the portrait of Molloy: In his greatcoat with his bowler hat tied to the button hole of his coat with a shoelace. Of Molloy dragging himself along on his crutches. Molloy trying to slash his wrists with his pocket knife that does not cut. Molloy, that grandiose Beckettian figure, crawling on the ground pulling himself forward with his crutches.

And of Molloy in his mother's bed. Beckett does not tell us if he is wearing a night bonnet but in the tableau that I have in my own head of him in his mother's bed—Molloy "becoming" his own mother—I see him with such a night bonnet and a long white nightgown.

And there is also the marvelous tableau of the pathetic Malone in his bed pulling his possessions towards him with a hook at the end of a long stick.

And The Unnamable—ah, the incredible tableau of The Unnamable—fixed in space like a sun, tears running down his face and with all of Beckett's previous creatures orbiting like planets around him. They are all there: Murphy, Molloy,

Malone and the pseudo-couple Mercier and Camier. What a sublime surrealistic painting. There is also in the same novel, Worm, planted in a pot in front of a restaurant with the menu stuck on top of his head.

And Pim and Pam and Pem crawling naked in the mud of How It Is with a sack full of sardine and tuna fish cans tied around their necks. Salvador Dali could not have done better. These are indeed striking images. And there are so many others. Certain paintings — I mean now, real paintings by the great masters, those hanging in museums — once we have seen them can never be forgotten: The two young boys of Carravagio eating grapes. The self-portrait of Rembrandt wearing a turban. Velasquez's La Meninas. El Greco's elongated figures. Courbet's The Origin of the World. Cézanne's The Luberon Mountain. Van Gogh's sunflower or his green Christ or the three pairs of shoes. Picasso's Les Demoiselles d'Avignon. Clyfford Still's Black Canvas and so many other such great paintings that stay with us even though others may be our favorites. Standing in front of these paintings it is the form, the composition, the colors that move us and stay with us rather than the represented subject and the meaning of that subject, if there is a subject.

This is even more so when looking at an abstract painting. It is the geometry, the colors or lack of colors that touches us since there is no real subject, no story, no melodrama in the painting and therefore no reference to the real world.

All of Beckett's novels and plays are made of such tableaux — strange, somber, sad, often absurd, disturbing and yes, funny, but always beautifully constructed tableaux. The work of Samuel Beckett is extremely visual. That is why even some of his fiction has been adapted to the stage, for example, The Lost Ones.

As one follows the evolution of these tableaux in Beckett's work, one discovers that it parallels the evolution of painting in the 20 century. From neo-impressionism, to expressionism, to cubism, to surrealism, to abstract expressionism, to the optic and geometric experiments in the plastic arts of the last few decades — all these modes and styles of painting are present in Beckett's own tableaux. From the concrete to the abstract. From realism and surrealism to unrealism and abstract geometry.

This visual deconstruction and reconstruction of the world is performed in three movements, three precise Beckettian periods, as one says of the various styles of an artist.

The first period consists of the works written [but not necessarily published] between 1929 and 1945, the early works written in English: The surrealist period.

The second and central period — and the most important and richest — embraces the works written between 1945 and 1965 and includes the shift to the French language and the experiments in theater: The abstract expressionist period.

The third period – 1965 to 1989 – consists of the later shorter works in both fiction and for the theater: The minimalist and conceptualist period.

I call the first period "the lies of reality." More Pricks than Kicks, Murphy and Watt — all of which undermine the conventions of realism — are the major works of that period.

The second period represents "the truths of fiction." Molloy, Malone Dies, The Unnamable and Texts for Nothing, but also Waiting for Godot, Endgame and Krapp's Last Tape, are the major works here — works that gradually become more and more self-reflexive and non-referential.

The works of the third period point to "the impossibility of fiction" — these are all the later texts and short plays. For fiction Enough, Imagination Dead Imagine, Ping, The Lost Ones, Ill Seen Ill Said, Company, Worstward Ho, Lessness, Stirrings Still, and in the theater Not I, Ghost Trio, Ohio Impromptu, What Where, Catastrophe and the magnificent Quads, 1 and 2.

In these later works, literature becomes more and more conceptual as it empties itself of its own subject — no more fable, no more story, no more anecdote.

Whether working in fiction or in the theater, the evolution of Beckett's tableaux in words undergoes the same changes, the same transformation, the same form of deconstruction as takes place in some paintings, moving from the concrete to the abstract to become, finally, pure geometry, pure visual poetry, as in Quad 1 and 2.

It is interesting to note the relationship of Beckett's theater to his fiction. It seems that every time he found himself cornered into a fictional impasse, every time he pushed the work of fiction further into abstraction by removing from it the traditional elements of fiction such as plot, character and setting as well as story, he needed to step back somewhat to be able go forward again, and that's when he would write a play. After he finished Malone Dies in 1947, he wrote Waiting for Godot. [I'm giving here the English titles but these were written first in French]. After he wrote the thirteen Texts For Nothing in 1950, which are the ultimate deconstruction of fiction, Beckett stepped back again and wrote Endgame and Krapp's Last Tape. After he finished How It Is he wrote Play.

Basically, what all this accounts for is that Beckett's fiction pushed the monologue further and further into aloneness and lessnessness, and in order to be able to go on he needed to return to the dialogue, essential to theater even if there is only one character on stage as in Krapp's Last Tape [the tape recorder being the interlocutor] or the voice on tape in Eh Joe and in Rockaby, whereby the character dialogues with himself or herself. There are two key works in the evolution of Beckett's oeuvre which serve as transition between the three periods that I have indicated: Mercier and Camier marks not only the passage from English into French but also the passage from a third person narrative to the first person; the passage from the city landscape to the countryside landscape; and the passage from surrealistic to expressionistic tableaux — from the concrete to the abstract.

The novels and stories of the first period are situated in still recognizable settings: a city landscape, Dublin, London. Streets are named, houses are pictured, even nature is described — albeit ironically. But rather than realistic depictions, the "staging", one might say, these scenes are surreal. Of course Beckett was writing this fiction during the 1930's when Surrealism was the dominant mode in art.

In More Pricks Than Kicks, for instance, the scene where

we see the drunken protagonist, Belacqua Shuah, lying in the middle of the street, curled up in the fetal position in his own vomit, is a true surrealistic tableau. Or when Belacqua and his girl friend, Ruby, attempt a double suicide on top of a mountain while getting drunk on Irish whiskey and eventually make love rather than killing themselves is again a very surrealistic tableau.

And I have already mentioned Murphy tied naked with seven scarves to his rocking chair, and the remnants of Murphy being sweep away with the dirt on the floor of a pub at the end of the novel. I hope you have noticed that I am not trying to make comparisons between Beckett's tableaux and existing paintings, though as James Knowlson has pointed out in his biography of Beckett, Damned to Fame, one could certainly find sources in museums for some of Beckett's visual inventions.

The tableaux in the novel Watt bring us to the brink of disintegration of reality and meaning. There is, in fact, a painting in that novel — an actual painting — that puzzles Watt to the point of bringing tears of incomprehension to his eyes. The painting that is described in the novel may be Beckett's best explanation of his own work, and Watt's puzzlement in front of that painting corresponds to the confusion a reader may feel confronting Beckett's work. It is worth quoting the entire passage in order to give a better sense of how Beckett reveals, not without some verbal playfulness and humour, the aesthetics of his own work as an artiste-peintre, while at the same time warning us not to wonder too much about its meaning nor to try and see more than there is before our eyes:

The only other object in Erskine's room was a picture, hanging on the wall, from a nail. A circle, obviously described by a compass, and broken at its lowest point, occupied the middle foreground, of this picture. Was it receding? Watt had that impression. In the eastern background appeared a point, or dot. The circumference was black. The point was blue, but blue! The rest was white. How the effect of perspective was obtained Watt did not know. But it was obtained. By what means the illusion of movement in space and, it almost seemed, in time was given, Watt could not say. But it was given. Watt wondered how long it would be before the point and the circle entered together upon the same plane.

Or had they not done so already, or almost? And was it not rather the circle that was in the background, and the point that was in the foreground? Watt wondered if they had sighted each other, or were blindly flying thus, harried by some force of merely mechanical mutual attraction, or the playthings of chance. He wondered if they would eventually pause and converse, and perhaps even mingle, or keep steadfast on their ways, like ships in the night, prior to the invention of wireless telegraphy. Who knows, they might even collide. This is confirmed by the text entitled Imagination Dead Imagine, which opens with these words:

No trace anywhere of life, you say, pah, no difficulty there, imagination not dead yet, yes, dead, good, imagination dead imagine. Islands, waters, azure, verdure, one glimpse and vanished, endlessly, omit. No trace of life, no more nature. Beckett's fiction, very much like abstract painting, eliminates the subjects from his work, the traditional subjects of painting: Man and Nature. The little that is left of Man and Nature is perhaps best seen in the striking tableau of the novel How It Is where naked bodies crawl like reptiles in a landscape of mud. Little by little then, Beckett's fiction moves towards total reduction and abstraction but not to end in a vacuum or descend into total silence, as so many critics have suggested, but rather to become pure geometry, pure visual poetry.

I hope I have succeeded in showing you how the evolution of Beckett's work, from 1929 to 1989, follows that of the plastic arts of the same period. The first tableaux correspond, to a great extent, to the paintings of the 1930's — neo-impressionism, cubism, surrealism — and certainly there is a resemblance between the tableaux Beckett created with words in his early novels and the paintings of Magritte, Delvaux, de Chirico, Dali and other surrealist artists.

Following World War Two, humanity was confronted with both a crisis of conscience and, especially, a crisis of communication — the difficulty inherent in trying to explain and reconcile such barbaric acts taking place in a supposedly civilized society. The result was that the arts moved towards abstraction, briefly emptying themselves of their traditional subjects: Man and Nature in painting and sculpture, the melody in music, and the anecdote in literature.

It was as if the arts wanted to get rid of the illusions that had sustained them and, in so doing, to re-examine their own medium — in the case of literature its own language, that "rumor transmissible ad infinitum in either direction".

Shortly thereafter, though, by the end of the 1960's and into the 1970's, without rejecting abstraction completely, the arts reconstituted themselves into geometrical and optical forms, into conceptualism and minimalism. The short texts that Beckett wrote towards the end of his life, as well as the short plays, are in fact minimalistic and conceptual, but especially geometrical.

The best example of this is the mouth of Not I, especially as it was viewed on television. The bodiless mouth that becomes a monstrous organism is perhaps the most striking of Samuel Beckett's tableaux. I don't know how many of you have seen this play but I can assure you that once you do, you will never forget this tableau.

I don't think I am mistaken when I say that the literary work of Beckett parallels the evolution of painting of the last 70 years or so, and his own interest in painting is evinced by his profound essays on abstract expressionism and the work of Bram van Velde, Masson, Kandanski, Tal Coat, Jack Yeats, Avigdor Arikha and others, in which essays he insists on what he calls the dual confrontations of l'objet-obstacle and l'oeil-obstacle.

What he means is that the object itself prevents us from seeing it clearly, and that the eye itself is an obstacle to clear perception of the object. Beckett calls this "the agony of perceived-ness", which he exemplified so well in the film he made appropriately called Film, starring Buster Keaton. This agony of perceived-ness brings us back to the definition Beckett gave of language: Language is what gets us where we want to go and prevents us from getting there. Language as a vehicle of communication and as an obstacle to communication.

If it is true, as I hope I have shown, that Beckett's work parallels that of painting, one could also better appreciate the entire oeuvre of Beckett by following the evolution of music over the past 70 years, and of course the same applies to the evolution of philosophical thought and criticism during this same period. The work of Beckett can be understood in the light of Bergson's Evolutionism, Heiddeger's Phenomenology, Sartre's Existentialism, Foucault/Levi-Strauss/Deleuze's Structuralism and Derrida's Deconstruction.

It seems that Beckett was present at each moment during this evolution and always sensed what was happening and, in addition, anticipated what was going to happen. This, of course, is true of all great artists. They are always in advance of their time.

I hope that in presenting Beckett to you in this fashion, I did not give you the impression that his work is sad and depressing. Even though, like a magician, he makes the world and the beings who inhabit it disappear gradually from his work over time and — near the end — only the ruins of the world remain along with fragments of the human body [a woman buried to her neck in a mound of dirt; a disembodied mouth; an eye in a circle; a bodiless voice; a body without a voice], nevertheless his work seems to affirm that as long as there is a remnant of life, of breath, of movement, the human creature will continue to seek its place in the world but not necessarily understand the meaning of being in the world.

And so, if one avoids trying to seek the much too evident meaning of Beckett's work and instead concentrates on the form, the shape, the structure, the geometry of that work, one escapes despair. Personally, I do not see despair, anguish or suffering in Beckett's work as some critics do. On the contrary, for me his work is always an affirmation of being and of becoming, even if everything in the Beckettian world seems to disintegrate into nothingness and meaninglessness.

If Beckett did not keep the promise he made at the end of

one of the Texts for Nothing... And yet I have high hopes, I give you my word, high hopes. That one day I may tell a story, hear a story, yet another, with men, kinds of men as in the days when I play all regardless or nearly, worked and played.

...if Beckett never told us that story before he changed tense and entered the "long apres", then it is perhaps up to us to now tell it ourselves, to reconstruct the world from the devastated landscapes he has left with us and tell, in the real sense of that word, the story of our passage on this planet. Not to explain that passage but only to make it visible. Beckett certainly gave us a head start in this project, for if one learns anything from reading his work it is not to better understand but to better see, better listen and, especially, to say better and write better. To read the works of Beckett — to look at the magnificent tableaux he has created for us — is to learn to be oneself. It is in this sense that Beckett was a great artist and not the great thinker everyone wanted him to be.

Chapter 3

Language in 'Waiting for Godot'

Beckett's work is defined by the consciousness that words are incapable of expressing the inner self and by the simultaneous acceptance of the fact that language is intrinsic to the human situation and thus not a removable element. Beckett regards language as constitutive of the identity of the self it is on this conviction that his despair for the human condition and the power of his writing depend. Despair, because the self can only be approached asymptotically and expressed, words moving in an orbit without ever touching the centre, the essence power, because he sees in language's struggle to achieve expression the striving of the self to define its own identity. His attitude towards language is, then, the paradoxical acceptance of self-refutation as the condition for any artistic practice a recognition of the inherent inability of words to correspond to anything other than themselves together with the potentiality of expressing this very inability to express.

What Beckett is above all conscious of is the dialectical relationship between the object to be expressed (theme, subject matter) and the mode of expression (form of language, style). Regarding the latter as constitutive of the former, he foregrounds the comic absurdity of their dissociation into two non-interacting elements, whilst maintaining the dialectic through the overall theatrical form. However, because Beckett does not regard language as a self-sufficient system of concepts exoteric to the theme it is bound to express, the imposition of dramatic form is in turn problematized. Only a Naturalistic view of language as having a direct and unambiguous relation to the world can allow for an unproblematic organization of meaning at this level. By radically subverting such a notion of language Beckett sets all elements of his drama into a type of free-play. It is the movement within this free-play, taking in all previously fixed points (self, language, material reality, etc), which I have described as the dialectic in his work. In this context artistic expression can only be formless so long as the world it speaks about is itself formless: '... hence the quest for the art form that is capable of accommodating the formless. The only form that can do so is one in which the form itself is at issue'. In such a view, form, far from being a servile reflection of an external reality, establishes a much more complicated relationship with it form is granted a relative autonomy from the substance it expresses and thus actively intervenes in the artistic process by shaping the raw material and by subtly imposing an integral order upon it.

The 'formlessness' of any particular form is therefore merely phenomenal, because it actually masks a highly organized and disciplined structure. This-is particularly clear in Beckett's theatre where the almost physical experience of words as a natural and random flow obliterates the audience's elementary awareness that speech on stage is not spontaneous but part of a carefully structured text. Beckett feels that the domain of the writer-playwright is that of a form which creates meaning through its struggle to express meaning. He does not, therefore, resort to the formalistic demand for an art synonymous with form, but rather attempts to solve the problem of their relation by preserving the dialectic.

He is on record as saying that the world is a mess the implication is that, by its very nature, the world is the polar opposite of art, which is form, and thus destructive of the very thing that art holds itself to be. A corollary of this would be that any acceptance of a correspondence between art (form) and the world (substance) would refute the very existence and operation of art. He is naturally very careful, therefore, to make a distinction between the two, to ascribe to each of them certain autonomy, whilst always seeking to find the 'raison d'être' for the former:

The form and the chaos remain separate. The latter is not reduced to the former. That is why the form itself becomes a preoccupation, because it exists as a problem separate from the material it accommodates. To find a form that accommodates the mess, that is the task of the artist now.

In his essay on Proust Beckett describes style as pertaining to a particular authorial vision rather than to technique. In the case of the novelist Proust the quality of his language is the predominant factor, the element which incorporates and shapes his vision of the world. In drama, naturally, language cannot play the same absolute role theatre as a medium provides the playwright with a space to be covered with tangible and visual images, it does not merely serve a context within which the text is animated. Beckett has, of course, fully developed this stage potential in an ascetic dramaturgy organized around verbal constructs of condensed meaning and possessed of a unique ability to articulate visually both silence and absence on stage.

Yet Beckett's drama remains primarily one of language, of a language which does not pretend to convey the essence of things, which accepts the existence of the mess and which is aware of its own degradation. His choice of dramatic speech as the fundamental level of action, rather than its subordination to gestures, movements and setting, is therefore far more complicated than at first it seems to be. For whilst such a choice clearly does not entail his abandonment of 'pure' stage elements the power of his purely poetic images threatens to engulf them. And at the same time the choice posits the terms in which, out of its failure to express, language may be re-created. This commits him to an intrinsically self-defeating process. For whilst admitting language to be the primary reality, he is deeply suspicious of the words at his disposal they are unable either to communicate or to express, and so they can only fail, even though verbal expression may be a compulsive need. It is precisely this impulse to speak, this sense of an undefined compulsion to speak, which allows Beckett to attain the apparently impossible, namely the verbal and visual articulation of an unverbalized, undifferentiated self.

In Beckett's plays, for the first time, theatre's potential is extended so as materially to present abstraction and absence, not just as partial components of the main body of speech but as the very subject matter of the drama and as the constitutive elements of dramatic language. 'Self' is seen as a tendency away from any particular spatial and temporal context, away from the concreteness of being and sensation which resides in chaos, mess and rubbish. The only material dimension it is capable of grasping is by virtue of its voice, its capacity to speak even when the whole body is reduced to a head protruding from a dustbin, as in Endgame, or to a pair of lips, as in Not I. Words are the condition. and substance of consciousness and consciousness the only register of existence. For Beckett the self cannot be defined in positivist terms, that is merely temporally and spatially.

It strives to exist in an undefined place, outside history, to reach a still point, a world of solitude and peace. The tragedy of the human situation, in his eyes, lies in the fact that language frustrates the very movement which it instigates, by tying us to an inauthentic non-self in the material world. Language only permits the articulation of self in relation to what it is not. Beckett's urge towards stillness and nothingness is in reality an all-pervading desire to transcend the socio-historically determined human condition in order to attain the realm of the real self. The process which runs parallel to this desire in his drama is that whereby theatrical language tries to break logical sequences and associations so as to express the movement and fluidity of consciousness.

And for Beckett the only process which corresponds to it is inwards and downwards: 'The only possible spiritual development is in the sense of depth. The artistic tendency is not expansive, but a contraction. And art is the apotheosis of solitude. There is no communication because there are no vehicles of communication.' Beckett's denial of the possibility of communication stems from his awareness that absolute meaning is absent from a world which is in itself the absence of the absolute. Language-as-communication therefore tends to become 'private' because the lack of any absolute external criteria to which it might be compared makes it inherently self-referential. Reality cannot, then, be artistically depicted, even in terms of a sterile description of external characteristics. Beckett's conviction that the subject's perception of a particular object destroys its relation to the object by transforming the object into a mere intellectual pretext, negates the possibility of experiential knowledge and the validity of experiential testimony. His rejection of Naturalism in art stems from a radical repudiation of its very basis, the assumption that the human mind is capable of capturing and accurately registering phenomena exterior to it. The cause of the absence of absolute meaning is precisely the intellect's inability to establish continuity with the world. The myth of the existence of a unique and totalized world collapses from the very moment that the relationship between reality and mind is disrupted. The two fragments start moving in parallel orbits without ever re-establishing their time-honoured continuity. Beckett's work is a testimony to what kind of human existence is possible within the gap created by the disruption of this previously unquestioned unity.

To a very large extent traditional Western thinking has been based upon attempts to formulate a principle of congruity between Cosmos and Logos. Truth has been identified with WHAT IS, that is with presence testified through the senses in this tradition WHAT IS NOT cannot be expressed because it is non-recognizable and unexplorable within the paradigm. According to Parmenides 'it is the same thing to think and to be,' and 'that which it is possible to think is identical with that which can be.' These statements delineate the nature of the world by ascribing to it a series of characteristics and simultaneously establishing man's relation to it.

If visibility and tangibility constitute reality, then absence is non-existence. If to be is synonymous with to think, then the world is intelligible to man, who by using his mind discovers meaning the path he follows is that of a strict causality already implicit in the initial assumption that equates presence with existence. Man thinks and speaks in harmony with this meaningful causal world of 'objective' phenomena thus verbal expression, being the extension of reality, reinforces the bipolar unity. Beckett's refusal of such tenets along with his rejection of Naturalist theatre effectively places him in a very different philosophical tradition a tradition which makes language its central and crucial concern. It is to this extent that the work of linguist Ferdinand de Saussure can help us in understanding the dynamics of Beckett's work. At the beginning of the present century he defined language as a system of differences, in which a series of binary oppositions sustains the verbal system, with oppositions between presence and absence and positive and negative being the most determinate ones.

Within these pairs of antithetical notions the one pole 'is apprehended as positively having a certain feature while the other is apprehended as deprived of the feature in question'. In Waiting for Godot Beckett embodies these specific binary oppositions in the very structure of the play. Didi and Gogo stand in opposition to Godot much as presence stands in opposition to absence in the Saussurean system. In line with our expectations Beckett thus deals with the structure and operation of language both at the level of dramatic speech and at the level of dramatic form, using the Saussurean model of presence and absence as a metaphor for his more traditional, sceptical view of perception. Only insofar as they can be seen can Didi and Gogo be sure about their own presence, their own existence. In the first of his 'Three Dialogues witrh Georges Duthuit' Beckett identifies nature as a composite of perceiver and perceived Waiting for Godot is built upon such a composite. Didi feels lonely when Gogo sleeps because so long as the perceiver (Gogo) does not see, then the perceived (Didi) cannot be sure if he lives.

Hence the violence of Didi's outburst to the boy in the second act: 'You're sure you saw me, you won't come and tell me tomorrow that you never saw me!'. Presence is always, however, dependent on absence the latter verifies the existence of the former because it is the very element which constitutes consciousness. Such a relationship, Saussure would argue, is inherent in any language which opposes person (I or thou) to non-person (he or it), the sign of an absence which can never embody itself as presence. Didi/Gogo are in a binary relationship with Godot incapable of dissociation because they are referential one to another. The play is predicated upon this awareness, either by means of direct references to their relation with him (Estragon: 'We're not tied!... Vladimir: But to whom. By whom? Estragon: To your man'.) or by incorporating the awareness into the texture of their dialogue. In this latter respect words seem to carry them away from the painful knowledge that they depend on Godot. Words enable them to recover from the consciousness of their difference from Godot at the moment of their utterance but their sense of difference cannot be removed because it is intrinsic to the very language they employ, woven into their very being.

Godot lives outside space in a feedom uncontrolled by temporal restrictions. He is an abstraction existing in the peace of Nothingness. He does nothing. Didi and Gogo are deprived of these specific features. As they move towards the zero point at which they would overlap with the opposite term, they still do something they wait, think, speak and move. Didi and Gogo are tangible presences compared with the zero point of Godot they are obviously 'positive'. The repetition of the word 'nothing' ('nothing to be done,' 'nothing to show' etc.) does not, then, express their actual situation, so much as their desire to become the nothing. The arrival of Godot would collapse the gulf between desire and actuality because it would render the two poles synonymous: presence would be absence, the positive would be zero.

Since Godot does not come, only language remains to articulate their difference from the desired absence-negativity. The circular structure of the play epitomizes the asymptotic and futile movement of the self towards a state of 'authentic being'. This structure challenges the basic assumption of the absolute world that nothingness is equal to non-existence and therefore cannot be experienced. The audience experiences the presence of absence in the lonely gestures of Didi and Gogo, in their tautologous utterances and in the long silences which condense what has, necessarily (given Beckett's views on language), remained unsaid. The recurrence of the phrase 'We are waiting for Godot,' which becomes synonymous with 'We are waiting for nothing,' establishes absence as the very element constitutive of Didi and Gogo's condition of existence. If, as Democritus says in one of Beckett's favourite quotations, 'Nothing is more real than nothing,' then it is impossible for man to make any positive statement.

When reality is not measured by time and is not limited by spatial boundaries but lies in an infinite time and an abstract space, then words can never be definite about a meaning which must perpetually elude them. The lack of a 'positive' meaning, or rather the existence of a reality difficult or impossible to articulate verbally, compels language to enter a process of self-repudiation. A word like 'unhappy,' for example, a word which inevitably bears an enormous sentimental burden, is too definite to remain unrefuted:

Estragon: I'm unhappy.
Vladimir: Not really! Since when?
Estragon: I'd forgotten.
Vladimi: Extraordinary the tricks that memory plays!

In this simple exchange each line obliterates the preceding one. Their language is constructed out of an abiding awareness of the nothing, their acceptance of an essential negativity which nullifies any hope of absolute meaning. These innocent, 'clarifying' questions disclose the hollowness of certain words which were basic to a world of 'inner spirit' but which now seem absurd: 'Vladimir:... Two thieves crucified at the same time as our Saviour. One - Estragon: Our what? Vladimir: Our Saviour'. The absence of any internal logic in this world or of belief in a supernatural power able to impose a spiritual order upon the mess makes man especially suspicious about those words which have been particularly heavily invested with meaning. At the same time this 'negative' consciousness entails a tormenting recognition on the part of Didi and Gogo of the uncertainty of their particular situation. They attempt to defer this uncertainty by resorting to a series of repetitions which give them the happy illusion of temporary affirmations yet these very repetitions are soon refuted by the recurrence of the specific word with which they began: 'Vladimir: Say, I am happy. Estragon: I am happy. Vladimir: So am I. Estragon: So am I. Vladimir: We are happy. Estragon: We are happy. (silence)'... The consolation that the recurrence of the same word appears to offer as something conceptually and audibly familiar is easily transformed into a menace for both speaker and listener the simplest words become grotesque and forbidding. Repetition, the factor which permits language to establish itself as a code, is used by Beckett as the means whereby it may be repudiated as a system of definite concepts.

In Waiting for Godot the catalysts of speech are 'Silence' and 'Pause,' the very elements which undermine the emotions to which the characters lay claim and which prevent them occupying any decisive area of commitment. Silence breaks the continuity of words and conveys meaning in its totality. The silences in Beckett's plays effectively 'bracket' the terms an audience might adopt in order to understand them the meaning is communicated by the intervals between words. In Didi and Gogo's dialogue about the dead voices the silences are evenly distributed, atomizing the exchange into fragments of cross-talk. The empty stage is filled for a moment with the presence of dead people, worn out voices, fragmented whispers, murmurs and rustlings, and this sudden proliferation of the thoughts, speech, and noises of dead people suffocates Didi and Gogo because they themselves are emblematic of that dead humanity.

Beckett stages the sounds of silence, the other side of language, and Didi and Gogo, in their yearning for authenticity, aspire to the point of overlap, to the zero, to the point where all difference is obliterated. It is a form of death-wish. The dead voices are heard inside their silences talking of the past, of dreams and hopes presence is once again commensurate with absence. Their words report what they hear, describe it, even criticise it. But absence is clearly part of their own language and is read out loud by them for the audience. Silence performs the structural function of integrating the dialogue in this respect it becomes as explicit as speech itself. The causal logic which says that 'what is not' cannot be experienced is here being radically subverted thought is no longer the servant of material presence and the conclusion is no longer dependent upon the premise. The terminal juxtaposition of 'Let's go' and the stage direction 'They do not move' disrupts the causality between language and gesture. Beckett has the body ignore and annul the language which normally instigates its physical action, once more emphatically relating the discontinuity to that between the basic levels of dramatic form.

Even when utterances appear to have a degree of connection with the stage directions there is a linguistic wit threatening to separate them. The words 'just the same' in the following extract play this role, mocking the attempt being made to establish difference, preference and temporal sequence: Pozzo: (having lit his pipe). The second is never so sweet... (he takes the pipe out of his mouth, contemplates it)... as the first, I mean. (He puts the pipe back in his mouth.) But it's sweet just the same. As words gradually acquire more and more independence from their task of inducing causality they are liberated to interact solely with one another. Didi and Gogo play incessantly with words they treat the same word as its opposite, they find synonyms, they use scientific terms because they sound bombastic, they rhyme. But at the same time they dismantle language into fragments of religious, moral and scientific thought. Biblical quotations ('Hope deferred maketh the something sick') are cited not for their meaning but for the gratification offered by their shape, their musical feeling and their evasive nostalgia.

By parodying the pretentious rhetoric and logic of conventional philosophical thinking they demystify Logos by questioning the very elements it is presumed to be endowed with: clarity, intelligibility, rationality, causality. The myth of meaning is demolished. To be replaced with what? The third of the Duthuit dialogues is unequivocal: 'The much to express, the little to express, the ability to express much, the ability to express little, merge in a common anxiety to express as much as possible, or as truly as possible, or as finely as possible, to the best of one's ability. It is above all, as commentators on the play have often stated, in Lucky's repetitious, bombastic, pseudo-scientific speech that Beckett congeals the disarticulation of the rational language inaugurated by Didi's playful dealings with quotations.

Here unmediated speech is used against the mediated language representative of conventional literary, religious and scientific discourses. Lucky's speech is not, however, merely anti-intellectual, however much it may situate the intellect as the domain responsible for the mind's appropriation of feelings and sensations. For Beckett the problem does not so much reside in the split between the mind and the body which language initiates, but rather in the specific mode of articulation of different discourses with each other for the synthesis of a rational Logos. Lucky systematically disconnects these various discourses from their 'spinal cord,' from their point of convergence: a conception of the world in terms defined by the presence of an absolute. The fragmentation and repetition of his speech reflect the linguisticintellectual chaos which results from the 'absolute absence of the absolute.' The 'absolute' organizes human Logos by imposing an internal order Lucky's speech deconstructs that unity, and with it the congruity of man with the absolute by which it is determined.

The speech starts with a hypothetical statement about the existence of a personal God, outside time, living in divine 'apathia' (non-responsiveness), divine 'aphasia' (speechlessness), and divine 'athambia' (lack of the capacity for amazement). This personal God loves us dearly, with some exceptions, but he does not communicate with us, cannot feel anything for us, and finally condemns us 'for reasons unknown'. In this respect he is utterly absent from that humanity which, deprived of the meaning its attachment to any absolute could provide, is scattered in pieces across philosophical, religious and scientific domains. Despite its apparent haphazardness, however, the speech is carefully structured around recurrent phrases and words. The particular phrase 'for reasons unknown' recurs more often than any other it functions as an effective condensation of Lucky's message to the audience - the impossibility of reasoning when causes are unintelligible. Beckett once said that 'there is an endless verbal germination, maturation, putrefaction, the cyclic dynamism of the intermediate,' and Lucky's speech is based precisely upon such a circular movement of language from its initial stage of exemplary articulation (scientific hypothesis) to its final decay (childish gibberish).

Human Logos might, we infer, progress towards its perfection insofar as it were able to reflect the internal unity of a world inspired by the absolute, but 'the personal God' (whether absent or present) is neither charitable, intelligent nor in the least bit interested in humanity: Logos as progress is subverted by Logos as regress. Lucky's reduction of speech to a chaotic juxtaposition of irrelevant words expresses the decay of one kind of order, but his 'think' also embodies the germination of another kind in Andrew Kennedy's words, 'the deteriorating syntax releases, as through fission, isolated word clusters which sound like the lost "true voice" in the speech'. In the event, however, even this 'true' voice in its linguistic anarchy fades away 'There is an end to his thinking' as Pozzo says. In Act II we find out that this has become a permanent condition for the dumb Lucky.

Lucky, the slave, has by this time lost the last index of his humanity, the ability to articulate words and thoughts, and definitively regressed to the animal condition which his role as slave implies. But, astonishingly enough, Lucky's deterioration is not accompanied by an concomitant increase in Pozzo's status as master. Pozzo has not only gone blind he is less articulate than he was in Act I. His loss of articulacy goes hand in hand with his loss of sight both are emblematic of Pozzo's having himself entered a world in which time and space are meaningless. For to be blind is to be unconscious of whether or not you are perceived by Godot, the timeless/ spaceless witness, whose coming would soothe the anxieties of uncertainty and confirm humanity's existence. Where there is hope for Didi and Gogo, for Pozzo there is only despair. Even if he is perceived by Lucky he can never be reassured that this is the case because Lucky is not in a position to articulate his presence. Furthermore, to be blind is to live in a void, to be unable to perceive either the passage of time or the change of place. The notion of time is even more meaningless than the notion of space because it can in no way be empirically experienced. Time division is arbitrary because it is established in terms of purely subjective criteria it is the result of a general concensus to accept a certain timing system as the most suitable for given social purposes. Hence Pozzo's outburst to Vladimir: Pozzo: (suddenly furious) have you not done tormenting me with your accursed time! It's abominable! When!... One day... like any other day, one day he went dumb, one day I went blind, one day we'll go deaf, one day we were born, one day we shall die, the same day, the same second,...

For the Pozzo who experiences the flow of time as a raw material there is nothing 'natural' in the names those with sight give to their time divisions. For him words like 'yesterday and 'today' do not correspond to any physical reality. Time is not for him equal to the hours, days and years which are the mere notation of its passing, its arbitrarily defined time-signs. Here Beckett penetrates to what really undermines the myth of a 'natural' language, the acceptance of the notion of the 'arbitrariness' of the sign. Pozzo's experience is of stopped time because in the absence of accredited divisions time cannot be experienced as a movement.

He reacts violently to the use of words like 'yesterday' and 'tomorrow' because language as expression has for him ceased to be related to experience in an unproblematically 'natural' manner. If space and time have been dismantled, so too has causality, and with it discourses structured around a coherent internal principle of the validity and efficiency of reasoning. Blind Pozzo, deprived of the experience of those essential notions sustaining rational discourse, is no longer articulate. In the past he derived authority from his eloquence, from his lyricism and from his ability to reason. These three qualities constitute what in Happy days finds its verbal and visual quintessence: the 'old style'.

The Pozzo of Act I seems to be a living embodiment of the 'old style'. He explains (!) the twilight in a lyrical spirit which cannot conceal his fundamentally positivist preconceptions. His speech is larded with phrases which carry a residual poetical feeling ('touch of autumn in the air this evening,' for example) and by witticisms of an ambiguous kind. This vocabulary is enriched with a variety of synonyms noisily put together so as to select the 'right one'. Thus 'impress' is rejected for 'mollify' and this in turn for 'cod' so that he may 'accurately' explain why Lucky 'does not make himself comfortable,' in other words why he suffers. For Pozzo even suffering can be attributed to the free choice of the victim through the distorting effects of reasoning: 'Why he doesn't make himself comfortable? Lets try and get it clear. Has he not the right to? Certainly he has.

It follows that he doesn't want to. There's reasoning for you'. By disclosing the ground against which 'reasoning' figures, Beckett shatters the illusion that causality is a straightforward and 'objective' mental process and demonstrates the contrary, namely that rational discourse effectively distorts reality because it claims to reflect it. This is the unacceptable face of 'the old style' as reflected in the theatrical language of nineteenth century realism. Pozzo's wit, lyricism and rationality are wiped out by his experience of approaching the zero degree. But even this experience can be dynamic, as Vladimir and Estragon have shown, for it can lead to the attempt to articulate new meanings in new ways.

In this respect Waiting for Godot inaugurates the project which underpins all of Beckett's subsequent drama: to present the search for self and meaning in terms of a dramatic language which derives its power from its own self-questioning coupled with its 'obligation to express'. At every level of organization we encounter 'the dynamism of the intermediate'. There are no fixed frames of reference. We are from the start trapped in the realm of human existence, oscillating between the poles of difference, between presence and absence, between self and other, at once longing for and fearing the apotheosis of the zero. It is in accordance with Beckett's views on such matters, as epitomized and dramatized in Waiting for Godot, that value should be seen to reside not so much in any result of the process as in the process itself.

Chapter 4

Introduction to Theater of Absurd

I. The West

'The Theatre of the Absurd' is a term coined by the critic Martin Esslin for the work of a number of playwrights, mostly written in the 1950s and 1960s. The term is derived from an essay by the French philosopher Albert Camus. In his 'Myth of Sisyphus', written in 1942, he first defined the human situation as basically meaningless and absurd. The 'absurd' plays by Samuel Beckett, Arthur Adamov, Eugene Ionesco, Jean Genet, Harold Pinter and others all share the view that man is inhabiting a universe with which he is out of key. Its meaning is indecipherable and his place within it is without purpose. He is bewildered, troubled and obscurely threatened.

The origins of the Theatre of the Absurd are rooted in the avant-garde experiments in art of the 1920s and 1930s. At the same time, it was undoubtedly strongly influenced by the traumatic experience of the horrors of the Second World War, which showed the total impermanence of any values, shook the validity of any conventions and highlighted the precariousness of human life and its fundamental meaninglessness and arbitrariness. The trauma of living from 1945 under threat of nuclear annihilation also seems to have been an important factor in the rise of the new theatre.

At the same time, the Theatre of the Absurd also seems to have been a reaction to the disappearance of the religious dimension form contemporary life. The Absurd Theatre can be seen as an attempt to restore the importance of myth and ritual to our age, by making man aware of the ultimate realities of his condition, by instilling in him again the lost sense of cosmic wonder and primeval anguish. The Absurd Theatre hopes to achieve this by shocking man out of an existence that has become trite, mechanical and complacent. It is felt that there is mystical experience in confronting the limits of human condition.

As a result, absurd plays assumed a highly unusual, innovative form, directly aiming to startle the viewer, shaking him out of this comfortable, conventional life of everyday concerns. In the meaningless and Godless post-Second-World-War world, it was no longer possible to keep using such traditional art forms and standards that had ceased being convincing and lost their validity. The Theatre of the Absurd openly rebelled against conventional theatre. Indeed, it was anti-theatre. It was surreal, illogical, conflictless and plotless. The dialogue seemed total gobbledygook. Not unexpectedly, the Theatre of the Absurd first met with incomprehension and rejection.

One of the most important aspects of absurd drama was its distrust of language as a means of communication. Language had become a vehicle of conventionalised, stereotyped, meaningless exchanges. Words failed to express the essence of human experience, not being able to penetrate beyond its surface. The Theatre of the Absurd constituted first and foremost an onslaught on language, showing it as a very unreliable and insufficient tool of communication. Absurd drama uses conventionalised speech, clichés, slogans and technical jargon, which is distorts, parodies and breaks down.

By ridiculing conventionalised and stereotyped speech patterns, the Theatre of the Absurd tries to make people aware of the possibility of going beyond everyday speech conventions and communicating more authentically. Conventionalised speech acts as a barrier between ourselves and what the world is really about: in order to come into direct contact with natural reality, it is necessary to discredit and discard the false crutches of conventionalised language. Objects are much more important than language in absurd theatre: what happens transcends what is being said about it.

It is the hidden, implied meaning of words that assume primary importance in absurd theatre, over an above what is being actually said. The Theatre of the Absurd strove to communicate an undissolved totality of perception - hence it had to go beyond language.

Absurd drama subverts logic. It relishes the unexpected and the logically impossible. According to Sigmund Freud, there is a feeling of freedom we can enjoy when we are able to abandon the straitjacket of logic. In trying to burst the bounds of logic and language the absurd theatre is trying to shatter the enclosing walls of the human condition itself.

Our individual identity is defined by language, having a name is the source of our separateness - the loss of logical language brings us towards a unity with living things. In being illogical, the absurd theatre is anti-rationalist: it negates rationalism because it feels that rationalist thought, like language, only deals with the superficial aspects of things. Nonsense, on the other hand, opens up a glimpse of the infinite. It offers intoxicating freedom, brings one into contact with the essence of life and is a source of marvellous comedy.

There is no dramatic conflict in the absurd plays. Dramatic conflicts, clashes of personalities and powers belong to a world where a rigid, accepted hierarchy of values forms a permanent establishment. Such conflicts, however, lose their meaning in a situation where the establishment and outward reality have become meaningless. However frantically characters perform, this only underlines the fact that nothing happens to change their existence. Absurd dramas are lyrical statements, very much like music: they communicate an atmosphere, an experience of archetypal human situations. The Absurd Theatre is a theatre of situation, as against the more conventional theatre of sequential events. It presents a pattern of poetic images. In doing this, it uses visual elements, movement, light. Unlike conventional theatre, where language rules supreme, in the Absurd Theatre language is only one of many components of its multidimensional poetic imagery.

The Theatre of the Absurd is totally lyrical theatre which uses abstract scenic effects, many of which have been taken over and modified from the popular theatre arts: mime, ballet, acrobatics, conjuring, music-hall clowning. Much of its inspiration comes from silent film and comedy, as well as the tradition of verbal nonsense in early sound film (Laurel and Hardy, W C Fields, the Marx Brothers). It emphasises the importance of objects and visual experience: the role of language is relatively secondary. It owes a debt to European pre-war surrealism: its literary influences include the work of Franz Kafka. The Theatre of the Absurd is aiming to create a ritual-like, mythological, archetypal, allegorical vision, closely related to the world of dreams.

Some of the Predecessors of Absurd Drama

- In the realm of verbal nonsense: François Rabelais, Lewis Carroll and Edward Lear. Many serious poets occasionally wrote nonsense poetry (Johnson, Charles Lamb, Keats, Hugo, Byron, Thomas Hood). One of the greatest masters of nonsense poetry was the German poet Christian Morgernstern (1871-1914). Ionesco found the work of S J Perelman (i.e. the dialogues of the Marx Brothers' films) a great inspiration for his work.
- The world of allegory, myth and dream: The tradition of the world as a stage and life as a dream goes back to Elizabethan times. Baroque allegorical drama shows the world in terms of mythological archetypes: John Webster, Cyril Tourneur, Calderon, Jakob Biederman. With the decline of allegory, the element of fantasy prevails (Swift, Hugh Walpole).
- In some 18 and 19 Century works of literature we find sudden transformation of characters and nightmarish shifts of time and place (E T A Hoffman, Nerval, Aurevilly). Dreams are featured in many theatrical pieces, but it had to wait for Strindberg to produce the masterly transcriptions of dreams and obsessions that have become a direct source of the Absurd Theatre. Strindberg, Dostoyevsky, Joyce and Kafka created archetypes: by delving into their own

subconscious, they discovered the universal, collective significance of their own private obsessions. In the view of Mircea Eliade, myth has never completely disappeared on the level of individual experience. The Absurd Theatre sought to express the individual's longing for a single myth of general validity. The above-mentioned authors anticipated this.

Alfred Jarry is an important predecessor of the Absurd Theatre. His UBU ROI (1896) is a mythical figure, set amidst a world of grotesque archetypal images. Ubu Roi is a caricature, a terrifying image of the animal nature of man and his cruelty. (Ubu Roi makes himself King of Poland and kills and tortures all and sundry. The work is a puppet play and its décor of childish naivety underlines the horror.) Jarry expressed man's psychological states by objectifying them on the stage. Similarly, Franz Kafka's short stories and novels are meticulously exact descriptions of archetypal nightmares and obsessions in a world of convention and routine.

- 20 Century European avant-garde: For the French avant-garde, myth and dream was of utmost importance: the surrealists based much of their artistic theory on the teachings of Freud and his emphasis on the role of the subconscious. The aim of the avant-garde was to do away with art as a mere imitation of appearances. Apollinaire demanded that art should be more real than reality and deal with essences rather than appearances. One of the more extreme manifestations of the avant-garde was the Dadaist movement, which took the desire to do away with obsolete artistic conventions to the extreme. Some Dadaist plays were written, but these were mostly nonsense poems in dialogue form, the aim of which was primarily to 'shock the bourgeois audience'. After the First World War, German Expressionism attempted to project inner realities and to objectify thought and feeling. Some of Brecht's plays are close to Absurd Drama, both in their clowning and their music-hall humour and the preoccupation with the problem of identity of the self and its fluidity. French surrealism acknowledged the subconscious mind as a great, positive healing force. However, its contribution to the sphere of drama was meagre: indeed it can be said that the Absurd Theatre of the 1950s and 1960s was a Belated practical realisation of the principles formulated by the Surrealists as early as the 1930s. In this connection, of particular importance were the theoretical writings of Antonin Artaud. Artaud fully rejected realism in the theatre, cherishing a vision of a stage of magical beauty and mythical power. He called for a return to myth and magic and to the exposure of the deepest conflicts within the human mind. He demanded a theatre that would produce collective archetypes, thus creating a new mythology. In his view, theatre should pursue the aspects of the internal world. Man should be considered metaphorically in a wordless language of shapes, light, movement and gesture. Theatre should aim at expressing what language is incapable of putting into words. Artaud forms a bridge between the inter-war avant-garde and the post-Second-World-War Theatre of the Absurd.

Chapter 5

The Theatre of the Absurd- the West and the East

II. The East

At the time when the first absurd plays were being written and staged in Western Europe in the late 1940s and early 1950s, people in the East European countries suddenly found themselves thrown into a world where absurdity was an integral part of everyday living. Suddenly, you did not need to be an abstract thinker in order to be able to reflect upon absurdity: the experience of absurdity became part and parcel of everybody's existence.

Hitler's attempt to conquer Russia during the Second World War gave Russia a unique opportunity to extend its sphere of influence and at the same time to 'further the cause of [the Soviet brand of] socialism'. In the final years of the war, Stalin turned the war of the defeat of Nazism into the war of conquest of Central Europe and the war of the division of Europe. In pursuing Hitler's retreating troops, the Russian Army managed to enter the territory of the Central European countries and to remain there, with very few exceptions, until now. The might of the Russian Army made it possible for Stalin to establish rigidly ideological pro-Soviet regimes, hermetically sealed from the rest of Europe.

The Central European countries, whose pre-war political systems ranged from feudal monarchies (Rumania), semi-authoritarian states (Poland) through to a parliamentary Western-type democracy (Czechoslovakia) were now subjected to a militant Sovietisation. The countries were forced to undergo a major traumatic political and economic transformation. The Western Theatre of the Absurd highlighted man's fundamental bewilderment and confusion, stemming from the fact that man has no answers to the basic existential questions: why we are alive, why we have to die, why there is injustice and suffering. East European Soviet-type socialism proudly proclaimed that it had answers to all these questions and, moreover, that it was capable of eliminating suffering and setting all injustices right.

To doubt this was subversive. Officially, it was sufficient to implement a grossly simplified formula of Marxism to all spheres of life and Paradise on Earth would ensue. It became clear very soon that this simplified formula offered even fewer real answers than various esoteric and complex Western philosophical systems and that its implementation by force brought enormous suffering.

From the beginning it was clear that the simplified idea was absurd: yet it was made to dominate all spheres of life. People were expected to shape their lives according to its dictates and to enjoy it. It was, and still is, an offence to be sceptical about Soviet-type socialism if you are a citizen of an East-European country. The sheer fact that the arbitrary formula of simplified Marxism was made to dominate the lives of millions of people, forcing them to behave against their own nature, brought the absurdity of the formula into sharp focus for these millions. Thus the Soviet-type system managed to bring the experience of what was initially a matter of concern for only a small number of sensitive individuals in the West to whole nations in the East.

This is not to say that the absurdity of life as experienced in the East differs in any way from the absurdity of life as it is experienced in the West. In both parts of the world it stems from the ambiguity of man's position in the universe, from his fear of death and from his instinctive yearning for the Absolute. It is just that official East-European practices, based on a contempt for the fundamental existential questions and on a primitive and arrogant faith in the power of a simplified idea, have created a reality which makes absurdity a primary and deeply-felt, intrinsic experience for anybody who comes in contact with that reality.

To put it another way: the western Theatre of the Absurd may be seen as the expression of frustration and anger of a handful of intellectuals over the fact that people seem to lead uninspired, second-rate and stereotyped existences, either by deliberate choice or because they do not know any better and have no idea how or ability by which to help themselves. Although such anger may sound smug and condescending, it is really mixed with despair. And when we look at Eastern Europe, we realise that these intellectuals are justified in condemning lives of mediocrity, even though many people in the West seem to lead such lives quite happily and without any awareness of the absurdity. In Eastern Europe, second-rateness has been elevated to a single, sacred, governing principle. There, mediocrity rules with a rod of iron. Thus it can be seen clearly what it can achieve. As a result, unlike in the West, may people in the East seem to have discovered that it is very uncomfortable to live under the command of second-rateness.

(The fact that mediocrity is harmful to life comes across so clearly in Eastern Europe either because East-European second-rateness is much harsher than the mild, West-European, consumerist mediocrity, or simply because it is a single, totalitarian second-rateness, obligatory for all. A single version of a simple creed cannot suit all, its insufficiencies immediately show. This is not the case if everybody is allowed to choose their own simplified models and prejudices which suit their individual needs, the way it is in the West - thus their insufficiencies are not immediately noticeable.)

The rise of the Theatre of the Absurd in the East is connected with the period of relative relaxation of the East European regimes after Stalin's death. In the first decade after the communist take-over of power, it would have been impossible for anyone to write anything even distantly based on his experiences of life after the take-over without endangering his personal safety. The arts, as indeed all other spheres of life, were subject to rigid political control and reduced to serving blatant ideological and propagandistic aims. This was the period when feature films were made about happy workers in a steelworks, or about a village tractor driver who after falling in love with his tractor becomes a member of the communist party, etc. All the arts assumed rigidly conservative, 19-Century realist forms, to which a strong political bias was added. 20 -Century developments, in particular the inter-war experiments with structure and form in painting and poetry were outlawed as bourgeois decadence.

In the years after Stalin's death in 1953, the situation slowly improved. The year 1956 saw two major attempts at liberalisation within the Soviet Bloc: the Hungarian revolution was defeated, while the Polish autumn managed to introduce a measure of normalcy into the country which lasted for several years. Czechoslovakia did not see the first thaw until towards the end of the 1950s: genuine liberalisation did not start gaining momentum until 1962-63. Hence it was only in the 1960s that the first absurdist plays could be written and staged in Eastern Europe. Even so, the Theatre of the Absurd remained limited to only two East European countries, those that were the most liberal at the time: Poland and Czechoslovakia.

The East European Absurd Theatre was undoubtedly inspired by Western absurd drama, yet it differed from it considerably in form, meaning and impact. Although East European authors and theatre producers were quite well acquainted with many West-European absurd plays from the mid to late 1950s onwards, nevertheless (with very few exceptions) these plays were not performed or even translated in Eastern Europe until the mid-1960s. The reasons for this were several. First, West-European absurd drama was regarded by East-European officialdom as the epitome of West-European bourgeois capitalist decadence and, as a result, East European theatrical producers would be wary of trying to stage a condemned play - such an act would blight their career once and for all, ensuring that they would never work in theatre again. The western absurdist plays were regarded a nihilistic and anti-realistic, especially after Kenneth Tynan had attacked Ionesco as the apostle of anti-realism: this attach was frequently used by the East European officialdom for condemning Western absurd plays.

Secondly, after a decade or more of staple conservative realistic bias, there were fears among theatrical producers that the West European absurd plays might be regarded as far too avantgarde and esoteric by the general public. Thirdly, there was an atmosphere of relative optimism in Eastern Europe in the late 1950s and the 1960s. It was felt that although life under Stalin's domination had been terrible, the bad times were now past after the dictator's death and full liberalisation was only a matter of time. The injustices and deficiencies of the East European systems were seen as due to human frailty rather than being a perennial metaphysical condition: it was felt that sincere and concerted human effort was in the long run going to be able to put all wrongs right. In a way, this was a continuation of the simplistic Stalinist faith in man's total power over his predicament. From this point of view, it was felt that most Western absurdist plays were too pessimistic, negative and destructive. It was argued (perhaps partially for official consumption) that the East European absurdist plays, unlike their Western counterparts, constituted constructive criticism.

The line of argument of reformist, pro-liberalisation Marxists in Czechoslovakia in the early 1960s ran as follows: The Western Theatre of the Absurd recorded the absurdity of human existence as an immutable condition. It was a by-product of the continuing disintegration of capitalism. Western absurd plays were irrelevant in Eastern Europe, since socialist society had already found all answers concerning man's conduct and the meaning of life in general. Unlike its Western counterpart, East European absurd drama was communicating constructive criticism of the deformation of Marxism by the Stalinists. All that the East-European absurdist plays were trying to do was to remove minor blemishes on the face of the Marxist model - and that was easily done.

It was only later that some critics were able to point out that West European absurd dram was not in fact nihilistic and destructive and that it played the same constructive roles as East European drama attempted to play. At this stage, it was realised that the liberal Marxist analysis of East European absurd drama was incorrect: just as with its Western counterpart, the East European absurdist theatre could be seen as a comment on the human condition in general - hence its relevance also for the West.

On the few occasions that Western absurdist plays were actually staged in Eastern Europe, the East European audiences found the plays highly relevant. A production of Waiting for Godot in Poland in 1956 and in Slovakia in 1969, for instance, both became something nearing a political demonstration. Both the Polish and Slovak audiences stressed that for them, this was a play about hope - hope against hope.

The tremendous impact of these productions in Eastern Europe can be perhaps compared with the impact of Waiting for Godot on the inmates of a Californian penitentiary, when it was staged there in 1957. Like the inmates of a gaol, people in Eastern Europe are possibly also freer of the numbing concerns of everyday living than the average Western man in the street. Since they live under pressure, this somehow brings them closer to the bare essentials of life and they are therefore more receptive to the works that deal with archetypal existential situations than is the case with an ordinary Wes-European citizen.

On the whole, East European absurd drama has been far less abstract and esoteric than its West European counterpart. Moreover, while the West European drama is usually considered as having spent itself by the end of the 1960s, several East European authors have been writing highly original plays in the absurdisy mould, well into the 1970s.

The main difference between the West European and the East European plays is that while the West European plays deal with a predicament of an individual or a group of individuals in a situation stripped to the bare, and often fairly abstract and metaphysical essentials, the East European plays mostly show and individual trapped within the cogwheels of a social system. The social context of the West European absurd plays is usually subdued and theoretical: in the East European plays it is concrete, menacing and fairly realistic: it is usually covered by very transparent metaphors. The social context is shown as a kind of Catch-22 system - it is a set of circumstances whose joint impact crushes the individual. The absurdity of the social system is highlighted and frequently shown as the result of the actions of stupid, misguided or evil people - this condemnation is of course merely implicit. Although the fundamental absurdity of the life feature in these plays is not intended to be metaphysically conditioned - these are primarily pieces of social satire - on reflection, the viewer will realise that there is fundamentally no difference between the 'messages' of the West European and the East European plays - except that the East European plays may be able to communicate these ideas more pressingly and more vividly to their audiences, because of their first-hand everyday experience of the absurdity that surrounds them.

At the end of the 1960s, the situation in Eastern Europe changed for the worse. After the invasion of Czechoslovakia in 1968, it became apparent that Russia would not tolerate a fuller liberalisation of the East European countries. Czechoslovakia was thrown into a harsh, neo-Stalinist mould, entering the time capsule of stagnating immobility, in which it has remained ever since. Since it had been primarily artists and intellectuals that were spearheading the liberalising reforms of the 1960s, the arts were now subjected to a vicious purge. Many well-known artists and intellectuals were turned into non-persons practically overnight: some left or were later forced to lea the country.

All the Czechoslovak absurdist playwrights fell into the non-person category. It is perhaps quite convincing evidence of the social relevance of their plays that the establishment feared them so much it felt the need to outlaw them. Several of the banned authors have continued writing, regardless of the fact that their plays cannot be staged in Czechoslovakia at present. They have been published and produced in the West.

As in the 1960s, these authors are still deeply socially conscious: for instance, Václav Havel, in the words of Martin

Esslin, 'one of the most promising European playwrights of today', is a courageous defender of basic human values and one of the most important (and most thoughtful) spokespersons of the non-establishment groupings in Czechoslovakia. By contrast, the Polish absurdist playwrights have been able to continue working in Poland undisturbed since the early 1960s, their plays having been normally published and produced within the country even throughout he 1970s.

It is perhaps quite interesting that even the Western absurd dramatists have gradually developed a need to defend basic human values. They have been showing solidarity with their East European colleagues. Ionesco was always deeply distrustful of politics and the clichéd language of the political establishment. Harold Pinter, who took part in a radio production of one of Václav Havel's plays from the 1970s several years ago, has frequently spoken in support of the East European writers and playwrights. Samuel Beckett has written a short play dedicated to Havel, which was staged in France in 1984 during a ceremony at the University of Toulouse, which awarded Havel an honorary doctorate.

Chapter 6

Absurdity of Absurd: Samuel Beckett's Waiting for Godot

What does Absurd mean ?When I searched the glossaries,I found the word to be out of harmony. But yet the definitions trying hard to explain the term, just to end in total Absurdity (assuming for a while that we know the meaning of the word),as they talk in total sense, the nonsense about it and of course that means they fail(in their attempt).But considering the term to be linked with literature (and other forms of art too!),when I searched for more I came across the lines that states that no literary criticism in which I include the attempts to explain the literary terms can take the literary work itself,or to be more specific it literary criticism is not substitute for reading the work itself,as it the piece of work is the most exactly and precisely,the thought conveyed or explained. So, I reached the idea that to understand absurd.I must view an absurd work by an artist, rather than poring over the talks about it. Hence as a literary student what first came to my mind at this instant is none, but WAITING FOR GODOT by Samuel Beckett,the so called absurd play structured around Godot,the axis all absurdity as till the date none could declare with confidence who or what Godot is !

What I found in the dustbin of my memories about this godot is: "On 19 Nov 1957, a group of worried actors were preparing to face their audience. The actors were members of the company of the San Francisco Actors Workshop. The audience consisted of fourteen hundred convicts at the San Quentin penitentiary. No live play had been preformed at San

Quentin since Sarah Bernhardt appeared there in 1913.Now,fourty four years later,the play that had been chosen,largely because no woman appeared in it, was Samuel Becketts WAITING FOR GODOT. "Beckett real triumph,came when WAITING FOR GODOT which appeared in book form in 1952,was first produced on 5 January 1953, at the little Theatre de Babylone (now defunct),

And I found also some lines of this play:

ESTRGON:Didi.

VLADIMIR:Yes.

ESTRGON:I cant go on like this.

VLADIMIR: Thats what you think.

ESTRAGON:If we parted?That might be better of us.

VLADIMIR:Well hang ourselves tomorrow.(Pause)Unless Godot comes.

ESTRAGON:And if comes?

VLADIMIR:Well be saved

It is said about Beckett that when he was asked that what he meant by Godot he answered "If I knew,I would have said so in the play". WAITING FOR GODOT does not tell a story it explores a static situation.So it is clear from the very beginning that Beckett tried to create a character with out a character as he himself doesnt know him Godot, and again the movement of plot tends to zero,i.e. there is absolutely no plot. Previously it was taken for granted that if there exits a literary piece then there must be either a story(or plot) to tellor any character to be represented.But did exactly opposite to revolutionize his concept.He presents a character whom he himself does not know and tell a plot which is nothing but variations in arrangements and sequences of few events with negligible movement or action:nothing happens, nobody comes nobody goes.

But can be the term Absurd assigned to merely these qualities of the play? No, there are still more as mentioned by critics.In an essay on Kalfka,Ionesco defined his understanding of the term as Absurd is that which is devoid of purpose. And the purposeless becomes evident when the more things change, the more they are the same.And this is done by creating uncommon situations in the play by Breckett. For instance the boy who carries message of Godot to Estragon and Vladimir fails to recognize them on each day of his reappearance."The French version explicitly states that the boy who appears in the second act is the same boy as the one in the first act, yet the boy denies that he has even seen the two tramps before, and insists that this is the first time he has acted as Godots messenger.And this is done while waiting which is interpreted by Martin Esslin as Waiting is to experience the action of time, which is constant change. And yet, as nothing real ever happens, the change is itself an illusion.The ceaseless activity of time is a self defeating purposeless.

And thus by this purposelessness Beckett tries to prove the absurdity of his play.But is this really absurd ? If we view it from some different point of views we can suddenly find something contradicting. It is because we know the fact that truth is never real,and what we define for a situation becomes a truth for us, for that moment. So is the case of abnormality or normality of a situation. When any action is most common that becomes normal for us and this is the very base of our understanding.We understand what is most common and general.We understand something uncommon by referring it to some common things or actions we understand.So our very base of understanding is based upon some general truth or common events,the state which we call normal.

Now when we something out of order in a play (e.g. WAITIG FOR GODOT),we interpret it in terms of those commons of our memory.But on this view we analyze, can uncommon or absurdity be perceived by us directly without any aid or reference to our definition of normality ? It is similar to what Rene Wellek tried to explain in his essay ATTACK ON LITERATURE by citing an example of Samuel Becketts ENDGAME.Becket has portrayed a character in END GAME who was looking for the voice of his silence.The artists dissatisfaction with language can only be expressed by language.Pause may be a device to express the inexpressible,but pause cant be prolonged indefinitely,can not be simply silence as such. It needs contrast, it needs a beginning and an end. This statement suggests the importance of contrast and this is as true in case of absurdity and non-absurdity as it is true in the case of silence and music.

In this light we can reach decision that there is no sense of absurdity with out the normality. But how this is true in case of Godot can be analysed as follows:

Beckett tries hard to achieve absurdity by doing through his characters, the abnormal things (or at least normal things in abnormal sequence), still there remains the elements of non-absurdity in every corner of the play. The boy who doesnt recognize the two tramps bring message from the same Godot (It never happens ever that Godot brings a message from the boy or the tramps bring message from the boy to godot or tramps speak out the message that the boy brings from the Godot for them or Godot never receives message from tramps and so many can be the absurd case).It was only one angle of interpretation of the situation.

Other interpretations can be many in numbers:Godot waits for tramps or tramps dont wait for Godot while they say they waited. etc. When I mean to say is that whatever action is done in the play has there fore the elements of non-absurdity.We could have recognized them if what we call absurdity would be the most normal and what we now feel normal would have been absurd.In fact we cant express absurdity itself and this is the deceiving nature of Absurdity, because the moment we speak out something it becomes a little different from what we originally meant to express. Words, the medium of fiction,are a fabrication of man's intellect.They are a part of human lie. And for this reason any literature needs that medium to be expressed, that becomes deceptive.So Roland Barthes of France says therefore that Literature is a system of deceptive signification emphatically signifying,but never finally signified.

There fore what ever actions Beckett tried to fabricated in to the play, stands till today between in the limits of absurd and non-absurd and how this action is nearer to any of these two limits depends on what words are used and how they are used to define the limits.

Thats why the play of the supposedly esoteric avant-grade make so imidiate and so deep an impact on an audience of convicts,where as the critics could not easily accepted the play as an art in the beginning.

Martin Esslin writes: because it confronted them the prisoners with a situation in some ways analogous to their own ? Perhaps. Or perhaps because they were un sophisticated enough to come to the theater without any preconceived notions and readymade expectations,so that they avoided the mistake that trapped so many established critics who condemned the play for its lack of plot,development, characterizations, suspense or plain common sense. And of course this is what we see as the attempt to define absurd with non-absurd.Similarly many other attempts have been made in the past and present to create uncommon out of common.For example the Dadaist Movement. Attempts have been made not only to widen the realm of art,but to abolish the boundery between the art and the non-art. In music, noises of machines or the streets are used in painting, collage uses stuck-on news papers, buttons, medals and so on, or found objects soup cans, bicycle wheels, electric bulbs, any piece of junksare exhibited. the newest fad is earth works, holes or trenches in the ground, tracks through a corn field, square sheets of leads in snow. A sculptor, Christo wrapped a million square feet of Australian coastline in plastic. At 1972 Bicnnale in Venice, a painter,Gino de Dominicis, exhibited a mongoloid picked up from the streets as a work of art.In poetry poems have been concocted by the Dadaists by drawing news paper clippings from a bag at random more recently poems have been produced by computer and a shuffle novel (by Marc Saporta) has appeared, in which every page can be replaced by another in any order.

Similarly we can cite the example of Pop-Culture now so popular by the young generations,which was once considered as absurd.So what conclusion we reached can be seen in the light of that contrast theory of silence and music told in this essay in the beginning, that what ever we want to express (may it be Silence or Absurdity) we need words to express. But a word can never be a thing.So we can either achieve a situation or express it, but we can not do both because, if we try to do, the situation wont be the same.This is what we can imply when we speak of absurdity i.e. we cant be totally absured in expression as there is no proper medium exists.

Chapter 7

Plot Synopsis

THE plot of Samuel Beckett's Waiting for Godot is simple to relate. Two tramps are waiting by a sickly looking tree for the arrival of M. Godot. They quarrel, make up, contemplate suicide, try to sleep, eat a carrot and gnaw on some chicken bones. Two other characters appear, a master and a slave, who perform a grotesque scene in the middle of the play. A young boy arrives to say that M. Godot will not come today, but that he will come tomorrow. The play is a development of the title, Waiting for Godot. He does not come and the two tramps resume their vigil by the tree, which between the first and second day has sprouted a few leaves, the only symbol of a possible order in a thoroughly alienated world.

The two tramps of Beckett, in their total disposition and in their antics with hats and tight shoes, are reminiscent of Chaplin and the American burlesque comedy team. Pozzo and Lucky, the master and slave, are half vaudeville characters and half marionettes. The purely comic aspect of the play involves traditional routines that come from the entire history of farce, from the Romans and the Italians, and the red-nosed clown of the modern circus. The language of the play has gravity, intensity, and conciseness. The long speech of Lucky, a bravura passage that is seemingly meaningless, is strongly reminiscent of Joyce and certain effects in Finnegans Wake. But the play is far from being a pastiche. It has its own beauty and suggestiveness, and it makes its own comment on man's absurd hope and on the absurd insignificance of man.

The utter simplicity of the play, in the histrionic sense, places it in the classical tradition of French playwriting. It's close adherence to the three unities is a clue to the play's dramaturgy. The unity of place is a muddy plateau with one tree, a kind of gallows which invites the tramps to consider hanging themselves. This place is any place. It is perhaps best characterized as being the place where Godot is not. As the play unfolds we come to realize that M. Godot is not in any place comparable to the setting of the play.

He will not come out of one place into another. The unity of time is two days, but it might be any sequence of days in anyone's life. Time is equivalent to what is announced in the title: the act of waiting. Tame is really immobility, although a few minor changes do take place during the play: the tree grows leaves and one of the characters, Pozzo, becomes blind. The act of waiting is never over, and yet it mysteriously starts up again each day. The action, in the same way, describes a circle. Each day is the return to the beginning. Nothing is completed because nothing can be completed. The despair in the play, which is never defined as such but which pervades all the lack of action and gives the play its metaphysical colour, is the fact that the two tramps cannot not wait for Godot, and the corollary fact that he cannot come.

The rigorous use of the unities is demanded by the implacable interpretation of human life. The denouement of the play is another beginning. Vladimir asks his friend: Alors? On y va? ("Well? Shall we go?") And Estragon answers: Allons-y ("Yes, let's go.") But neither moves. And the curtain descends over their immobility. In scene after scene the permanent absurdity of the world is stressed. In the scene, for example, between the master and the slave, Lucky is held on a leash by Pozzo. He carries a heavy suitcase without ever thinking of dropping it. He is able to utter his long incoherent speech only when he has his hat on and when Pozzo commands him to think.

The unity of place, the particular site on the edge of a forest which the two tramps cannot leave, recalls Sartre's striking use of the unity of place in his first play, No Exit. There it is hell in the appearance of a Second Empire living-room that the three characters cannot leave. The curtain line of each play underscores the unity of place, the setting of which is prison. The Allons-y! of Godot corresponds to the Eh bien, continuons! ("Well, well, let's get on with it....") of No Exit. Sartre's hell is projected by use of some of the quid pro quos of a typical bedroom farce, whereas Beckett's unnamed plateau resembles the empty vaudeville stage. The two tramps in a seemingly improvised dialogue arouse laughter in their public, despite their alienation from the social norm and despite the total pessimism of their philosophy.

Many ingenious theories have been advanced to provide satisfactory interpretations for the characters of Beckett's play. Religious or mythical interpretations prevail. The two tramps Estragon (Gogo) and Vladimir (Didi) may be Everyman and his conscience. Gogo is less confident and at one moment is ready to hang himself. Vladimir is more hopeful, more even in temperament. One thinks of the medieval debate between the body and the soul, between the intellectual and the nonrational in man. Certain of their speeches about Christ might substantiate the theory that they are the two crucified thieves. Pozzo would seem to be the evil master, the exploiter. But perhaps he is Godot, or an evil incarnation of Godot. The most obvious interpretation of Godot is that he is God. As the name Pierrot comes from Pierre, so Godot may come from God. (One thinks also of the combination of God and Charlot, the name used by the French for Charlie Chaplin.)

Mr. Beckett himself has repudiated all theories of a symbolic nature. But this does not necessarily mean that it is useless to search for such clues. The fundamental imagery of the play is Christian. Even the tree recalls the Tree of Knowledge and the Cross. The life of the tramps at many points in the text seems synonymous with the fallen state of man. Their strange relationship is a kind of marriage. The play is a series of actions that are aborted and that give a despairing uniformity to its duration.

Samuel Beckett's Waiting for Godot

An empty road, a single tree, a friends company. These sickly rewards are the ones given to men, theorizes Samuel

Beckett in Waiting for Godot, when they wait for the arrival of God. Stark barren surroundings and perpetual loneliness are the only gift, in Beckett's mind, when one waits for a supernatural being who does not deign to visit mere mortals. This aloof and impersonal deity is symbolized in the aptly named character of Godot, who restricts the plot of the play. He keeps Vladimir and Estragon from taking action, strands the theme in an unending wait for supernatural meaning, and restricts the characters' development by keeping their thoughts turned towards the always-impending appointment.

Vladimir and Estragon are the pinnacle of human indecisiveness-while vowing several times to leave their barren and lifeless surroundings, they dare not flinch or move a muscle lest they offend Godot or miss a promised appointment. Mired by vows and politeness, they take no action with deep meaning, nor do they change their surroundings with the clarion call of thier existence. Instead, the feeble whistle of their purpose is lost in the oppressive, stifling silence of unanswered questions. By refusing to come or even acknowledge their arrival with more than a small messenger boy, Godot prevents any climax in the plot. In Beckett's estimation, the search for a caring God keeps humankind from making a difference in the world - the only purpose for life in the existentialist worldview.

Likewise, the play is shackled to a single, mind-numbing pattern by Godot's refusal to arrive. Certainly the arrival of their eagerly-awaited guest would bring the plot to a conclusion and perhaps allow the introduction of purpose and meaning. But without his star appearance, the play's theme is left wandering like the Israelites in the desert of normalcy - surviving only on the manna of Pozzo's ritual appearance. Just as the play's theme leads nowhere and circles back in on itself, Beckett believes that mankind's quest for an uncaring God will lead nowhere and will not provide more meaning for life.

The play's twin protagonists, Vladimir and Estragon, are similarly deprived of a chance to develop and grow. Estragon always reacts the same to Vladimir's news that they must continue waiting, and both keep their nervous habit of inspecting hats and boots. Only late in the play does Vladimir realize their impending doom, and it does not impress or even draw a reaction from his longtime friend. They are shallow two-dimensional characters, robbed of a chance to develop and grow by the continual wait for an appointment that wil never be kept, a time that will never be reached. Without the arrival of God in the character Godot, they are not free to take risks or even leave their surroundings for more stimulating climes.

Men are doomed, according to Beckett, to face the same fate as Vladimir and Estragon. Without the closure provided by God's arrival their action is held back, their meaning unfound, their personal development halted. And in the view of existentialists Mr. Godot will never keep his appointment, and curse all men to a pointless existence.

Chapter 8

Characters

Vladimir

One of the two main characters of the play. Estragon calls him Didi, and the boy addresses him as Mr. Albert. He seems to be the more responsible and mature of the two main characters. Vladimir: Vladimir is one of the two protagonists. He is a bum like Estragon, but retains a memory of most events. However, he is often unsure wnether his memory is playing tricks on him. Vladimir is friends with Estragon because Estragon provides him with the chance to remember past events. Vladimir is the one who makes Estragon wait with him for Mr. Godot's imminent arrival throughout the play. Vladimir has been compared to the intellect which provides for the body, represented by Estragon.

Estragon

The second of the two main characters. Vladimir calls him Gogo. He seems weak and helpless, always looking for Vladimir's protection. He also has a poor memory, as Vladimir has to remind him in the second act of the events that happened the previous night. Estragon is one of the two protagonists. He is a bum and sleeps in a ditch where he is beaten each night. He has no memory beyond what is immediately said to him, and relies on Vladimir to remember for him. Estragon is impatient and constantly wants to leave Vladimir, but is restrained from leaving by the fact that he needs Vladimir. It is Estragon's idea for the bums to pass their time by hanging themselves. Estragon has been compared to a body without an intellect, which therefore needs Vladimir to provide the intellect.

Pozzo

He passes by the spot where Vladimir and Estragon are waiting and provides a diversion. In the second act, he is blind and does not remember meeting Vladimir and Estragon the night before. Pozzo is the master who rules over Lucky. He stops and talks to the two bums in order to have some company. In the second act Pozzo is blind and requires their help. He, like Estragon, cannot remember people he has met. His transformation between the acts may represent the passage of time

Lucky

Pozzo's slave, who carries Pozzo's bags and stool. In Act I, he entertains by dancing and thinking. However, in Act II, he is dumb. Lucky is the slave of Pozzo. He is tied to Pozzo via a rope around his neck and he carries Pozzo's bags. Lucky is only allowed to speak twice during the entire play, but his long monologue is filled with incomplete ideas. He is silenced only by the other characters who fight with him to take of his hat. Lucky appears as a mute in the second act.

Boy

He appears at the end of each act to inform Vladimir that Godot will not be coming that night. In the second act, he insists that he was not there the previous night. The boy is a servant of Mr. Godot. He plays an identical role in both acts by coming to inform Vladimir and Estragon the Mr. Godot will not be able to make it that night, but will surely come the next day. The boy never remembers having met Vladimir and Estragon before. He has a brother who is mentioned but who never appears.

Godot

The man for whom Vladimir and Estragon wait unendingly. Godot never appears in the play. His name are character are often thought to refer to God, changing the play's title and subject to Waiting for Godot.

Chapter 9

Complete Text

ACT I

A country road. A tree.

Evening.

Estragon, sitting on a low mound, is trying to take off his boot. He pulls at it with both hands, panting.

He gives up, exhausted, rests, tries again.

As before.

Enter Vladimir.

ESTRAGON:

(*giving up again*). Nothing to be done.

VLADIMIR:

(*advancing with short, stiff strides, legs wide apart*). I'm beginning to come round to that opinion. All my life I've tried to put it from me, saying Vladimir, be reasonable, you haven't yet tried everything. And I resumed the struggle. (*He broods, musing on the struggle. Turning to Estragon.*) So there you are again.

ESTRAGON:

Am I?

VLADIMIR:

I'm glad to see you back. I thought you were gone forever.

ESTRAGON:

Me too.

VLADIMIR:

Together again at last! We'll have to celebrate this. But how? (*He reflects.*) Get up till I embrace you.

ESTRAGON:

(*irritably*). Not now, not now.

VLADIMIR:

(*hurt, coldly*). May one inquire where His Highness spent the night?
ESTRAGON:
In a ditch.
VLADIMIR:
(*admiringly*). A ditch! Where?
ESTRAGON:
(*without gesture*). Over there.
VLADIMIR:
And they didn't beat you?
ESTRAGON:
Beat me? Certainly they beat me.
VLADIMIR:
The same lot as usual?
ESTRAGON:
The same? I don't know.
VLADIMIR:
When I think of it... all these years... but for me... where would you be... (*Decisively.*) You'd be nothing more than a little heap of bones at the present minute, no doubt about it.
ESTRAGON:
And what of it?
VLADIMIR:
(*gloomily*). It's too much for one man. (*Pause. Cheerfully.*) On the other hand what's the gcod of losing heart now, that's what I say. We should have thought of it a million years ago, in the nineties.
ESTRAGON:
Ah stop blathering and help me off with this bloody thing.
VLADIMIR:
Hand in hand from the top of the Eiffel Tower, among the first. We were respectable in those days. Now it's too late. They wouldn't even let us up. (*Estragon tears at his boot.*) What are you doing?
ESTRAGON:
Taking off my boot. Did that never happen to you?
VLADIMIR:

Boots must be taken off every day, I'm tired telling you that. Why don't you listen to me?

ESTRAGON:

(*feebly*). Help me!

VLADIMIR:

It hurts?

ESTRAGON:

(*angrily*). Hurts! He wants to know if it hurts!

VLADIMIR:

(*angrily*). No one ever suffers but you. I don't count. I'd like to hear what you'd say if you had what I have.

ESTRAGON:

It hurts?

VLADIMIR:

(*angrily*). Hurts! He wants to know if it hurts!

ESTRAGON:

(*pointing*). You might button it all the same.

VLADIMIR:

(*stooping*). True. (*He buttons his fly.*) Never neglect the little things of life.

ESTRAGON:

What do you expect, you always wait till the last moment.

VLADIMIR:

(*musingly*). The last moment... (*He meditates.*) Hope deferred maketh the something sick, who said that?

ESTRAGON:

Why don't you help me?

VLADIMIR:

Sometimes I feel it coming all the same. Then I go all queer. (*He takes off his hat, peers inside it, feels about inside it, shakes it, puts it on again.*) How shall I say? Relieved and at the same time... (*he searches for the word*)... appalled. (*With emphasis.*) APPALLED. (*He takes off his hat again, peers inside it.*) Funny. (*He knocks on the crown as though to dislodge a foreign body, peers into it again, puts it on again.*)

Nothing to be done. (*Estragon with a supreme effort succeeds in pulling off his boot. He peers inside it, feels about inside it, turns it upside down, shakes it, looks on the ground to see if anything has *fallen out, finds nothing, feels inside it again, staring sightlessly before him.*) Well?

ESTRAGON:

Nothing.

VLADIMIR:

Show me.

ESTRAGON:

There's nothing to show.

VLADIMIR:

Try and put it on again.

ESTRAGON:

(*examining his foot*). I'll air it for a bit.

VLADIMIR:

There's man all over for you, blaming on his boots the faults of his feet. (*He takes off his hat again, peers inside it, feels about inside it, knocks on the crown, blows into it, puts it on again.*) This is getting alarming. (*Silence. Vladimir deep in thought, Estragon pulling at his toes.*) One of the thieves was saved. (*Pause.*) It's a reasonable percentage. (*Pause.*) Gogo.

ESTRAGON:

What?

VLADIMIR:

Suppose we repented.

ESTRAGON:

Repented what?

VLADIMIR:

Oh... (*He reflects.*) We wouldn't have to go into the details.

ESTRAGON:

Our being born?

Vladimir breaks into a hearty laugh which he immediately stifles, his hand pressed to his pubis, his face contorted.

VLADIMIR:

One daren't even laugh any more.

ESTRAGON:

Dreadful privation.

VLADIMIR:

Merely smile. (*He smiles suddenly from ear to ear, keeps smiling, ceases as suddenly.*) It's not the same thing. Nothing to be done. (*Pause.*) Gogo.

ESTRAGON:

(*irritably*). What is it?

VLADIMIR:

Did you ever read the Bible?

ESTRAGON:

The Bible... (*He reflects.*) I must have taken a look at it.

VLADIMIR:

Do you remember the Gospels?

ESTRAGON:

I remember the maps of the Holy Land. Coloured they were. Very pretty. The Dead Sea was pale blue. The very look of it made me thirsty. That's where we'll go, I used to say, that's where we'll go for our honeymoon. We'll swim. We'll be happy.

VLADIMIR:

You should have been a poet.

ESTRAGON:

I was. (*Gesture towards his rags.*) Isn't that obvious?

Silence.

VLADIMIR:

Where was I... How's your foot?

ESTRAGON:

Swelling visibly.

VLADIMIR:

Ah yes, the two thieves. Do you remember the story?

ESTRAGON:

No.

VLADIMIR:

Shall I tell it to you?

ESTRAGON:

No.

VLADIMIR:

It'll pass the time. (*Pause.*) Two thieves, crucified at the same time as our Saviour. One—

ESTRAGON:

Our what?

VLADIMIR:

Our Saviour. Two thieves. One is supposed to have been

saved and the other... (*he searches for the contrary of saved*)... damned.

ESTRAGON:

Saved from what?

VLADIMIR:

Hell.

ESTRAGON:

I'm going.

He does not move.

VLADIMIR:

And yet... (*pause*)... how is it –this is not boring you I hope– how is it that of the four Evangelists only one speaks of a thief being saved. The four of them were there –or thereabouts– and only one speaks of a thief being saved. (*Pause.*) Come on, Gogo, return the ball, can't you, once in a while?

ESTRAGON:

(*with exaggerated enthusiasm*). I find this really most extraordinarily interesting.

VLADIMIR:

One out of four. Of the other three, two don't mention any thieves at all and the third says that both of them abused him.

ESTRAGON:

Who?

VLADIMIR:

What?

ESTRAGON:

What's all this about? Abused who?

VLADIMIR:

The Saviour.

ESTRAGON:

Why?

VLADIMIR:

Because he wouldn't save them.

ESTRAGON:

From hell?

VLADIMIR:

Imbecile! From death.

ESTRAGON:

I thought you said hell.

VLADIMIR:

From death, from death.

ESTRAGON:

Well what of it?

VLADIMIR:

Then the two of them must have been damned.

ESTRAGON:

And why not?

VLADIMIR:

But one of the four says that one of the two was saved.

ESTRAGON:

Well? They don't agree and that's all there is to it.

VLADIMIR:

But all four were there. And only one speaks of a thief being saved. Why believe him rather than the others?

ESTRAGON:

Who believes him?

VLADIMIR:

Everybody. It's the only version they know.

ESTRAGON:

People are bloody ignorant apes.

He rises painfully, goes limping to extreme left, halts, gazes into distance off with his hand screening his eyes, turns, goes to extreme right, gazes into distance. Vladimir watches him, then goes and picks up the boot, peers into it, drops it hastily.

VLADIMIR:

Pah!

He spits. Estragon moves to centre, halts with his back to auditorium.

ESTRAGON:

Charming spot. (*He turns, advances to front, halts facing auditorium.*) Inspiring prospects. (*He turns to Vladimir.*) Let's go.

VLADIMIR:

We can't.

ESTRAGON:

Why not?
VLADIMIR:
We're waiting for Godot.
ESTRAGON:
(*despairingly*). Ah! (*Pause.*) You're sure it was here?
VLADIMIR:
What?
ESTRAGON:
That we were to wait.
VLADIMIR:
He said by the tree. (*They look at the tree.*) Do you see any others?
ESTRAGON:
What is it?
VLADIMIR:
I don't know. A willow.
ESTRAGON:
Where are the leaves?
VLADIMIR:
It must be dead.
ESTRAGON:
No more weeping.
VLADIMIR:
Or perhaps it's not the season.
ESTRAGON:
Looks to me more like a bush.
VLADIMIR:
A shrub.
ESTRAGON:
A bush.
VLADIMIR:
A—. What are you insinuating? That we've come to the wrong place?
ESTRAGON:
He should be here.
VLADIMIR:
He didn't say for sure he'd come.
ESTRAGON:

And if he doesn't come?
VLADIMIR:
We'll come back tomorrow.
ESTRAGON:
And then the day after tomorrow.
VLADIMIR:
Possibly.
ESTRAGON:
And so on.
VLADIMIR:
The point is—
ESTRAGON:
Until he comes.
VLADIMIR:
You're merciless.
ESTRAGON:
We came here yesterday.
VLADIMIR:
Ah no, there you're mistaken.
ESTRAGON:
What did we do yesterday?
VLADIMIR:
What did we do yesterday?
ESTRAGON:
Yes.
VLADIMIR:
Why... (*Angrily*.) Nothing is certain when you're about.
ESTRAGON:
In my opinion we were here.
VLADIMIR:
(*looking round*). You recognize the place?
ESTRAGON:
I didn't say that.
VLADIMIR:
Well?
ESTRAGON:
That makes no difference.
VLADIMIR:

All the same... that tree... (*turning towards auditorium*) that bog...

ESTRAGON:

You're sure it was this evening?

VLADIMIR:

What?

ESTRAGON:

That we were to wait.

VLADIMIR:

He said Saturday. (*Pause.*) I think.

ESTRAGON:

You think.

VLADIMIR:

I must have made a note of it. (*He fumbles in his pockets, bursting with miscellaneous rubbish.*)

ESTRAGON:

(*very insidious*). But what Saturday? And is it Saturday? Is it not rather Sunday? (*Pause.*) Or Monday? (*Pause.*) Or Friday?

VLADIMIR:

(*looking wildly about him, as though the date was inscribed in the landscape*). It's not possible!

ESTRAGON:

Or Thursday?

VLADIMIR:

What'll we do?

ESTRAGON:

If he came yesterday and we weren't here you may be sure he won't come again today.

VLADIMIR:

But you say we were here yesterday.

ESTRAGON:

I may be mistaken. (*Pause.*) Let's stop talking for a minute, do you mind?

VLADIMIR:

(*feebly*). All right. (*Estragon sits down on the mound. Vladimir paces agitatedly to and fro, halting from time to time to gaze into distance off. Estragon falls asleep.*

Vladimir halts finally before Estragon.) Gogo!... Gogo!... GOGO!

Estragon wakes with a start.

ESTRAGON:

(*restored to the horror of his situation*). I was asleep! (*Despairingly.*) Why will you never let me sleep?

VLADIMIR:

I felt lonely.

ESTRAGON:

I had a dream.

VLADIMIR:

Don't tell me!

ESTRAGON:

I dreamt that—

VLADIMIR:

DON'T TELL ME!

ESTRAGON:

(*gesture toward the universe*). This one is enough for you? (*Silence.*) It's not nice of you, Didi. Who am I to tell my private nightmares to if I can't tell them to you?

VLADIMIR:

Let them remain private. You know I can't bear that.

ESTRAGON:

(*coldly.*) There are times when I wonder if it wouldn't be better for us to part.

VLADIMIR:

You wouldn't go far.

ESTRAGON:

That would be too bad, really too bad. (*Pause.*) Wouldn't it, Didi, be really too bad? (*Pause.*) When you think of the beauty of the way. (*Pause.*) And the goodness of the wayfarers. (*Pause. Wheedling.*) Wouldn't it, Didi?

VLADIMIR:

Calm yourself.

ESTRAGON:

(*voluptuously.*) Calm... calm... The English say cawm. (*Pause.*) You know the story of the Englishman in the brothel?

VLADIMIR:

Yes.

ESTRAGON:

Tell it to me.

VLADIMIR:

Ah stop it!

ESTRAGON:

An Englishman having drunk a little more than usual proceeds to a brothel. The bawd asks him if he wants a fair one, a dark one or a red-haired one. Go on.

VLADIMIR:

STOP IT!

Exit Vladimir hurriedly. Estragon gets up and follows him as far as the limit of the stage. Gestures of Estragon like those of a spectator encouraging a pugilist. Enter Vladimir. He brushes past Estragon, crosses the stage with bowed head. Estragon takes a step towards him, halts.

ESTRAGON:

(*gently.*) You wanted to speak to me? (*Silence. Estragon takes a step forward.*) You had something to say to me? (*Silence. Another step forward.*) Didi...

VLADIMIR:

(*without turning*). I've nothing to say to you.

ESTRAGON:

(*step forward*). You're angry? (*Silence. Step forward*). Forgive me. (*Silence. Step forward. Estragon lays his hand on Vladimir's shoulder.*) Come, Didi. (*Silence.*) Give me your hand. (*Vladimir half turns.*) Embrace me! (*Vladimir stiffens.*) Don't be stubborn! (*Vladimir softens. They embrace. #*

Estragon recoils.) You stink of garlic!

VLADIMIR:

It's for the kidneys. (*Silence. Estragon looks attentively at the tree.*) What do we do now?

ESTRAGON:

Wait.

VLADIMIR:

Yes, but while waiting.

ESTRAGON:

What about hanging ourselves?

VLADIMIR:

Hmm. It'd give us an erection.

ESTRAGON:

(*highly excited*). An erection!

VLADIMIR:

With all that follows. Where it falls mandrakes grow. That's why they shriek when you pull them up. Did you not know that?

ESTRAGON:

Let's hang ourselves immediately!

VLADIMIR:

From a bough? (*They go towards the tree.*) I wouldn't trust it.

ESTRAGON:

We can always try.

VLADIMIR:

Go ahead.

ESTRAGON:

After you.

VLADIMIR:

No no, you first.

ESTRAGON:

Why me?

VLADIMIR:

You're lighter than I am.

ESTRAGON:

Just so!

VLADIMIR:

I don't understand.

ESTRAGON:

Use your intelligence, can't you?

Vladimir uses his intelligence.

VLADIMIR:

(*finally*). I remain in the dark.

ESTRAGON:

This is how it is. (*He reflects.*) The bough... the bough... (*Angrily.*) Use your head, can't you?

VLADIMIR:
You're my only hope.
ESTRAGON:
(*with effort*). Gogo light—bough not break—Gogo dead. Didi heavy—bough break—Didi alone. Whereas—
VLADIMIR:
I hadn't thought of that.
ESTRAGON:
If it hangs you it'll hang anything.
VLADIMIR:
But am I heavier than you?
ESTRAGON:
So you tell me. I don't know. There's an even chance. Or nearly.
VLADIMIR:
Well? What do we do?
ESTRAGON:
Don't let's do anything. It's safer.
VLADIMIR:
Let's wait and see what he says.
ESTRAGON:
Who?
VLADIMIR:
Godot.
ESTRAGON:
Good idea.
VLADIMIR:
Let's wait till we know exactly how we stand.
ESTRAGON:
On the other hand it might be better to strike the iron before it freezes.
VLADIMIR:
I'm curious to hear what he has to offer. Then we'll take it or leave it.
ESTRAGON:
What exactly did we ask him for?
VLADIMIR:
Were you not there?

ESTRAGON:
I can't have been listening.
VLADIMIR:
Oh... Nothing very definite.
ESTRAGON:
A kind of prayer.
VLADIMIR:
Precisely.
ESTRAGON:
A vague supplication.
VLADIMIR:
Exactly.
ESTRAGON:
And what did he reply?
VLADIMIR:
That he'd see.
ESTRAGON:
That he couldn't promise anything.
VLADIMIR:
That he'd have to think it over.
ESTRAGON:
In the quiet of his home.
VLADIMIR:
Consult his family.
ESTRAGON:
His friends.
VLADIMIR:
His agents.
ESTRAGON:
His correspondents.
VLADIMIR:
His books.
ESTRAGON:
His bank account.
VLADIMIR:
Before taking a decision.
ESTRAGON:
It's the normal thing.

VLADIMIR:
Is it not?
ESTRAGON:
I think it is.
VLADIMIR:
I think so too.
Silence.
ESTRAGON:
(*anxious*). And we?
VLADIMIR:
I beg your pardon?
ESTRAGON:
I said, And we?
VLADIMIR:
I don't understand.
ESTRAGON:
Where do we come in?
VLADIMIR:
Come in?
ESTRAGON:
Take your time.
VLADIMIR:
Come in? On our hands and knees.
ESTRAGON:
As bad as that?
VLADIMIR:
Your Worship wishes to assert his prerogatives?
ESTRAGON:
We've no rights any more?
Laugh of Vladimir, stifled as before, less the smile.
VLADIMIR:
You'd make me laugh if it wasn't prohibited.
ESTRAGON:
We've lost our rights?
VLADIMIR:
(*distinctly*). We got rid of them.
Silence. They remain motionless, arms dangling, heads sunk, sagging at the knees.

ESTRAGON:

(*feebly*). We're not tied? (*Pause.*) We're not—

VLADIMIR:

Listen!

They listen, grotesquely rigid. #

ESTRAGON:

I hear nothing.

VLADIMIR:

Hsst! (*They listen. Estragon loses his balance, almost falls. He clutches the arm of Vladimir, who totters. They listen, huddled together.*) Nor I.

Sighs of relief. They relax and separate.

ESTRAGON:

You gave me a fright.

VLADIMIR:

I thought it was he.

ESTRAGON:

Who?

VLADIMIR:

Godot.

ESTRAGON:

Pah! The wind in the reeds.

VLADIMIR:

I could have sworn I heard shouts.

ESTRAGON:

And why would he shout?

VLADIMIR:

At his horse.

Silence.

ESTRAGON:

(*violently*). I'm hungry!

VLADIMIR:

Do you want a carrot?

ESTRAGON:

Is that all there is?

VLADIMIR:

I might have some turnips.

ESTRAGON:

Give me a carrot. (*Vladimir rummages in his pockets, takes out a turnip and gives it to Estragon who takes a bite out of it. Angrily.*) It's a turnip!

VLADIMIR:

Oh pardon! I could have sworn it was a carrot. (*He rummages again in his pockets, finds nothing but turnips.*) All that's turnips. (*He rummages.*) You must have eaten the last. (*He rummages.*) Wait, I have it. (*He brings out a carrot and gives it to Estragon.*) There, dear fellow. #

(*Estragon wipes the carrot on his sleeve and begins to eat it.*) Make it last, that's the end of them.

ESTRAGON:

(*chewing*). I asked you a question.

VLADIMIR:

Ah.

ESTRAGON:

Did you reply?

VLADIMIR:

How's the carrot?

ESTRAGON:

It's a carrot.

VLADIMIR:

So much the better, so much the better. (*Pause.*) What was it you wanted to know?

ESTRAGON:

I've forgotten. (*Chews.*) That's what annoys me. (*He looks at the carrot appreciatively, dangles it between finger and thumb.*) I'll never forget this carrot. (*He sucks the end of it meditatively.*) Ah yes, now I remember.

VLADIMIR:

Well?

ESTRAGON:

(*his mouth full, vacuously*). We're not tied?

VLADIMIR:

I don't hear a word you're saying.

ESTRAGON:

(*chews, swallows*). I'm asking you if we're tied.

VLADIMIR:

Tied?
ESTRAGON:
Ti-ed.
VLADIMIR:
How do you mean tied?
ESTRAGON:
Down.
VLADIMIR:
But to whom? By whom?
ESTRAGON:
To your man.
VLADIMIR:
To Godot? Tied to Godot! What an idea! No question of it. (*Pause.*) For the moment.
ESTRAGON:
His name is Godot?
VLADIMIR:
I think so.
ESTRAGON:
Fancy that. (*He raises what remains of the carrot by the stub of leaf, twirls it before his eyes.*) Funny, the more you eat the worse it gets.
VLADIMIR:
With me it's just the opposite.
ESTRAGON:
In other words?
VLADIMIR:
I get used to the muck as I go along.
ESTRAGON:
(*after prolonged reflection*). Is that the opposite?
VLADIMIR:
Question of temperament.
ESTRAGON:
Of character.
VLADIMIR:
Nothing you can do about it.
ESTRAGON:
No use struggling.

VLADIMIR:
One is what one is.
ESTRAGON:
No use wriggling.
VLADIMIR:
The essential doesn't change.
ESTRAGON:
Nothing to be done. (*He proffers the remains of the carrot to Vladimir.*) Like to finish it?

A terrible cry, close at hand. Estragon drops the carrot. They remain motionless, then together make a sudden rush towards the wings. Estragon stops halfway, runs back, picks up the carrot, stuffs it in his pocket, runs to rejoin Vladimir who is waiting for him, stops again, runs back, picks up his boot, runs to rejoin Vladimir. Huddled together, shoulders hunched, cringing away from the menace, they wait. #

Enter Pozzo and Lucky. Pozzo drives Lucky by means of a rope passed round his neck, so that Lucky is the first to enter, followed by the rope which is long enough to let him reach the middle of the stage before Pozzo appears. Lucky carries a heavy bag, a folding stool, a picnic basket and a greatcoat, Pozzo a whip.

POZZO:
(*off*). On! (*Crack of whip. Pozzo appears. They cross the stage. Lucky passes before Vladimir and Estragon and exit. Pozzo at the sight of Vladimir and Estragon stops short. The rope tautens. Pozzo jerks at it violently.*) Back!

Noise of Lucky falling with all his baggage. Vladimir and Estragon turn towards him, half wishing half fearing to go to his assistance. Vladimir takes a step towards Lucky, Estragon holds him back by the sleeve.

VLADIMIR:
Let me go!
ESTRAGON:
Stay where you are!
POZZO:
Be careful! He's wicked. (*Vladimir and Estragon turn towards Pozzo.*) With strangers.
ESTRAGON:

(*undertone*). Is that him?
VLADIMIR:
Who?
ESTRAGON:
(*trying to remember the name*). Er...
VLADIMIR:
Godot?
ESTRAGON:
Yes.
POZZO:
I present myself: Pozzo.
VLADIMIR:
(*to Estragon*). Not at all!
ESTRAGON:
He said Godot.
VLADIMIR:
Not at all!
ESTRAGON:
(*timidly, to Pozzo*). You're not Mr. Godot, Sir?
POZZO:
(*terrifying voice*). I am Pozzo! (*Silence.*) Pozzo! (*Silence.*) Does that name mean nothing to you? (*Silence.*) I say does that name mean nothing to you?

Vladimir and Estragon look at each other questioningly.

ESTRAGON:
(*pretending to search*). Bozzo... Bozzo...
VLADIMIR:
(*ditto*). Pozzo... Pozzo...
POZZO:
PPPOZZZO!
ESTRAGON:
Ah! Pozzo... let me see... Pozzo...
VLADIMIR:
Is it Pozzo or Bozzo?
ESTRAGON:
Pozzo... no... I'm afraid I... no... I don't seem to...

Pozzo advances threateningly.

VLADIMIR:

(*conciliating*). I once knew a family called Gozzo. The mother had the clap.

ESTRAGON:

(*hastily*). We're not from these parts, Sir.

POZZO:

(*halting*). You are human beings none the less. (*He puts on his glasses.*) As far as one can see. (*He takes off his glasses.*) Of the same species as myself. (*He bursts into an enormous laugh.*) Of the same species as Pozzo! Made in God's image!

VLADIMIR:

Well you see—

POZZO:

(*peremptory*). Who is Godot?

ESTRAGON:

Godot?

POZZO:

You took me for Godot.

VLADIMIR:

Oh no, Sir, not for an instant, Sir.

POZZO:

Who is he?

VLADIMIR:

Oh he's a... he's a kind of acquaintance.

ESTRAGON:

Nothing of the kind, we hardly know him.

VLADIMIR:

True... we don't know him very well... but all the same...

ESTRAGON:

Personally, I wouldn't even know him if I saw him.

POZZO:

You took me for him.

ESTRAGON:

(*recoiling before Pozzo*). That's to say... you understand... the dusk... the strain... waiting... I confess... I imagined... for a second...

POZZO:

Waiting? So you were waiting for him?

VLADIMIR:

Well you see—

POZZO:

Here? On my land?

VLADIMIR:

We didn't intend any harm.

ESTRAGON:

We meant well.

POZZO:

The road is free to all.

VLADIMIR:

That's how we looked at it.

POZZO:

It's a disgrace. But there you are.

ESTRAGON:

Nothing we can do about it.

POZZO:

(*with magnanimous gesture*). Let's say no more about it. (*He jerks the rope.*) Up pig! (*Pause.*) Every time he drops he falls asleep. (*Jerks the rope.*) Up hog! (*Noise of Lucky getting up and picking up his baggage. Pozzo jerks the rope.*) Back! (*Enter Lucky backwards.*) Stop! (*Lucky stops.*) Turn! (*Lucky turns. To Vladimir and Estragon, affably.*) Gentlemen, I am happy to have met you. (*Before their incredulous expression.*) Yes yes, sincerely happy. (*He jerks the rope.*) Closer! (*Lucky advances.*) Stop! (*Lucky stops.*) Yes, the road seems long when one journeys all alone for... (*he consults his watch*)... yes... (*he calculates*)... yes, six hours, that's right, six hours on end, and never a soul in sight. (*To Lucky.*) Coat! (*Lucky puts down the bag, advances, gives the coat, goes back to his place, takes up the bag.*) Hold that! (*Pozzo holds out the whip. Lucky advances and, both his hands being occupied, takes the whip in his mouth, then goes back to his place. Pozzo begins to put on his coat, stops.*) Coat! (*Lucky puts down the bag, basket and stool, helps Pozzo on with his coat, goes back to his place and takes up bag, basket and stool.*) Touch of autumn in the air this evening. (*Pozzo finishes buttoning up his coat, stoops, inspects himself, straightens up.*) Whip! (*Lucky advances, stoops, Pozzo snatches the whip from his mouth, Lucky goes back to his place.*) Yes, gentlemen, I cannot go for long without the society of my likes (*he puts on his glasses and looks at the two likes*) even when the likeness is an imperfect one. (*He takes off his glasses.*) Stool! (*Lucky puts down bag and basket, advances, opens stool, puts it down, goes back to his place, takes up bag and basket.*) Closer! (*Lucky puts down bag and basket, advances, moves stool, goes back to his place, takes up bag and basket. Pozzo sits down, places the butt of his whip against Lucky's chest and pushes.*) Back! (*Lucky takes a step back.*) Further! (*Lucky takes another step back.*) Stop! (*Lucky stops. To Vladimir and Estragon.*) That is why, with your permission, I propose to dally with you a moment, before I venture any further. Basket! (*Lucky advances, gives the basket, goes back to his place.*) The fresh air stimulates the jaded appetite. (*He opens the basket, takes out a piece of chicken and a bottle of wine.*) Basket! (*Lucky advances, picks up the basket and goes back to his place.*) Further! (*Lucky takes a step back.*) He stinks. Happy days!

He drinks from the bottle, puts it down and begins to eat. Silence.

Vladimir and Estragon, cautiously at first, then more boldly, begin to circle about Lucky, inspecting him up and down. Pozzo eats his chicken voraciously, throwing away the bones after having sucked them. Lucky sags slowly, until bag and basket touch the ground, then straightens up with a start and begins to sag again. Rhythm of one sleeping on his feet.

ESTRAGON:
What ails him?
VLADIMIR:
He looks tired.
ESTRAGON:
Why doesn't he put down his bags?
VLADIMIR:
How do I know? (*They close in on him.*) Careful!
ESTRAGON:
Say something to him.
VLADIMIR:
Look!
ESTRAGON:
What?
VLADIMIR:

(*pointing*). His neck!

ESTRAGON:

(*looking at the neck*). I see nothing.

VLADIMIR:

Here.

Estragon goes over beside Vladimir.

ESTRAGON:

Oh I say!

VLADIMIR:

A running sore!

ESTRAGON:

It's the rope.

VLADIMIR:

It's the rubbing.

ESTRAGON:

It's inevitable.

VLADIMIR:

It's the knot.

ESTRAGON:

It's the chafing.

They resume their inspection, dwell on the face.

VLADIMIR:

(*grudgingly*). He's not bad looking.

ESTRAGON:

(*shrugging his shoulders, wry face.*) Would you say so?

VLADIMIR:

A trifle effeminate.

ESTRAGON:

Look at the slobber.

VLADIMIR:

It's inevitable.

ESTRAGON:

Look at the slaver.

VLADIMIR:

Perhaps he's a halfwit.

ESTRAGON:

A cretin.

VLADIMIR:

(*looking closer*). Looks like a goiter.
ESTRAGON:
(*ditto*). It's not certain.
VLADIMIR:
He's panting.
ESTRAGON:
It's inevitable.
VLADIMIR:
And his eyes!
ESTRAGON:
What about them?
VLADIMIR:
Goggling out of his head. #
ESTRAGON:
Looks like his last gasp to me.
VLADIMIR:
It's not certain. (*Pause.*) Ask him a question.
ESTRAGON:
Would that be a good thing?
VLADIMIR:
What do we risk?
ESTRAGON:
(*timidly*). Mister...
VLADIMIR:
Louder.
ESTRAGON:
(*louder*). Mister...
POZZO:
Leave him in peace! (*They turn toward Pozzo who, having finished eating, wipes his mouth with the back of his hand.*) Can't you see he wants to rest? Basket! (*He strikes a match and begins to light his pipe. Estragon sees the chicken bones on the ground and stares at them greedily. As Lucky does not move Pozzo throws the match angrily away and jerks the rope.*) Basket! (*Lucky starts, almost falls, recovers his senses, advances, puts the bottle in the basket and goes back to his place. Estragon stares at the bones. Pozzo strikes another match and lights his pipe.*) What can you expect, it's not his job. (*He pulls at his pipe, stretches*

out his legs.) Ah! That's better.

ESTRAGON:

(*timidly*). Please Sir...

POZZO:

What is it, my good man?

ESTRAGON:

Er... you've finished with the... er... you don't need the... er... bones, Sir?

VLADIMIR:

(*scandalized*). You couldn't have waited?

POZZO:

No no, he does well to ask. Do I need the bones? (*He turns them over with the end of his whip.*) No, personally I do not need them any more. (*Estragon takes a step towards the bones.*) But... (*Estragon stops short*)... but in theory the bones go to the carrier. He is therefore the one to ask. (*Estragon turns towards Lucky, hesitates.*) Go on, go on, don't be afraid, ask him, he'll tell you.

Estragon goes towards Lucky, stops before him.

ESTRAGON:

Mister... excuse me, Mister...

POZZO:

You're being spoken to, pig! Reply! (*To Estragon.*) Try him again.

ESTRAGON:

Excuse me, Mister, the bones, you won't be wanting the bones?

Lucky looks long at Estragon.

POZZO:

(*in raptures*). Mister! (*Lucky bows his head.*) Reply! Do you want them or don't you? (*Silence of Lucky. To Estragon.*) They're yours. (*Estragon makes a dart at the bones, picks them up and begins to gnaw them.*) I don't like it. I've never known him to refuse a bone before. (*He looks anxiously at Lucky.*) Nice business it'd be if he fell sick on me!

He puffs at his pipe.

VLADIMIR:

(*exploding*). It's a scandal!

Silence. Flabbergasted, Estragon stops gnawing, looks at Pozzo and Vladimir in turn. Pozzo outwardly calm. Vladimir embarrassed.

POZZO:

(*To Vladimir*). Are you alluding to anything in particular?

VLADIMIR:

(*stutteringly resolute*). To treat a man... (*gesture towards Lucky*)... like that... I think that... no... a human being... no... it's a scandal!

ESTRAGON:

(*not to be outdone*). A disgrace!

He resumes his gnawing.

POZZO:

You are severe. (*To Vladimir.*) What age are you, if it's not a rude question? (*Silence.*) Sixty? Seventy? (*To Estragon.*) What age would you say he was?

ESTRAGON:

Eleven.

POZZO:

I am impertinent. (*He knocks out his pipe against the whip, gets up.*) I must be getting on. Thank you for your society. (*He reflects.*) Unless I smoke another pipe before I go. What do you say? (*They say nothing.*) Oh I'm only a small smoker, a very small smoker, I'm not in the habit of smoking two pipes one on top of the other, it makes (*hand to heart, sighing*) my heart go pit-a-pat. (*Silence.*) It's the nicotine, one absorbs it in spite of one's precautions. (*Sighs.*) You know how it is. (*Silence.*) But perhaps you don't smoke? Yes? No? It's of no importance. (*Silence.*) But how am I to sit down now, without affectation, now that I have risen? Without appearing to –how shall I say– without appearing to falter. (*To Vladimir.*) I beg your pardon? (*Silence.*) Perhaps you didn't speak? (*Silence.*) It's of no importance. Let me see...

He reflects.

ESTRAGON:

Ah! That's better.

He puts the bones in his pocket.

VLADIMIR:

Let's go.

ESTRAGON:
So soon?
POZZO:
One moment! (*He jerks the rope.*) Stool! (*He points with his whip. Lucky moves the stool.*) More! There! (*He sits down. Lucky goes back to his place.*) Done it!
He fills his pipe.
VLADIMIR:
(*vehemently*). Let's go!
POZZO:
I hope I'm not driving you away. Wait a little longer, you'll never regret it.
ESTRAGON:
(*scenting charity*). We're in no hurry.
POZZO:
(*having lit his pipe*). The second is never so sweet... (*he takes the pipe out of his mouth, contemplates it*)... as the first I mean. (*He puts the pipe back in his mouth.*) But it's sweet just the same.
VLADIMIR:
I'm going.
POZZO:
He can no longer endure my presence. I am perhaps not particularly human, but who cares? (*To Vladimir.*) Think twice before you do anything rash. Suppose you go now while it is still day, for there is no denying it is still day. (*They all look up at the sky.*) Good.

(*They stop looking at the sky.*) What happens in that case– (*he takes the pipe out of his mouth, examines it*) –I'm out– (*he relights his pipe*) –in that case– (*puff*) –in that case– (*puff*) –what happens in that case to your appointment with this... Godet... Godot... Godin... anyhow you see who I mean, who has your future in his hands... (*pause*)... at least your immediate future?

VLADIMIR:
Who told you?
POZZO:
He speaks to me again! If this goes on much longer we'll soon be old friends.

ESTRAGON:

Why doesn't he put down his bags?

POZZO:

I too would be happy to meet him. The more people I meet the happier I become. From the meanest creature one departs wiser, richer, more conscious of one's blessings. Even you... (*he looks at them ostentatiously in turn to make it clear they are both meant*)... even you, who knows, will have added to my store.

ESTRAGON:

Why doesn't he put down his bags?

POZZO:

But that would surprise me.

VLADIMIR:

You're being asked a question.

POZZO:

(*delighted*). A question! Who? What? A moment ago you were calling me Sir, in fear and trembling. Now you're asking me questions. No good will come of this!

VLADIMIR:

(*to Estragon*). I think he's listening.

ESTRAGON:

(*circling about Lucky*). What?

VLADIMIR:

You can ask him now. He's on the alert.

ESTRAGON:

Ask him what?

VLADIMIR:

Why he doesn't put down his bags.

ESTRAGON:

I wonder.

VLADIMIR:

Ask him, can't you?

POZZO:

(*who has followed these exchanges with anxious attention, fearing lest the question get lost*). You want to know why he doesn't put down his bags, as you call them.

VLADIMIR:

That's it.

POZZO:

(*to Estragon*). You are sure you agree with that?

ESTRAGON:

He's puffing like a grampus.

POZZO:

The answer is this. (*To Estragon*). But stay still, I beg of you, you're making me nervous!

VLADIMIR:

Here.

ESTRAGON:

What is it?

VLADIMIR:

He's about to speak.

Estragon goes over beside Vladimir. Motionless, side by side, they wait.

POZZO:

Good. Is everybody ready? Is everybody looking at me? (*He looks at Lucky, jerks the rope. Lucky raises his head.*) Will you look at me, pig! (*Lucky looks at him.*) Good. (*He puts the pipe in his pocket, takes out a little vaporizer and sprays his throat, puts back the vaporizer in his pocket, clears his throat, spits, takes out the vaporizer again, sprays his throat again, puts back the vaporizer in his pocket.*) I am ready. Is everybody listening? Is everybody ready? (*He looks at them all in turn, jerks the rope.*) Hog! (*Lucky raises his head.*) I don't like talking in a vacuum. Good. Let me see.

He reflects.

ESTRAGON:

I'm going.

POZZO:

What was it exactly you wanted to know?

VLADIMIR:

Why he—

POZZO:

(*angrily*). Don't interrupt me! (*Pause. Calmer.*) If we all speak at once we'll never get anywhere. (*Pause.*) What was I saying? (*Pause. Louder.*) What was I saying?

Vladimir mimics one carrying a heavy burden. Pozzo looks at him, puzzled.

ESTRAGON:

(*forcibly*). Bags. (*He points at Lucky.*) Why? Always hold. (*He sags, panting.*) Never put down. (*He opens his hands, straightens up with relief.*) Why?

POZZO:

Ah! Why couldn't you say so before? Why he doesn't make himself comfortable? Let's try and get this clear. Has he not the right to? Certainly he has. It follows that he doesn't want to. There's reasoning for you. And why doesn't he want to? (*Pause.*) Gentlemen, the reason is this.

VLADIMIR:

(*to Estragon*). Make a note of this.

POZZO:

He wants to impress me, so that I'll keep him.

ESTRAGON:

What?

POZZO:

Perhaps I haven't got it quite right. He wants to mollify me, so that I'll give up the idea of parting with him. No, that's not exactly it either.

VLADIMIR:

You want to get rid of him?

POZZO:

He wants to cod me, but he won't.

VLADIMIR:

You want to get rid of him?

POZZO:

He imagines that when I see how well he carries I'll be tempted to keep him on in that capacity.

ESTRAGON:

You've had enough of him?

POZZO:

In reality he carries like a pig. It's not his job.

VLADIMIR:

You want to get rid of him?

POZZO:

He imagines that when I see him indefatigable I'll regret my decision. Such is his miserable scheme. As though I were short of slaves! (*All three look at Lucky.*) Atlas, son of Jupiter! (*Silence.*) Well, that's that, I think. Anything else?

Vaporizer.

VLADIMIR:

You want to get rid of him?

POZZO:

Remark that I might just as well have been in his shoes and he in mine. If chance had not willed otherwise. To each one his due.

VLADIMIR:

You waagerrim?

POZZO:

I beg your pardon?

VLADIMIR:

You want to get rid of him?

POZZO:

I do. But instead of driving him away as I might have done, I mean instead of simply kicking him out on his arse, in the goodness of my heart I am bringing him to the fair, where I hope to get a good price for him. The truth is you can't drive such creatures away. The best thing would be to kill them.

Lucky weeps.

ESTRAGON:

He's crying!

POZZO:

Old dogs have more dignity. (*He proffers his handkerchief to Estragon.*) Comfort him, since you pity him. (*Estragon hesitates.*) Come on. (*Estragon takes the handkerchief.*) Wipe away his tears, he'll feel less forsaken.

Estragon hesitates.

VLADIMIR:

Here, give it to me, I'll do it.

Estragon refuses to give the handkerchief.

Childish gestures.

POZZO:

Make haste, before he stops. (*Estragon approaches Lucky and makes to wipe his eyes. Lucky kicks him violently in the shins. Estragon drops the handkerchief, recoils, staggers about the stage howling with pain.*) Hanky!

Lucky puts down bag and basket, picks up handkerchief and gives it to Pozzo, goes back to his place, picks up bag and basket.

ESTRAGON:

Oh the swine! (*He pulls up the leg of his trousers.*) He's crippled me!

POZZO:

I told you he didn't like strangers.

VLADIMIR:

(*to Estragon*). Show me. (*Estragon shows his leg. To Pozzo, angrily.*) He's bleeding!

POZZO:

It's a good sign.

ESTRAGON:

(*on one leg*). I'll never walk again!

VLADIMIR:

(*tenderly*). I'll carry you. (*Pause.*) If necessary.

POZZO:

He's stopped crying. (*To Estragon.*) You have replaced him as it were. (*Lyrically.*) The tears of the world are a constant quantity. For each one who begins to weep, somewhere else another stops. The same is true of the laugh. (*He laughs.*) Let us not then speak ill of our generation, it is not any unhappier than its predecessors. (*Pause.*) Let us not speak well of it either. (*Pause.*) Let us not speak of it at all. (*Pause. Judiciously.*) It is true the population has increased.

VLADIMIR:

Try and walk.

Estragon takes a few limping steps, stops before Lucky and spits on him, then goes and sits down on the mound.

POZZO:

Guess who taught me all these beautiful things. (*Pause. Pointing to Lucky.*) My Lucky!

VLADIMIR:

(*looking at the sky.*) Will night never come?

POZZO:

But for him all my thoughts, all my feelings, would have been of common things. (*Pause. With extraordinary vehemence.*) Professional worries! (*Calmer.*) Beauty, grace, truth of the first water, I knew they were all beyond me. So I took a knook.

VLADIMIR:

(*startled from his inspection of the sky*). A knook?

POZZO:

That was nearly sixty years ago... (*he consults his watch*)... yes, nearly sixty. (*Drawing himself up proudly.*) You wouldn't think it to look at me, would you? Compared to him I look like a young man, no? (*Pause.*) Hat! (*Lucky puts down the basket and takes off his hat. His long white hair falls about his face. He puts his hat under his arm and picks up the basket.*) Now look. (*Pozzo takes off his hat.* [All four wear bowlers.] *He is completely bald. He puts on his hat again.*) Did you see?

VLADIMIR:

And now you turn him away? Such an old and faithful servant!

ESTRAGON:

Swine!

Pozzo more and more agitated.

VLADIMIR:

After having sucked all the good out of him you chuck him away like a... like a banana skin. Really...

POZZO:

(*groaning, clutching his head*). I can't bear it... any longer... the way he goes on... you've no idea... it's terrible... he must go... (*he waves his arms*)... I'm going mad... (*he collapses, his head in his hands*)... I can't bear it... any longer...

Silence. All look at Pozzo.

VLADIMIR:

He can't bear it.

ESTRAGON:

Any longer.

VLADIMIR:

He's going mad.

ESTRAGON:

It's terrible.

VLADIMIR:
(*to Lucky*). How dare you! It's abominable! Such a good master! Crucify him like that! After so many years! Really!
POZZO:
(*sobbing*). He used to be so kind... so helpful... and entertaining... my good angel... and now... he's killing me.
ESTRAGON:
(*to Vladimir*). Does he want to replace him?
VLADIMIR:
What?
ESTRAGON:
Does he want someone to take his place or not?
VLADIMIR:
I don't think so.
ESTRAGON:
What?
VLADIMIR:
I don't know.
ESTRAGON:
Ask him.
POZZO:
(*calmer*). Gentlemen, I don't know what came over me. Forgive me. Forget all I said. (*More and more his old self.*) I don't remember exactly what it was, but you may be sure there wasn't a word of truth in it. (*Drawing himself up, striking his chest.*) Do I look like a man that can be made to suffer? Frankly? (*He rummages in his pockets.*) What have I done with my pipe?
VLADIMIR:
Charming evening we're having.
ESTRAGON:
Unforgettable.
VLADIMIR:
And it's not over.
ESTRAGON:
Apparently not.
VLADIMIR:
It's only beginning.
ESTRAGON:

It's awful.
VLADIMIR:
Worse than the pantomime.
ESTRAGON:
The circus.
VLADIMIR:
The music-hall.
ESTRAGON:
The circus.
POZZO:
What can I have done with that briar?
ESTRAGON:
He's a scream. He's lost his dudeen.
Laughs noisily.
VLADIMIR:
I'll be back.
He hastens towards the wings.
ESTRAGON:
End of the corridor, on the left.
VLADIMIR:
Keep my seat.
Exit Vladimir.
POZZO:
(*on the point of tears*). I've lost my Kapp and Peterson!
ESTRAGON:
(*convulsed with merriment*). He'll be the death of me!
POZZO:
You didn't see by any chance– (*He misses Vladimir.*) Oh! He's gone! Without saying goodbye! How could he! He might have waited!
ESTRAGON:
He would have burst.
POZZO:
Oh! (*Pause.*) Oh well then of course in that case...
ESTRAGON:
Come here.
POZZO:
What for?

ESTRAGON:
You'll see.
POZZO:
You want me to get up?
ESTRAGON:
Quick! (*Pozzo gets up and goes over beside Estragon. Estragon points off.*) Look!
POZZO:
(*having put on his glasses*). Oh I say!
ESTRAGON:
It's all over.
Enter Vladimir, somber. He shoulders Lucky out of his way, kicks over the stool, comes and goes agitatedly.
POZZO:
He's not pleased.
ESTRAGON:
(*to Vladimir*). You missed a treat. Pity.
Vladimir halts, straightens the stool, comes and goes, calmer.
POZZO:
He subsides. (*Looking round.*) Indeed all subsides. A great calm descends. (*Raising his hand.*) Listen! Pan sleeps.
VLADIMIR:
Will night never come?
All three look at the sky.
POZZO:
You don't feel like going until it does?
ESTRAGON:
Well you see—
POZZO:
Why it's very natural, very natural. I myself in your situation, if I had an appointment with a Godin... Godet... Godot... anyhow, you see who I mean, I'd wait till it was black night before I gave up. (*He looks at the stool.*) I'd very much like to sit down, but I don't quite know how to go about it.
ESTRAGON:
Could I be of any help?
POZZO:
If you asked me perhaps.

ESTRAGON:
What?
POZZO:
If you asked me to sit down.
ESTRAGON:
Would that be a help?
POZZO:
I fancy so.
ESTRAGON:
Here we go. Be seated, Sir, I beg of you.
POZZO:
No no, I wouldn't think of it! (*Pause. Aside.*) Ask me again.
ESTRAGON:
Come come, take a seat I beseech you, you'll get pneumonia.
POZZO:
You really think so?
ESTRAGON:
Why it's absolutely certain.
POZZO:
No doubt you are right. (*He sits down.*) Done it again! (*Pause.*) Thank you, dear fellow. (*He consults his watch.*) But I must really be getting along, if I am to observe my schedule.
VLADIMIR:
Time has stopped.
POZZO:
(*cuddling his watch to his ear*). Don't you believe it, Sir, don't you believe it. (*He puts his watch back in his pocket.*) Whatever you like, but not that.
ESTRAGON:
(*to Pozzo*). Everything seems black to him today.
POZZO:
Except the firmament. (*He laughs, pleased with this witticism.*) But I see what it is, you are not from these parts, you don't know what our twilights can do. Shall I tell you? (*Silence. Estragon is fiddling with his boot again, Vladimir with his hat.*) I can't refuse you. (*Vaporizer.*) A little attention, if you

please. (*Vladimir and Estragon continue their fiddling, Lucky is half asleep. Pozzo cracks his whip feebly.*) What's the matter with this whip? (*He gets up and cracks it more vigorously, finally with success. Lucky jumps. Vladimir's hat, Estragon's boot, Lucky's hat, fall to the ground. Pozzo throws down the whip.*) Worn out, this whip. (*He looks at Vladimir and Estragon.*) What was I saying?

VLADIMIR:

Let's go.

ESTRAGON:

But take the weight off your feet, I implore you, you'll catch your death.

POZZO:

True. (*He sits down. To Estragon.*) What is your name?

ESTRAGON:

Adam.

POZZO:

(*who hasn't listened*). Ah yes! The night. (*He raises his head.*) But be a little more attentive, for pity's sake, otherwise we'll never get anywhere. (*He looks at the sky.*) Look! (*All look at the sky except Lucky who is dozing off again. Pozzo jerks the rope.*) Will you look at the sky, pig! (*Lucky looks at the sky.*) Good, that's enough. (*They stop looking at the sky.*) What is there so extraordinary about it? Qua sky. It is pale and luminous like any sky at this hour of the day. (*Pause.*) In these latitudes. (*Pause.*) When the weather is fine. (*Lyrical.*) An hour ago (*he looks at his watch, prosaic*) roughly (*lyrical*) after having poured forth even since (*he hesitates, prosaic*) say ten o'clock in the morning (*lyrical*) tirelessly torrents of red and white light it begins to lose its effulgence, to grow pale (*gesture of the two hands lapsing by stages*) pale, ever a little paler, a little paler until (*dramatic pause, ample gesture of the two hands flung wide apart*) pppfff! finished! it comes to rest. But– (*hand raised in admonition*)– but behind this veil of gentleness and peace, night is charging (*vibrantly*) and will burst upon us (*snaps his fingers*) pop! like that! (*his inspiration leaves him*) just when we least expect it. (*Silence. Gloomily.*) That's how it is on this bitch of an earth.

Long silence.

ESTRAGON:
So long as one knows.
VLADIMIR:
One can bide one's time.
ESTRAGON:
One knows what to expect.
VLADIMIR:
No further need to worry.
ESTRAGON:
Simply wait.
VLADIMIR:
We're used to it.
He picks up his hat, peers inside it, shakes it, puts it on.
POZZO:
How did you find me? (*Vladimir and Estragon look at him blankly.*) Good? Fair? Middling? Poor? Positively bad?
VLADIMIR:
(*first to understand*). Oh very good, very very good.
POZZO:
(*to Estragon*). And you, Sir?
ESTRAGON:
Oh tray bong, tray tray tray bong.
POZZO:
(*fervently*). Bless you, gentlemen, bless you! (*Pause.*) I have such need of encouragement! (*Pause.*) I weakened a little towards the end, you didn't notice?
VLADIMIR:
Oh perhaps just a teeny weeny little bit.
ESTRAGON:
I thought it was intentional.
POZZO:
You see my memory is defective.
Silence.
ESTRAGON:
In the meantime, nothing happens.
POZZO:
You find it tedious?
ESTRAGON:

Somewhat.

POZZO:

(*to Vladimir*). And you, Sir?

VLADIMIR:

I've been better entertained.

Silence. Pozzo struggles inwardly.

POZZO:

Gentlemen, you have been... civil to me.

ESTRAGON:

Not at all!

VLADIMIR:

What an idea!

POZZO:

Yes yes, you have been correct. So that I ask myself is there anything I can do in my turn for these honest fellows who are having such a dull, dull time.

ESTRAGON:

Even ten francs would be a help.

VLADIMIR:

We are not beggars!

POZZO:

Is there anything I can do, that's what I ask myself, to cheer them up? I have given them bones, I have talked to them about this and that, I have explained the twilight, admittedly. But is it enough, that's what tortures me, is it enough?

ESTRAGON:

Even five.

VLADIMIR:

(*to Estragon, indignantly*). That's enough!

ESTRAGON:

I couldn't accept less.

POZZO:

Is is enough? No doubt. But I am liberal. It's my nature. This evening. So much the worse for me. (*He jerks the rope. Lucky looks at him.*) For I shall suffer, no doubt about that. (*He picks up the whip.*) What do you prefer? Shall we have him dance, or sing, or recite, or think, or—

ESTRAGON:

Who?

POZZO:

Who! You know how to think, you two?

VLADIMIR:

He thinks?

POZZO:

Certainly. Aloud. He even used to think very prettily once, I could listen to him for hours. Now... (*he shudders*). So much the worse for me. Well, would you like him to think something for us?

ESTRAGON:

I'd rather he dance, it'd be more fun.

POZZO:

Not necessarily.

ESTRAGON:

Wouldn't it, Didi, be more fun?

VLADIMIR:

I'd like well to hear him think.

ESTRAGON:

Perhaps he could dance first and think afterwards, if it isn't too much to ask him.

VLADIMIR:

(*to Pozzo*). Would that be possible?

POZZO:

By all means, nothing simpler. It's the natural order.

He laughs briefly.

VLADIMIR:

Then let him dance.

Silence.

POZZO:

Do you hear, hog?

ESTRAGON:

He never refuses?

POZZO:

He refused once. (*Silence.*) Dance, misery!

Lucky puts down bag and basket, advances towards front, turns to Pozzo. Lucky dances. He stops.

ESTRAGON:

Is that all?
POZZO:
Encore!
Lucky executes the same movements, stops.
ESTRAGON:
Pooh! I'd do as well myself. (*He imitates Lucky, almost falls.*) With a little practice.
POZZO:
He used to dance the farandole, the fling, the brawl, the jig, the fandango and even the hornpipe. He capered. For joy. Now that's the best he can do. Do you know what he calls it?
ESTRAGON:
The Scapegoat's Agony.
VLADIMIR:
The Hard Stool.
POZZO:
The Net. He thinks he's entangled in a net.
VLADIMIR:
(*squirming like an aesthete*). There's something about it...
Lucky makes to return to his burdens.
POZZO:
Woaa!
Lucky stiffens.
ESTRAGON:
Tell us about the time he refused.
POZZO:
With pleasure, with pleasure. (*He fumbles in his pockets.*) Wait. (*He fumbles.*) What have I done with my spray? (*He fumbles.*) Well now isn't that... (*He looks up, consternation on his features. Faintly.*) I can't find my pulverizer!
ESTRAGON:
(*faintly*). My left lung is very weak! (*He coughs feebly. In ringing tones.*) But my right lung is as sound as a bell!
POZZO:
(*normal voice*). No matter! What was I saying. (*He ponders.*) Wait. (*Ponders.*) Well now isn't that... (*He raises his head.*) Help me!
ESTRAGON:

Wait!

VLADIMIR:

Wait!

POZZO:

Wait!

All three take off their hats simultaneously, press their hands to their foreheads, concentrate.

ESTRAGON:

(*triumphantly*). Ah!

VLADIMIR:

He has it.

POZZO:

(*impatient*). Well?

ESTRAGON:

Why doesn't he put down his bags?

VLADIMIR:

Rubbish!

POZZO:

Are you sure?

VLADIMIR:

Damn it haven't you already told us?

POZZO:

I've already told you?

ESTRAGON:

He's already told us?

VLADIMIR:

Anyway he has put them down.

ESTRAGON:

(*glance at Lucky*). So he has. And what of it?

VLADIMIR:

Since he has put down his bags it is impossible we should have asked why he does not do so.

POZZO:

Stoutly reasoned!

ESTRAGON:

And why has he put them down?

POZZO:

Answer us that.

VLADIMIR:
In order to dance.
ESTRAGON:
True!
POZZO:
True!
Silence. They put on their hats.
ESTRAGON:
Nothing happens, nobody comes, nobody goes, it's awful!
VLADIMIR:
(*to Pozzo*). Tell him to think.
POZZO:
Give him his hat.
VLADIMIR:
His hat?
POZZO:
He can't think without his hat.
VLADIMIR:
(*to Estragon*). Give him his hat.
ESTRAGON:
Me! After what he did to me! Never!
VLADIMIR:
I'll give it to him.
He does not move.
ESTRAGON:
(*to Pozzo*). Tell him to go and fetch it.
POZZO:
It's better to give it to him.
VLADIMIR:
I'll give it to him.
He picks up the hat and tenders it at arm's length to Lucky, who does not move.
POZZO:
You must put it on his head.
ESTRAGON:
(*to Pozzo*). Tell him to take it.
POZZO:
It's better to put it on his head.

VLADIMIR:

I'll put it on his head.

He goes round behind Lucky, approaches him cautiously, puts the hat on his head and recoils smartly. Lucky does not move. Silence.

ESTRAGON:

What's he waiting for?

POZZO:

Stand back! (*Vladimir and Estragon move away from Lucky. Pozzo jerks the rope. Lucky looks at Pozzo.*) Think, pig! (*Pause. Lucky begins to dance.*) Stop! (*Lucky stops.*) Forward! (*Lucky advances.*) Stop! (*Lucky stops.*) Think!

Silence.

LUCKY:

On the other hand with regard to—

POZZO:

Stop! (*Lucky stops.*) Back! (*Lucky moves back.*) Stop! (*Lucky stops.*) Turn! (*Lucky turns towards auditorium.*) Think!

During Lucky's tirade the others react as follows.

- Vladimir and Estragon all attention, Pozzo dejected and disgusted.
- Vladimir and Estragon begin to protest, Pozzo's sufferings increase.
- Vladimir and Estragon attentive again, Pozzo more and more agitated and groaning.
- *Vladimir and Estragon protest violently. Pozzo jumps up, pulls on the rope. General outcry. Lucky pulls on the rope, staggers, shouts his text. All three throw themselves on Lucky who struggles and shouts his text.*

LUCKY:

Given the existence as uttered forth in the public works of Puncher and Wattmann of a personal God quaquaquaqua with white beard quaquaquaqua outside time without extension who from the heights of divine apathia divine athambia divine aphasia loves us dearly with some exceptions for reasons unknown but time will tell and suffers like the divine Miranda with those who for reasons unknown but time will tell are plunged in torment plunged in fire whose fire flames if that continues and who can doubt it will fire the firmament that is to say blast hell to heaven so blue still and calm so calm with a calm which even though intermittent is better than nothing but not so fast and considering what is more that as a result of the labors left unfinished crowned by the Acacacacademy of Anthropopopometry of Essy-in-Possy of Testew and Cunard it is established beyond all doubt all other doubt than that which clings to the labors of men that as a result of the labors unfinished of Testew and Cunnard it is established as hereinafter but not so fast for reasons unknown that as a result of the public works of Puncher and Wattmann it is established beyond all doubt that in view of the labors of Fartov and Belcher left unfinished for reasons unknown of Testew and Cunard left unfinished it is established what many deny that man in Possy of Testew and Cunard that man in Essy that man in short that man in brief in spite of the strides of alimentation and defecation wastes and pines wastes and pines and concurrently simultaneously what is more for reasons unknown in spite of the strides of physical culture the practice of sports such as tennis football running cycling swimming flying floating riding gliding conating camogie skating tennis of all kinds dying flying sports of all sorts autumn summer winter winter tennis of all kinds hockey of all sorts penicillin and succedanea in a word I resume flying gliding golf over nine and eighteen holes tennis of all sorts in a word for reasons unknown in Feckham Peckham Fulham Clapham namely concurrently simultaneously what is more for reasons unknown but time will tell fades away I resume Fulham Clapham in a word the dead loss per head since the death of Bishop Berkeley being to the tune of one inch four ounce per head approximately by and large more or less to the nearest decimal good measure round figures stark naked in the stockinged feet in Connemara in a word for reasons unknown no matter what matter the facts are there and considering what is more much more grave that in the light of the labors lost of Steinweg and Peterman it appears what is more much more grave that in the light the light the light of the labors lost of Steinweg and Peterman that in the plains in the mountains by the seas by the rivers running water running fire the air is the same and then the earth namely the air and then the earth in the great cold the great dark the air and the earth abode of stones in the great cold alas alas in the year of their Lord six hundred and something the air the earth the sea the earth abode of stones in the great deeps the great cold on sea on land and in the air I resume for reasons unknown in spite of the tennis the facts are there but time will tell I resume alas alas on on in short in fine on on abode of stones who can doubt it I resume but not so fast I resume the skull fading fading fading and concurrently simultaneously what is more for reasons unknown in spite of the tennis on on the beard the flames the tears the stones so blue so calm alas alas on on the skull the skull the skull the skull in Connemara in spite of the tennis the labors abandoned left unfinished graver still abode of stones in a word I resume alas alas abandoned unfinished the skull the skull in Connemara in spite of the tennis the skull alas the stones Cunard (*mêlée, final vociferations*)

... tennis... the stones... so calm... Cunard... unfinished...

POZZO:

His hat!

Vladimir seizes Lucky's hat. Silence of Lucky. He falls. Silence. Panting of the victors.

ESTRAGON:

Avenged!

Vladimir examines the hat, peers inside it.

POZZO:

Give me that! (*He snatches the hat from Vladimir, throws it on the ground, tramples on it.*) There's an end to his thinking!

VLADIMIR:

But will he be able to walk?

POZZO:

Walk or crawl! (*He kicks Lucky.*) Up pig!

ESTRAGON:

Perhaps he's dead.

VLADIMIR:

You'll kill him.

POZZO:

Up scum! (*He jerks the rope.*) Help me!

VLADIMIR:

How?

POZZO:

Raise him up!

Vladimir and Estragon hoist Lucky to his feet, support him an instant, then let him go. He falls.

ESTRAGON:

He's doing it on purpose!

POZZO:

You must hold him. (*Pause.*) Come on, come on, raise him up.

ESTRAGON:

To hell with him!

VLADIMIR:

Come on, once more.

ESTRAGON:

What does he take us for?

They raise Lucky, hold him up.

POZZO:

Don't let him go! (*Vladimir and Estragon totter.*) Don't move! (*Pozzo fetches bag and basket and brings them towards Lucky.*) Hold him tight! (*He puts the bag in Lucky's hand. Lucky drops it immediately.*) Don't let him go! (*He puts back the bag in Lucky's hand. Gradually, at the feel of the bag, Lucky recovers his senses and his fingers finally close round the handle.*) Hold him tight! (*As before with basket.*) #

Now! You can let him go. (*Vladimir and Estragon move away from Lucky who totters, reels, sags, but succeeds in remaining on his feet, bag and basket in his hands. Pozzo steps back, cracks his whip.*) Forward! (*Lucky totters forward.*) Back! (*Lucky totters back.*) Turn! (*Lucky turns.*) Done it! He can walk.

(*Turning to Vladimir and Estragon.*) Thank you, gentlemen, and let me... (*he fumbles in his pockets*)... let me wish you... (*fumbles*)... wish you... (*fumbles*)... what have I done with my watch? (*Fumbles.*) A genuine half-hunter, gentlemen, with deadbeat escapement! (*Sobbing.*) Twas my granpa gave it to me! (*He searches on the ground, Vladimir and Estragon likewise.*

Pozzo turns over with his foot the remains of Lucky's hat.) Well now isn't that just—

VLADIMIR:

Perhaps it's in your fob.

POZZO:

Wait! (*He doubles up in an attempt to apply his ear to his stomach, listens. Silence.*) I hear nothing. (*He beckons them to approach, Vladimir and Estragon go over to him, bend over his stomach.*) Surely one should hear the tick-tick.

VLADIMIR:

Silence!

All listen, bent double. #

ESTRAGON:

I hear something.

POZZO:

Where?

VLADIMIR:

It's the heart.

POZZO:

(*disappointed*). Damnation!

VLADIMIR:

Silence!

ESTRAGON:

Perhaps it has stopped.

They straighten up.

POZZO:

Which of you smells so bad?

ESTRAGON:

He has stinking breath and I have stinking feet.

POZZO:

I must go.

ESTRAGON:

And your half-hunter?

POZZO:

I must have left it at the manor.

Silence.

ESTRAGON:

Then adieu.

POZZO:
Adieu.
VLADIMIR:
Adieu.
POZZO:
Adieu.
Silence. No one moves.
VLADIMIR:
Adieu.
POZZO:
Adieu.
ESTRAGON:
Adieu.
Silence.
POZZO:
And thank you.
VLADIMIR:
Thank *you*.
POZZO:
Not at all.
ESTRAGON:
Yes yes.
POZZO:
No no.
VLADIMIR:
Yes yes.
ESTRAGON:
No no.
Silence.
POZZO:
I don't seem to be able... (*long hesitation*)... to depart.
ESTRAGON:
Such is life.
Pozzo turns, moves away from Lucky towards the wings, paying out the rope as he goes.
VLADIMIR:
You're going the wrong way.
POZZO:

I need a running start. (*Having come to the end of the rope, i.e., off stage, he stops, turns and cries.*) Stand back! (*Vladimir and Estragon stand back, look towards Pozzo. Crack of whip.*) On! On!

ESTRAGON:

On!

VLADIMIR:

On!

Lucky moves off.

POZZO:

Faster! (*He appears, crosses the stage preceded by Lucky. Vladimir and Estragon wave their hats. Exit Lucky.*) On! On! (*On the point of disappearing in his turn he stops and turns. The rope tautens. Noise of Lucky falling off.*) Stool! (*Vladimir fetches stool and gives it to Pozzo who throws it to Lucky.*) Adieu!

VLADIMIR and ESTRAGON:

(*waving*). Adieu! Adieu!

POZZO:

Up! Pig! (*Noise of Lucky getting up.*) On! (*Exit Pozzo.*) Faster! On! Adieu! Pig! Yip! Adieu!

Long silence.

VLADIMIR:

That passed the time.

ESTRAGON:

It would have passed in any case.

VLADIMIR:

Yes, but not so rapidly.

Pause.

ESTRAGON:

What do we do now?

VLADIMIR:

I don't know.

ESTRAGON:

Let's go.

VLADIMIR:

We can't.

ESTRAGON:

Why not?

VLADIMIR:

We're waiting for Godot.
ESTRAGON:
(*despairingly*). Ah!
Pause.
VLADIMIR:
How they've changed!
ESTRAGON:
Who?
VLADIMIR:
Those two.
ESTRAGON:
That's the idea, let's make a little conversation.
VLADIMIR:
Haven't they?
ESTRAGON:
What?
VLADIMIR:
Changed.
ESTRAGON:
Very likely. They all change. Only we can't.
VLADIMIR:
Likely! It's certain. Didn't you see them?
ESTRAGON:
I suppose I did. But I don't know them.
VLADIMIR:
Yes you do know them.
ESTRAGON:
No I don't know them.
VLADIMIR:
We know them, I tell you. You forget everything. (*Pause. To himself.*) Unless they're not the same...
ESTRAGON:
Why didn't they recognize us then?
VLADIMIR:
That means nothing. I too pretended not to recognize them. And then nobody ever recognizes us.
ESTRAGON:
Forget it. What we need– Ow! (*Vladimir does not react.*) Ow!

VLADIMIR:
(*to himself*). Unless they're not the same...
ESTRAGON:
Didi! It's the other foot!
He goes hobbling towards the mound.
VLADIMIR:
Unless they're not the same...
BOY:
(*off*). Mister!
Estragon halts. Both look towards the voice.
ESTRAGON:
Off we go again.
VLADIMIR:
Approach, my child.
Enter Boy, timidly. He halts.
BOY:
Mister Albert... ?
VLADIMIR:
Yes.
ESTRAGON:
What do you want?
VLADIMIR:
Approach!
The Boy does not move.
ESTRAGON:
(*forcibly*). Approach when you're told, can't you?
The Boy advances timidly, halts.
VLADIMIR:
What is it?
BOY:
Mr. Godot...
VLADIMIR:
Obviously... (*Pause.*) Approach.
ESTRAGON:
(*violently*). Will you approach! (*The Boy advances timidly.*) What kept you so late?
VLADIMIR:
You have a message from Mr. Godot?

BOY:
Yes Sir.
VLADIMIR:
Well, what is it?
ESTRAGON:
What kept you so late?
The Boy looks at them in turn, not knowing to which he should reply.
VLADIMIR:
(*to Estragon*). Let him alone.
ESTRAGON:
(*violently*). You let me alone. (*Advancing, to the Boy.*) Do you know what time it is?
BOY:
(*recoiling*). It's not my fault, Sir.
ESTRAGON:
And whose is it? Mine?
BOY:
I was afraid, Sir.
ESTRAGON:
Afraid of what? Of us? (*Pause.*) Answer me!
VLADIMIR:
I know what it is, he was afraid of the others.
ESTRAGON:
How long have you been here?
BOY:
A good while, Sir.
VLADIMIR:
You were afraid of the whip?
BOY:
Yes Sir.
VLADIMIR:
The roars?
BOY:
Yes Sir.
VLADIMIR:
The two big men.
BOY:

Yes Sir.

VLADIMIR:

Do you know them?

BOY:

No Sir.

VLADIMIR:

Are you a native of these parts? (*Silence.*) Do you belong to these parts?

BOY:

Yes Sir.

ESTRAGON:

That's all a pack of lies. (*Shaking the Boy by the arm.*) Tell us the truth!

BOY:

(*trembling*). But it is the truth, Sir!

VLADIMIR:

Will you let him alone! What's the matter with you? #

(*Estragon releases the Boy, moves away, covering his face with his hands. Vladimir and the Boy observe him. Estragon drops his hands. His face is convulsed.*) What's the matter with you?

ESTRAGON:

I'm unhappy.

VLADIMIR:

Not really! Since when?

ESTRAGON:

I'd forgotten.

VLADIMIR:

Extraordinary the tricks that memory plays! (*Estragon tries to speak, renounces, limps to his place, sits down and begins to take off his boots. To Boy.*) Well?

BOY:

Mr. Godot—

VLADIMIR:

I've seen you before, haven't I?

BOY:

I don't know, Sir.

VLADIMIR:

You don't know me?

BOY:
No Sir.
VLADIMIR:
It wasn't you came yesterday?
BOY:
No Sir.
VLADIMIR:
This is your first time?
BOY:
Yes Sir.
Silence.
VLADIMIR:
Words words. (*Pause.*) Speak.
BOY:
(*in a rush*). Mr. Godot told me to tell you he won't come this evening but surely tomorrow.
Silence.
VLADIMIR:
Is that all?
BOY:
Yes Sir.
Silence.
VLADIMIR:
You work for Mr. Godot?
BOY:
Yes Sir.
VLADIMIR:
What do you do?
BOY:
I mind the goats, Sir.
VLADIMIR:
Is he good to you?
BOY:
Yes Sir.
VLADIMIR:
He doesn't beat you?
BOY:
No Sir, not me.

VLADIMIR:
Whom does he beat?
BOY:
He beats my brother, Sir.
VLADIMIR:
Ah, you have a brother?
BOY:
Yes Sir.
VLADIMIR:
What does he do?
BOY:
He minds the sheep, Sir.
VLADIMIR:
And why doesn't he beat you?
BOY:
I don't know, Sir.
VLADIMIR:
He must be fond of you.
BOY:
I don't know, Sir.
Silence.
VLADIMIR:
Does he give you enough to eat? (*The Boy hesitates.*) Does he feed you well?
BOY:
Fairly well, Sir.
VLADIMIR:
You're not unhappy? (*The Boy hesitates.*) Do you hear me?
BOY:
Yes Sir.
VLADIMIR:
Well?
BOY:
I don't know, Sir.
VLADIMIR:
You don't know if you're unhappy or not?
BOY:
No Sir.

VLADIMIR:

You're as bad as myself. (*Silence.*) Where do you sleep?

BOY:

In the loft, Sir.

VLADIMIR:

With your brother?

BOY:

Yes Sir.

VLADIMIR:

In the hay?

BOY:

Yes Sir.

Silence.

VLADIMIR:

All right, you may go.

BOY:

What am I to tell Mr. Godot, Sir?

VLADIMIR:

Tell him... (*he hesitates*)... tell him you saw us. (*Pause.*) You did see us, didn't you?

BOY:

Yes Sir.

He steps back, hesitates, turns and exit running. The light suddenly fails. In a moment it is night. The moon rises at back, mounts in the sky, stands still, shedding a pale light on the scene.

VLADIMIR:

At last! (*Estragon gets up and goes towards Vladimir, a boot in each hand. He puts them down at edge of stage, straightens and contemplates the moon.*) #

What are you doing?

ESTRAGON:

Pale for weariness.

VLADIMIR:

Eh?

ESTRAGON:

Of climbing heaven and gazing on the likes of us.

VLADIMIR:

Your boots, what are you doing with your boots?

ESTRAGON:
(*turning to look at the boots*). I'm leaving them there. (*Pause.*) Another will come, just as... as... as me, but with smaller feet, and they'll make him happy.
VLADIMIR:
But you can't go barefoot!
ESTRAGON:
Christ did.
VLADIMIR:
Christ! What has Christ got to do with it. You're not going to compare yourself to Christ!
ESTRAGON:
All my life I've compared myself to him.
VLADIMIR:
But where he lived it was warm, it was dry!
ESTRAGON:
Yes. And they crucified quick.
Silence.
VLADIMIR:
We've nothing more to do here.
ESTRAGON:
Nor anywhere else.
VLADIMIR:
Ah Gogo, don't go on like that. Tomorrow everything will be better.
ESTRAGON:
How do you make that out?
VLADIMIR:
Did you not hear what the child said?
ESTRAGON:
No.
VLADIMIR:
He said that Godot was sure to come tomorrow. (*Pause.*) What do you say to that?
ESTRAGON:
Then all we have to do is to wait on here.
VLADIMIR:
Are you mad? We must take cover. (*He takes Estragon by*

the arm.) Come on. *He draws Estragon after him. Estragon yields, then resists. They halt.*

ESTRAGON:

(*looking at the tree*). Pity we haven't got a bit of rope.

VLADIMIR:

Come on. It's cold.

He draws Estragon after him. As before.

ESTRAGON:

Remind me to bring a bit of rope tomorrow.

VLADIMIR:

Yes. Come on.

He draws him after him. As before.

ESTRAGON:

How long have we been together all the time now?

VLADIMIR:

I don't know. Fifty years maybe.

ESTRAGON:

Do you remember the day I threw myself into the Rhone?

VLADIMIR:

We were grape harvesting.

ESTRAGON:

You fished me out.

VLADIMIR:

That's all dead and buried.

ESTRAGON:

My clothes dried in the sun.

VLADIMIR:

There's no good harking back on that. Come on.

He draws him after him. As before.

ESTRAGON:

Wait!

VLADIMIR:

I'm cold!

ESTRAGON:

Wait! (*He moves away from Vladimir.*) I sometimes wonder if we wouldn't have been better off alone, each one for himself. (*He crosses the stage and sits down on the mound.*) We weren't made for the same road.

VLADIMIR:
(*without anger*). It's not certain.
ESTRAGON:
No, nothing is certain.
Vladimir slowly crosses the stage and sits down beside Estragon.
VLADIMIR:
We can still part, if you think it would be better.
ESTRAGON:
It's not worthwhile now.
Silence.
VLADIMIR:
No, it's not worthwhile now.
Silence.
ESTRAGON:
Well, shall we go?
VLADIMIR:
Yes, let's go.
They do not move.
Curtain.
ACT II
Next day. Same time.
Same place.
Estragon's boots front centre, heels together, toes splayed.
Lucky's hat at same place.
The tree has four or five leaves.

Enter Vladimir agitatedly. He halts and looks long at the tree, then suddenly begins to move feverishly about the stage. He halts before the boots, picks one up, examines it, sniffs it, manifests disgust, puts it back carefully.

Comes and goes. Halts extreme right and gazes into distance off, shading his eyes with his hand. Comes and goes. Halts extreme left, as before. Comes and goes. Halts suddenly and begins to sing loudly.

VLADIMIR:
A dog came in–
Having begun too high he stops, clears his throat, resumes:
A dog came in the kitchen
And stole a crust of bread.

Then cook up with a ladle
And beat him till he was dead.
Then all the dogs came running
And dug the dog a tomb–

He stops, broods, resumes:

Then all the dogs came running
And dug the dog a tomb
And wrote upon the tombstone
For the eyes of dogs to come:
A dog came in the kitchen
And stole a crust of bread.
Then cook up with a ladle
And beat him till he was dead.
Then all the dogs came running
And dug the dog a tomb–

He stops, broods, resumes.

Then all the dogs came running
And dug the dog a tomb–

He stops, broods. Softly.

And dug the dog a tomb ..

He remains a moment silent and motionless, then begins to move feverishly about the stage. He halts before the tree, comes and goes, before the boots, comes and goes, halts extreme right, gazes into distance, extreme left, gazes into distance. Enter Estragon right, barefoot, head bowed. He slowly crosses the stage. Vladimir turns and sees him.

VLADIMIR:

You again! (*Estragon halts but does not raise his head. Vladimir goes towards him.*) Come here till I embrace you.

ESTRAGON:

Don't touch me!

Vladimir holds back, pained.

VLADIMIR:

Do you want me to go away? (*Pause.*) Gogo! (*Pause. Vladimir observes him attentively.*) Did they beat you? (*Pause.*) Gogo! (*Estragon remains silent, head bowed.*) Where did you spend the night?

ESTRAGON:

Don't touch me! Don't question me! Don't speak to me! Stay with me!

VLADIMIR:

Did I ever leave you?

ESTRAGON:

You let me go.

VLADIMIR:

Look at me. (*Estragon does not raise his head. Violently.*) Will you look at me!

Estragon raises his head. They look long at each other, then suddenly embrace, clapping each other on the back. End of the embrace. Estragon, no longer supported, almost falls.

ESTRAGON:

What a day!

VLADIMIR:

Who beat you? Tell me.

ESTRAGON:

Another day done with.

VLADIMIR:

Not yet.

ESTRAGON:

For me it's over and done with, no matter what happens. (*Silence.*) I heard you singing.

VLADIMIR:

That's right, I remember.

ESTRAGON:

That finished me. I said to myself, He's all alone, he thinks I'm gone for ever, and he sings.

VLADIMIR:

One is not master of one's moods. All day I've felt in great form. (*Pause.*) I didn't get up in the night, not once!

ESTRAGON:

(*sadly*). You see, you piss better when I'm not there.

VLADIMIR:

I missed you... and at the same time I was happy. Isn't that a strange thing?

ESTRAGON:

(*shocked*). Happy?

VLADIMIR:

Perhaps it's not quite the right word.

ESTRAGON:

And now?

VLADIMIR:

Now?... (*Joyous.*) There you are again... (*Indifferent.*) There we are again... (*Gloomy.*) There I am again.

ESTRAGON:

You see, you feel worse when I'm with you. I feel better alone too.

VLADIMIR:

(*vexed*). Then why do you always come crawling back?

ESTRAGON:

I don't know.

VLADIMIR:

No, but I do. It's because you don't know how to defend yourself. I wouldn't have let them beat you.

ESTRAGON:

You couldn't have stopped them.

VLADIMIR:

Why not?

ESTRAGON:

There was ten of them.

VLADIMIR:

No, I mean before they beat you. I would have stopped you from doing whatever it was you were doing.

ESTRAGON:

I wasn't doing anything.

VLADIMIR:

Then why did they beat you?

ESTRAGON:

I don't know.

VLADIMIR:

Ah no, Gogo, the truth is there are things that escape you that don't escape me, you must feel it yourself.

ESTRAGON:

I tell you I wasn't doing anything.

VLADIMIR:

Perhaps you weren't. But it's the way of doing it that counts, the way of doing it, if you want to go on living.

ESTRAGON:

I wasn't doing anything.

VLADIMIR:

You must be happy too, deep down, if you only knew it.

ESTRAGON:

Happy about what?

VLADIMIR:

To be back with me again.

ESTRAGON:

Would you say so?

VLADIMIR:

Say you are, even if it's not true.

FSTRAGON:

What am I to say?

VLADIMIR:

Say, I am happy.

ESTRAGON:

I am happy.

VLADIMIR:

So am I.

ESTRAGON:

So am I.

VLADIMIR:

We are happy.

ESTRAGON:

We are happy. (*Silence.*) What do we do now, now that we are happy?

VLADIMIR:

Wait for Godot. (*Estragon groans. Silence.*) Things have changed here since yesterday.

ESTRAGON:

And if he doesn't come?

VLADIMIR:

(*after a moment of bewilderment*). We'll see when the time comes. (*Pause.*) I was saying that things have changed here since yesterday.

ESTRAGON:
Everything oozes.
VLADIMIR:
Look at the tree.
ESTRAGON:
It's never the same pus from one second to the next.
VLADIMIR:
The tree, look at the tree.
Estragon looks at the tree.
ESTRAGON:
Was it not there yesterday?
VLADIMIR:
Yes of course it was there. Do you not remember? We nearly hanged ourselves from it. But you wouldn't. Do you not remember?
ESTRAGON:
You dreamt it.
VLADIMIR:
Is it possible you've forgotten already?
ESTRAGON:
That's the way I am. Either I forget immediately or I never forget.
VLADIMIR:
And Pozzo and Lucky, have you forgotten them too?
ESTRAGON:
Pozzo and Lucky?
VLADIMIR:
He's forgotten everything!
ESTRAGON:
I remember a lunatic who kicked the shins off me. Then he played the fool.
VLADIMIR:
That was Lucky.
ESTRAGON:
I remember that. But when was it?
VLADIMIR:
And his keeper, do you not remember him?
ESTRAGON:

He gave me a bone.

VLADIMIR:

That was Pozzo.

ESTRAGON:

And all that was yesterday, you say?

VLADIMIR:

Yes of course it was yesterday.

ESTRAGON:

And here where we are now?

VLADIMIR:

Where else do you think? Do you not recognize the place?

ESTRAGON:

(*suddenly furious*). Recognize! What is there to recognize? All my lousy life I've crawled about in the mud! And you talk to me about scenery! (*Looking wildly about him.*) Look at this muckheap! I've never stirred from it!

VLADIMIR:

Calm yourself, calm yourself.

ESTRAGON:

You and your landscapes! Tell me about the worms!

VLADIMIR:

All the same, you can't tell me that this (*gesture*) bears any resemblance to... (*he hesitates*)... to the Macon country for example. You can't deny there's a big difference.

ESTRAGON:

The Macon country! Who's talking to you about the Macon country?

VLADIMIR:

But you were there yourself, in the Macon country.

ESTRAGON:

No I was never in the Macon country! I've puked my puke of a life away here, I tell you! Here! In the Cackon country!

VLADIMIR:

But we were there together, I could swear to it! Picking grapes for a man called... (*he snaps his fingers*)... can't think of the name of the man, at a place called... (*snaps his fingers*)... can't think of the name of the place, do you not remember?

ESTRAGON:

(*a little calmer*). It's possible. I didn't notice anything.
VLADIMIR:
But down there everything is red!
ESTRAGON:
(*exasperated*). I didn't notice anything, I tell you!
Silence. Vladimir sighs deeply.
VLADIMIR:
You're a hard man to get on with, Gogo.
ESTRAGON:
It'd be better if we parted.
VLADIMIR:
You always say that and you always come crawling back.
ESTRAGON:
The best thing would be to kill me, like the other.
VLADIMIR:
What other? (*Pause.*) What other?
ESTRAGON:
Like billions of others.
VLADIMIR:
(*sententious*). To every man his little cross. (*He sighs.*) Till he dies. (*Afterthought.*) And is forgotten.
ESTRAGON:
In the meantime let us try and converse calmly, since we are incapable of keeping silent.
VLADIMIR:
You're right, we're inexhaustible.
ESTRAGON:
It's so we won't think.
VLADIMIR:
We have that excuse.
ESTRAGON:
It's so we won't hear.
VLADIMIR:
We have our reasons.
ESTRAGON:
All the dead voices.
VLADIMIR:
They make a noise like wings.

ESTRAGON:
Like leaves.
VLADIMIR:
Like sand.
ESTRAGON:
Like leaves.
Silence.
VLADIMIR:
They all speak at once.
ESTRAGON:
Each one to itself.
Silence.
VLADIMIR:
Rather they whisper.
ESTRAGON:
They rustle.
VLADIMIR:
They murmur.
ESTRAGON:
They rustle.
Silence.
VLADIMIR:
What do they say?
ESTRAGON:
They talk about their lives.
VLADIMIR:
To have lived is not enough for them.
ESTRAGON:
They have to talk about it.
VLADIMIR:
To be dead is not enough for them.
ESTRAGON:
It is not sufficient.
Silence.
VLADIMIR:
They make a noise like feathers.
ESTRAGON:
Like leaves.

VLADIMIR:
Likes ashes.
ESTRAGON:
Like leaves.
Long silence.
VLADIMIR:
Say something!
ESTRAGON:
I'm trying.
Long silence.
VLADIMIR:
(*in anguish*). Say anything at all!
ESTRAGON:
What do we do now?
VLADIMIR:
Wait for Godot.
ESTRAGON:
Ah!
Silence.
VLADIMIR:
This is awful!
ESTRAGON:
Sing something.
VLADIMIR:
No no! (*He reflects.*) We could start all over again perhaps.
ESTRAGON:
That should be easy.
VLADIMIR:
It's the start that's difficult.
ESTRAGON:
You can start from anything.
VLADIMIR:
Yes, but you have to decide.
ESTRAGON:
True.
Silence.
VLADIMIR:
Help me!

ESTRAGON:
I'm trying.
Silence.
VLADIMIR:
When you seek you hear.
ESTRAGON:
You do.
VLADIMIR:
That prevents you from finding.
ESTRAGON:
It does.
VLADIMIR:
That prevents you from thinking.
ESTRAGON:
You think all the same.
VLADIMIR:
No no, it's impossible.
ESTRAGON:
That's the idea, let's contradict each another.
VLADIMIR:
Impossible.
ESTRAGON:
You think so?
VLADIMIR:
We're in no danger of ever thinking any more.
ESTRAGON:
Then what are we complaining about?
VLADIMIR:
Thinking is not the worst.
ESTRAGON:
Perhaps not. But at least there's that.
VLADIMIR:
That what?
ESTRAGON:
That's the idea, let's ask each other questions.
VLADIMIR:
What do you mean, at least there's that?
ESTRAGON:

That much less misery.
VLADIMIR:
True.
ESTRAGON:
Well? If we gave thanks for our mercies?
VLADIMIR:
What is terrible is to *have* thought.
ESTRAGON:
But did that ever happen to us?
VLADIMIR:
Where are all these corpses from?
ESTRAGON:
These skeletons.
VLADIMIR:
Tell me that.
ESTRAGON:
True.
VLADIMIR:
We must have thought a little.
ESTRAGON:
At the very beginning.
VLADIMIR:
A charnel-house! A charnel-house!
ESTRAGON:
You don't have to look.
VLADIMIR:
You can't help looking.
ESTRAGON:
True.
VLADIMIR:
Try as one may.
ESTRAGON:
I beg your pardon?
VLADIMIR:
Try as one may.
ESTRAGON:
We should turn resolutely towards Nature.
VLADIMIR:

We've tried that.
ESTRAGON:
True.
VLADIMIR:
Oh it's not the worst, I know.
ESTRAGON:
What?
VLADIMIR:
To have thought.
ESTRAGON:
Obviously.
VLADIMIR:
But we could have done without it.
ESTRAGON:
Que voulez-vous?
VLADIMIR:
I beg your pardon?
ESTRAGON:
Que voulez-vouz.
VLADIMIR:
Ah! que voulez-vous. Exactly.
Silence.
ESTRAGON:
That wasn't such a bad little canter.
VLADIMIR:
Yes, but now we'll have to find something else.
ESTRAGON:
Let me see.
He takes off his hat, concentrates.
VLADIMIR:
Let me see. (*He takes off his hat, concentrates. Long silence.*) Ah!
They put on their hats, relax.
ESTRAGON:
Well?
VLADIMIR:
What was I saying, we could go on from there.
ESTRAGON:

What were you saying when?

VLADIMIR:

At the very beginning.

ESTRAGON:

The very beginning of WHAT?

VLADIMIR:

This evening... I was saying... I was saying...

ESTRAGON:

I'm not a historian.

VLADIMIR:

Wait... we embraced... we were happy... happy... what do we do now that we're happy... go on waiting... waiting... let me think... it's coming... go on waiting... now that we're happy... let me see... ah! The tree!

ESTRAGON:

The tree?

VLADIMIR:

Do you not remember?

ESTRAGON:

I'm tired.

VLADIMIR:

Look at it.

They look at the tree.

ESTRAGON:

I see nothing.

VLADIMIR:

But yesterday evening it was all black and bare. And now it's covered with leaves.

ESTRAGON:

Leaves?

VLADIMIR:

In a single night.

ESTRAGON:

It must be the Spring.

VLADIMIR:

But in a single night!

ESTRAGON:

I tell you we weren't here yesterday. Another of your

nightmares.

VLADIMIR:

And where were we yesterday evening according to you?

ESTRAGON:

How would I know? In another compartment. There's no lack of void.

VLADIMIR:

(*sure of himself*). Good. We weren't here yesterday evening. Now what did we do yesterday evening?

ESTRAGON:

Do?

VLADIMIR:

Try and remember.

ESTRAGON:

Do... I suppose we blathered.

VLADIMIR:

(*controlling himself*). About what?

ESTRAGON:

Oh... this and that I suppose, nothing in particular. (*With assurance.*) Yes, now I remember, yesterday evening we spent blathering about nothing in particular. That's been going on now for half a century.

VLADIMIR:

You don't remember any fact, any circumstance?

ESTRAGON:

(*weary*). Don't torment me, Didi.

VLADIMIR:

The sun. The moon. Do you not remember?

ESTRAGON:

They must have been there, as usual.

VLADIMIR:

You didn't notice anything out of the ordinary?

ESTRAGON:

Alas!

VLADIMIR:

And Pozzo? And Lucky?

ESTRAGON:

Pozzo?

VLADIMIR:
The bones.
ESTRAGON:
They were like fishbones.
VLADIMIR:
It was Pozzo gave them to you.
ESTRAGON:
I don't know.
VLADIMIR:
And the kick.
ESTRAGON:
That's right, someone gave me a kick.
VLADIMIR:
It was Lucky gave it to you.
ESTRAGON:
And all that was yesterday?
VLADIMIR:
Show me your leg.
ESTRAGON:
Which?
VLADIMIR:
Both. Pull up your trousers. (*Estragon gives a leg to Vladimir, staggers. Vladimir takes the leg. They stagger.*) Pull up your trousers.
ESTRAGON:
I can't.
Vladimir pulls up the trousers, looks at the leg, lets it go. Estragon almost falls.
VLADIMIR:
The other. (*Estragon gives the same leg.*) The other, pig! (*Estragon gives the other leg. Triumphantly.*) There's the wound! Beginning to fester!
ESTRAGON:
And what about it?
VLADIMIR:
(*letting go the leg*). Where are your boots?
ESTRAGON:
I must have thrown them away.

VLADIMIR:
When?
ESTRAGON:
I don't know.
VLADIMIR:
Why?
ESTRAGON:
(*exasperated*). I don't know why I don't know!
VLADIMIR:
No, I mean why did you throw them away?
ESTRAGON:
(*exasperated*). Because they were hurting me!
VLADIMIR:
(*triumphantly, pointing to the boots*). There they are! (*Estragon looks at the boots.*) At the very spot where you left them yesterday!

Estragon goes towards the boots, inspects them closely.

ESTRAGON:
They're not mine.
VLADIMIR:
(*stupefied*). Not yours!
ESTRAGON:
Mine were black. These are brown.
VLADIMIR:
You're sure yours were black?
ESTRAGON:
Well they were a kind of gray.
VLADIMIR:
And these are brown. Show me.
ESTRAGON:
(*picking up a boot*). Well they're a kind of green.
VLADIMIR:
Show me. (*Estragon hands him the boot. Vladimir inspects it, throws it down angrily.*) Well of all the—
ESTRAGON:
You see, all that's a lot of bloody—
VLADIMIR:
Ah! I see what it is. Yes, I see what's happened.

ESTRAGON:
All that's a lot of bloody—
VLADIMIR:
It's elementary. Someone came and took yours and left you his.
ESTRAGON:
Why?
VLADIMIR:
His were too tight for him, so he took yours.
ESTRAGON:
But mine were too tight.
VLADIMIR:
For you. Not for him.
ESTRAGON:
(*having tried in vain to work it out*). I'm tired! (*Pause.*) Let's go.
VLADIMIR:
We can't.
ESTRAGON:
Why not?
VLADIMIR:
We're waiting for Godot.
ESTRAGON:
Ah! (*Pause. Despairing.*) What'll we do, what'll we do!
VLADIMIR:
There's nothing we can do.
ESTRAGON:
But I can't go on like this!
VLADIMIR:
Would you like a radish?
ESTRAGON:
Is that all there is?
VLADIMIR:
There are radishes and turnips.
ESTRAGON:
Are there no carrots?
VLADIMIR:
No. Anyway you overdo it with your carrots.

ESTRAGON:

Then give me a radish. (*Vladimir fumbles in his pockets, finds nothing but turnips, finally brings out a radish and hands it to Estragon who examines it, sniffs it.*) It's black!

VLADIMIR:

It's a radish.

ESTRAGON:

I only like the pink ones, you know that!

VLADIMIR:

Then you don't want it?

ESTRAGON:

I only like the pink ones!

VLADIMIR:

Then give it back to me.

Estragon gives it back.

ESTRAGON:

I'll go and get a carrot.

He does not move.

VLADIMIR:

This is becoming really insignificant.

ESTRAGON:

Not enough.

Silence.

VLADIMIR:

What about trying them.

ESTRAGON:

I've tried everything.

VLADIMIR:

No, I mean the boots.

ESTRAGON:

Would that be a good thing?

VLADIMIR:

It'd pass the time. (*Estragon hesitates.*) I assure you, it'd be an occupation.

ESTRAGON:

A relaxation.

VLADIMIR:

A recreation.

ESTRAGON:
A relaxation.
VLADIMIR:
Try.
ESTRAGON:
You'll help me?
VLADIMIR:
I will of course.
ESTRAGON:
We don't manage too badly, eh Didi, between the two of us?
VLADIMIR:
Yes yes. Come on, we'll try the left first.
ESTRAGON:
We always find something, eh Didi, to give us the impression we exist?
VLADIMIR:
(*impatiently*). Yes yes, we're magicians. But let us persevere in what we have resolved, before we forget. (*He picks up a boot.*) Come on, give me your foot. (*Estragon raises his foot.*) The other, hog! (*Estragon raises the other foot.*) Higher! #

(*Wreathed together they stagger about the stage. Vladimir succeeds finally in getting on the boot.*) Try and walk. (*Estragon walks.*) Well?
ESTRAGON:
It fits.
VLADIMIR:
(*taking string from his pocket*). We'll try and lace it.
ESTRAGON:
(*vehemently*). No no, no laces, no laces!
VLADIMIR:
You'll be sorry. Let's try the other. (*As before.*) Well?
ESTRAGON:
(*grudgingly*). It fits too.
VLADIMIR:
They don't hurt you?
ESTRAGON:
Not yet.
VLADIMIR:

Then you can keep them.
ESTRAGON:
They're too big.
VLADIMIR:
Perhaps you'll have socks some day.
ESTRAGON:
True.
VLADIMIR:
Then you'll keep them?
ESTRAGON:
That's enough about these boots.
VLADIMIR:
Yes, but—
ESTRAGON:
(*violently*). Enough! (*Silence.*) I suppose I might as well sit down.
He looks for a place to sit down, then goes and sits down on the mound.
VLADIMIR:
That's where you were sitting yesterday evening.
ESTRAGON:
If I could only sleep.
VLADIMIR:
Yesterday you slept.
ESTRAGON:
I'll try.
He resumes his foetal posture, his head between his knees.
VLADIMIR:
Wait. (*He goes over and sits down beside Estragon and begins to sing in a loud voice.*)
Bye bye bye bye
Bye bye– #
ESTRAGON:
(*looking up angrily*). Not so loud!
VLADIMIR:
(*softly*).
Bye bye bye bye
Bye bye bye bye

Bye bye bye bye

Bye bye...

Estragon sleeps. Vladimir gets up softly, takes off his coat and lays it across Estragon's shoulders, then starts walking up and down, swinging his arms to keep himself warm. Estragon wakes with a start, jumps up, casts about wildly. Vladimir runs to him, puts his arms around him.) There... there... Didi is here... don't be afraid...

ESTRAGON:

Ah!

VLADIMIR:

There... there... it's all over.

ESTRAGON:

I was falling—

VLADIMIR:

It's all over, it's all over.

ESTRAGON:

I was on top of a—

VLADIMIR:

Don't tell me! Come, we'll walk it off.

He takes Estragon by the arm and walks him up and down until Estragon refuses to go any further.

ESTRAGON:

That's enough. I'm tired.

VLADIMIR:

You'd rather be stuck there doing nothing?

ESTRAGON:

Yes.

VLADIMIR:

Please yourself.

He releases Estragon, picks up his coat and puts it on.

ESTRAGON:

Let's go.

VLADIMIR:

We can't.

ESTRAGON:

Why not?

VLADIMIR:

We're waiting for Godot.

ESTRAGON:

Ah! (*Vladimir walks up and down.*) Can you not stay still?

VLADIMIR:

I'm cold.

ESTRAGON:

We came too soon.

VLADIMIR:

It's always at nightfall.

ESTRAGON:

But night doesn't fall.

VLADIMIR:

It'll fall all of a sudden, like yesterday.

ESTRAGON:

Then it'll be night.

VLADIMIR:

And we can go.

ESTRAGON:

Then it'll be day again. (*Pause. Despairing.*) What'll we do, what'll we do!

VLADIMIR:

(*halting, violently*). Will you stop whining! I've had about my bellyful of your lamentations!

ESTRAGON:

I'm going.

VLADIMIR:

(*seeing Lucky's hat*). Well!

ESTRAGON:

Farewell.

VLADIMIR:

Lucky's hat. (*He goes towards it.*) I've been here an hour and never saw it. (*Very pleased.*) Fine!

ESTRAGON:

You'll never see me again.

VLADIMIR:

I knew it was the right place. Now our troubles are over. (*He picks up the hat, contemplates it, straightens it.*) Must have been a very fine hat. (*He puts it on in place of his own which he hands to Estragon.*) Here.

ESTRAGON:

What?

VLADIMIR:

Hold that.

Estragon takes Vladimir's hat. Vladimir adjusts Lucky's hat on his head. Estragon puts on Vladimir's hat in place of his own which he hands to Vladimir. Vladimir takes Estragon's hat. Estragon adjusts Vladimir's hat on his head. Vladimir puts on Estragon's hat in place of Lucky's which he hands to Estragon. Estragon takes Lucky's hat. Vladimir adjusts Estragon's hat on his head. Estragon puts on Lucky's hat in place of Vladimir's which he hands to Vladimir. Vladimir takes his hat, Estragon adjusts Lucky's hat on his head. Vladimir puts on his hat in place of Estragon's which he hands to Estragon. Estragon takes his hat. Vladimir adjusts his hat on his head. Estragon puts on his hat in place of Lucky's which he hands to Vladimir. Vladimir takes Lucky's hat. Estragon adjusts his hat on his head. Vladimir puts on Lucky's hat in place of his own which he hands to Estragon. Estragon takes Vladimir's hat. Vladimir adjusts Lucky's hat on his head. Estragon hands Vladimir's hat back to Vladimir who takes it and hands it back to Estragon who takes it and hands it back to Vladimir who takes it and throws it down.

How does it fit me?

ESTRAGON:

How would I know?

VLADIMIR:

No, but how do I look in it?

He turns his head coquettishly to and fro, minces like a mannequin.

ESTRAGON:

Hideous.

VLADIMIR:

Yes, but not more so than usual?

ESTRAGON:

Neither more nor less.

VLADIMIR:

Then I can keep it. Mine irked me. (*Pause.*) How shall I say? (*Pause.*) It itched me.

He takes off Lucky's hat, peers into it, shakes it, knocks on the crown, puts it on again.

ESTRAGON:

I'm going.

Silence.

VLADIMIR:

Will you not play?

ESTRAGON:

Play at what?

VLADIMIR:

We could play at Pozzo and Lucky.

ESTRAGON:

Never heard of it.

VLADIMIR:

I'll do Lucky, you do Pozzo. (*He imitates Lucky sagging under the weight of his baggage. Estragon looks at him with stupefaction.*) Go on.

ESTRAGON:

What am I to do?

VLADIMIR:

Curse me!

ESTRAGON:

(*after reflection*). Naughty!

VLADIMIR:

Stronger!

ESTRAGON:

Gonococcus! Spirochete!

Vladimir sways back and forth, doubled in two.

VLADIMIR:

Tell me to think.

ESTRAGON:

What?

VLADIMIR:

Say, Think, pig!

ESTRAGON:

Think, pig!

Silence.

VLADIMIR:

I can't.

ESTRAGON:

That's enough of that.

VLADIMIR:

Tell me to dance.

ESTRAGON:

I'm going.

VLADIMIR:

Dance, hog! (*He writhes. Exit Estragon left, precipitately.*) I can't! (*He looks up, misses Estragon.*) Gogo! (*He moves wildly about the stage. Enter Estragon left, panting. He hastens towards Vladimir, falls into his arms.*) There you are again at last!

ESTRAGON:

I'm accursed!

VLADIMIR:

Where were you? I thought you were gone for ever.

ESTRAGON:

They're coming!

VLADIMIR:

Who?

ESTRAGON:

I don't know.

VLADIMIR:

How many?

ESTRAGON:

I don't know.

VLADIMIR:

(*triumphantly*). It's Godot! At last! Gogo! It's Godot! We're saved! Let's go and meet him! (*He drags Estragon towards the wings. Estragon resists, pulls himself free, exit right.*) Gogo! Come back! (*Vladimir runs to extreme left, scans the horizon. Enter Estragon right, he hastens towards Vladimir, falls into his arms.*) There you are again again!

ESTRAGON:

I'm in hell!

VLADIMIR:

Where were you?

ESTRAGON:

They're coming there too!

VLADIMIR:

We're surrounded! (*Estragon makes a rush towards back.*) Imbecile! There's no way out there. (*He takes Estragon by the arm and drags him towards front. Gesture towards front.*) There! Not a soul in sight! Off you go! Quick! (*He pushes Estragon towards auditorium. Estragon recoils in horror.*) You won't? (*He contemplates auditorium.*) Well I can understand that. Wait till I see. (*He reflects.*) Your only hope left is to disappear.

ESTRAGON:

Where?

VLADIMIR:

Behind the tree. (*Estragon hesitates.*) Quick! Behind the tree. (*Estragon goes and crouches behind the tree, realizes he is not hidden, comes out from behind the tree.*) Decidedly this tree will not have been the slightest use to us.

ESTRAGON:

(*calmer*). I lost my head. Forgive me. It won't happen again. Tell me what to do.

VLADIMIR:

There's nothing to do.

ESTRAGON:

You go and stand there. (*He draws Vladimir to extreme right and places him with his back to the stage.*) There, don't move, and watch out. (*Vladimir scans horizon, screening his eyes with his hand. Estragon runs and takes up same position extreme left. They turn their heads and look at each other.*) Back to back like in the good old days. (*They continue to look at each other for a moment, then resume their watch. Long silence.*) Do you see anything coming?

VLADIMIR:

(*turning his head*). What?

ESTRAGON:

(*louder*). Do you see anything coming?

VLADIMIR:

No.

ESTRAGON:

Nor I.

They resume their watch. Silence.

VLADIMIR:
You must have had a vision.
ESTRAGON:
(*turning his head*). What?
VLADIMIR:
(*louder*). You must have had a vision.
ESTRAGON:
No need to shout!
They resume their watch. Silence.
VLADIMIR and ESTRAGON:
(*turning simultaneously*). Do you—
VLADIMIR:
Oh pardon!
ESTRAGON:
Carry on.
VLADIMIR:
No no, after you.
ESTRAGON:
No no, you first.
VLADIMIR:
I interrupted you.
ESTRAGON:
On the contrary.
They glare at each other angrily.
VLADIMIR:
Ceremonious ape!
ESTRAGON:
Punctilious pig!
VLADIMIR:
Finish your phrase, I tell you!
ESTRAGON:
Finish your own!
Silence. They draw closer, halt.
VLADIMIR:
Moron!
ESTRAGON:
That's the idea, let's abuse each other.
They turn, move apart, turn again and face each other.

VLADIMIR:
Moron!
ESTRAGON:
Vermin!
VLADIMIR:
Abortion!
ESTRAGON:
Morpion!
VLADIMIR:
Sewer-rat!
ESTRAGON:
Curate!
VLADIMIR:
Cretin!
ESTRAGON:
(*with finality*). Crritic!
VLADIMIR:
Oh!
He wilts, vanquished, and turns away.
ESTRAGON:
Now let's make it up.
VLADIMIR:
Gogo!
ESTRAGON:
Didi!
VLADIMIR:
Your hand!
ESTRAGON:
Take it!
VLADIMIR:
Come to my arms!
ESTRAGON:
Yours arms?
VLADIMIR:
My breast!
ESTRAGON:
Off we go!
They embrace.

They separate. Silence.

VLADIMIR:

How time flies when one has fun!

Silence.

ESTRAGON:

What do we do now?

VLADIMIR:

While waiting.

ESTRAGON:

While waiting.

Silence.

VLADIMIR:

We could do our exercises.

ESTRAGON:

Our movements.

VLADIMIR:

Our elevations.

ESTRAGON:

Our relaxations.

VLADIMIR:

Our elongations.

ESTRAGON:

Our relaxations.

VLADIMIR:

To warm us up.

ESTRAGON:

To calm us down.

VLADIMIR:

Off we go.

Vladimir hops from one foot to the other. Estragon imitates him.

ESTRAGON:

(*stopping*). That's enough. I'm tired.

VLADIMIR:

(*stopping*). We're not in shape. What about a little deep breathing?

ESTRAGON:

I'm tired breathing.

VLADIMIR:

You're right. (*Pause.*) Let's just do the tree, for the balance.

ESTRAGON:

The tree?

Vladimir does the tree, staggering about on one leg.

VLADIMIR:

(*stopping*). Your turn.

Estragon does the tree, staggers.

ESTRAGON:

Do you think God sees me?

VLADIMIR:

You must close your eyes.

Estragon closes his eyes, staggers worse.

ESTRAGON:

(*stopping, brandishing his fists, at the top of his voice.*) God have pity on me!

VLADIMIR:

(*vexed*). And me?

ESTRAGON:

On me! On me! Pity! On me!

Enter Pozzo and Lucky. Pozzo is blind. Lucky burdened as before. Rope as before, but much shorter, so that Pozzo may follow more easily. Lucky wearing a different hat. At the sight of Vladimir and Estragon he stops short. Pozzo, continuing on his way, bumps into him.

VLADIMIR:

Gogo!

POZZO:

(*clutching onto Lucky who staggers*). What is it? Who is it?

Lucky falls, drops everything and brings down Pozzo with him. They lie helpless among the scattered baggage.

ESTRAGON:

Is it Godot?

VLADIMIR:

At last! (*He goes towards the heap.*) Reinforcements at last!

POZZO:

Help!

ESTRAGON:

Is it Godot?

VLADIMIR:
We were beginning to weaken. Now we're sure to see the evening out.
POZZO:
Help!
ESTRAGON:
Do you hear him?
VLADIMIR:
We are no longer alone, waiting for the night, waiting for Godot, waiting for... waiting. All evening we have struggled, unassisted. Now it's over. It's already tomorrow.
POZZO:
Help!
VLADIMIR:
Time flows again already. The sun will set, the moon rise, and we away... from here.
POZZO:
Pity!
VLADIMIR:
Poor Pozzo!
ESTRAGON:
I knew it was him.
VLADIMIR:
Who?
ESTRAGON:
Godot.
VLADIMIR:
But it's not Godot.
ESTRAGON:
It's not Godot?
VLADIMIR:
It's not Godot.
ESTRAGON:
Then who is it?
VLADIMIR:
It's Pozzo.
POZZO:

Here! Here! Help me up!
VLADIMIR:
He can't get up.
ESTRAGON:
Let's go.
VLADIMIR:
We can't.
ESTRAGON:
Why not?
VLADIMIR:
We're waiting for Godot.
ESTRAGON:
Ah!
VLADIMIR:
Perhaps he has another bone for you.
ESTRAGON:
Bone?
VLADIMIR:
Chicken. Do you not remember?
ESTRAGON:
It was him?
VLADIMIR:
Yes.
ESTRAGON:
Ask him.
VLADIMIR:
Perhaps we should help him first.
ESTRAGON:
To do what?
VLADIMIR:
To get up.
ESTRAGON:
He can't get up?
VLADIMIR:
He wants to get up.
ESTRAGON:
Then let him get up.
VLADIMIR:

He can't.
ESTRAGON:
Why not?
VLADIMIR:
I don't know.
Pozzo writhes, groans, beats the ground with his fists.
ESTRAGON:
We should ask him for the bone first. Then if he refuses we'll leave him there.
VLADIMIR:
You mean we have him at our mercy?
ESTRAGON:
Yes.
VLADIMIR:
And that we should subordinate our good offices to certain conditions?
ESTRAGON:
What?
VLADIMIR:
That seems intelligent all right. But there's one thing I'm afraid of.
POZZO:
Help!
ESTRAGON:
What?
VLADIMIR:
That Lucky might get going all of a sudden. Then we'd be ballocksed.
ESTRAGON:
Lucky?
VLADIMIR:
The one that went for you yesterday.
ESTRAGON:
I tell you there was ten of them.
VLADIMIR:
No, before that, the one that kicked you.
ESTRAGON:
Is he there?

VLADIMIR:
As large as life. (*Gesture towards Lucky.*) For the moment he is inert. But he might run amuck any minute.
POZZO:
Help!
ESTRAGON:
And suppose we gave him a good beating, the two of us.
VLADIMIR:
You mean if we fell on him in his sleep?
ESTRAGON:
Yes.
VLADIMIR:
That seems a good idea all right. But could we do it? Is he really asleep? (*Pause.*) No, the best would be to take advantage of Pozzo's calling for help—
POZZO:
Help!
VLADIMIR:
To help him—
ESTRAGON:
We help *him*?
VLADIMIR:
In anticipation of some tangible return.
ESTRAGON:
And suppose he—
VLADIMIR:
Let us not waste our time in idle discourse! (*Pause. Vehemently.*) Let us do something, while we have the chance! It is not every day that we are needed. Not indeed that we personally are needed. Others would meet the case equally well, if not better. To all mankind they were addressed, those cries for help still ringing in our ears! But at this place, at this moment of time, all mankind is us, whether we like it or not. Let us make the most of it, before it is too late! Let us represent worthily for once the foul brood to which a cruel fate consigned us! What do you say?

(*Estragon says nothing.*) It is true that when with folded arms we weigh the pros and cons we are no less a credit to our species. The tiger bounds to the help of his congeners without the least reflection, or else he slinks away into the depths of the thickets. But that is not the question. What are we doing here, *that* is the question. And we are blessed in this, that we happen to know the answer. Yes, in this immense confusion one thing alone is clear. We are waiting for Godot to come—

ESTRAGON:

Ah!

POZZO:

Help!

VLADIMIR:

Or for night to fall. (*Pause.*) We have kept our appointment and that's an end to that. We are not saints, but we have kept our appointment. How many people can boast as much?

ESTRAGON:

Billions.

VLADIMIR:

You think so?

ESTRAGON:

I don't know.

VLADIMIR:

You may be right.

POZZO:

Help!

VLADIMIR:

All I know is that the hours are long, under these conditions, and constrain us to beguile them with proceedings which –how shall I say– which may at first sight seem reasonable, until they become a habit. You may say it is to prevent our reason from foundering. No doubt. But has it not long been straying in the night without end of the abyssal depths? That's what I sometimes wonder. You follow my reasoning?

ESTRAGON:

(*aphoristic for once*). We are all born mad. Some remain so.

POZZO:

Help! I'll pay you!

ESTRAGON:
How much?
POZZO:
One hundred francs!
ESTRAGON:
It's not enough.
VLADIMIR:
I wouldn't go so far as that.
ESTRAGON:
You think it's enough?
VLADIMIR:
No, I mean so far as to assert that I was weak in the head when I came into the world. But that is not the question.
POZZO:
Two hundred!
VLADIMIR:
We wait. We are bored. (*He throws up his hand.*) No, don't protest, we are bored to death, there's no denying it. Good. A diversion comes along and what do we do? We let it go to waste. Come, let's get to work! (*He advances towards the heap, stops in his stride.*) In an instant all will vanish and we'll be alone once more, in the midst of nothingness!

He broods.

POZZO:
Two hundred!
VLADIMIR:
We're coming!

He tries to pull Pozzo to his feet, fails, tries again, stumbles, falls, tries to get up, fails.

ESTRAGON:
What's the matter with you all?
VLADIMIR:
Help!
ESTRAGON:
I'm going.
VLADIMIR:
Don't leave me! They'll kill me!
POZZO:

Where am I?
VLADIMIR:
Gogo!
POZZO:
Help!
VLADIMIR:
Help!
ESTRAGON:
I'm going.
VLADIMIR:
Help me up first, then we'll go together.
ESTRAGON:
You promise?
VLADIMIR:
I swear it!
ESTRAGON:
And we'll never come back?
VLADIMIR:
Never!
ESTRAGON:
We'll go to the Pyrenees.
VLADIMIR:
Wherever you like.
ESTRAGON:
I've always wanted to wander in the Pyrenees.
VLADIMIR:
You'll wander in them.
ESTRAGON:
(*recoiling*). Who farted?
VLADIMIR:
Pozzo.
POZZO:
Here! Here! Pity!
ESTRAGON:
It's revolting!
VLADIMIR:
Quick! Give me your hand!
ESTRAGON:

I'm going. (*Pause. Louder.*) I'm going.

VLADIMIR:

Well I suppose in the end I'll get up by myself. (*He tries, fails.*) In the fullness of time.

ESTRAGON:

What's the matter with you?

VLADIMIR:

Go to hell.

ESTRAGON:

Are you staying there?

VLADIMIR:

For the time being.

ESTRAGON:

Come on, get up, you'll catch a chill.

VLADIMIR:

Don't worry about me.

ESTRAGON:

Come on, Didi, don't be pig-headed!

He stretches out his hand which Vladimir makes haste to seize.

VLADIMIR:

Pull!

Estragon pulls, stumbles, falls. Long silence.

POZZO:

Help!

VLADIMIR:

We've arrived.

POZZO:

Who are you?

VLADIMIR:

We are men.

Silence.

ESTRAGON:

Sweet mother earth!

VLADIMIR:

Can you get up?

ESTRAGON:

I don't know.

VLADIMIR:

Try.
ESTRAGON:
Not now, not now.
Silence.
POZZO:
What happened?
VLADIMIR:
(*violently*). Will you stop it, you! Pest! He can think of nothing but himself!
ESTRAGON:
What about a little snooze?
VLADIMIR:
Did you hear him? He wants to know what happened!
ESTRAGON:
Don't mind him. Sleep.
Silence.
POZZO:
Pity! Pity!
ESTRAGON:
(*with a start*). What is it?
VLADIMIR:
Were you asleep?
ESTRAGON:
I must have been.
VLADIMIR:
It's this bastard Pozzo at it again.
ESTRAGON:
Make him stop it. Kick him in the crotch.
VLADIMIR:
(*striking Pozzo*). Will you stop it! Crablouse! (*Pozzo extricates himself with cries of pain and crawls away. He stops, saws the air blindly, calling for help. Vladimir, propped on his elbow, observes his retreat.*) He's off! (*Pozzo collapses.*) He's down!
ESTRAGON:
What do we do now?
VLADIMIR:
Perhaps I could crawl to him.
ESTRAGON:

Don't leave me!
VLADIMIR:
Or I could call to him.
ESTRAGON:
Yes, call to him.
VLADIMIR:
Pozzo! (*Silence.*) Pozzo! (*Silence.*) No reply.
ESTRAGON:
Together.
VLADIMIR and ESTRAGON:
Pozzo! Pozzo!
VLADIMIR:
He moved.
ESTRAGON:
Are you sure his name is Pozzo?
VLADIMIR:
(*alarmed*). Mr. Pozzo! Come back! We won't hurt you!
Silence.
ESTRAGON:
We might try him with other names.
VLADIMIR:
I'm afraid he's dying.
ESTRAGON:
It'd be amusing.
VLADIMIR:
What'd be amusing?
ESTRAGON:
To try him with other names, one after the other. It'd pass the time. And we'd be bound to hit on the right one sooner or later.
VLADIMIR:
I tell you his name is Pozzo.
ESTRAGON:
We'll soon see. (*He reflects.*) Abel! Abel!
POZZO:
Help!
ESTRAGON:
Got it in one!

VLADIMIR:
I begin to weary of this motif.
ESTRAGON:
Perhaps the other is called Cain. Cain! Cain!
POZZO:
Help!
ESTRAGON:
He's all humanity. (*Silence.*) Look at the little cloud.
VLADIMIR:
(*raising his eyes*). Where?
ESTRAGON:
There. In the zenith.
VLADIMIR:
Well? (*Pause.*) What is there so wonderful about it?
Silence.
ESTRAGON:
Let's pass on now to something else, do you mind?
VLADIMIR:
I was just going to suggest it.
ESTRAGON:
But to what?
VLADIMIR:
Ah!
Silence.
ESTRAGON:
Suppose we got up to begin with?
VLADIMIR:
No harm trying.
They get up.
ESTRAGON:
Child's play.
VLADIMIR:
Simple question of will-power.
ESTRAGON:
And now?
POZZO:
Help!
ESTRAGON:

Let's go.
VLADIMIR:
We can't.
ESTRAGON:
Why not?
VLADIMIR:
We're waiting for Godot.
ESTRAGON:
Ah! (*Despairing.*) What'll we do, what'll we do!
POZZO:
Help!
VLADIMIR:
What about helping him?
ESTRAGON:
What does he want?
VLADIMIR:
He wants to get up.
ESTRAGON:
Then why doesn't he?
VLADIMIR:
He wants us to help him get up.
ESTRAGON:
Then why don't we? What are we waiting for?
They help Pozzo to his feet, let him go. He falls.
VLADIMIR:
We must hold him. (*They get him up again. Pozzo sags between them, his arms round their necks.*) #
Feeling better?
POZZO:
Who are you?
VLADIMIR:
Do you not recognize us?
POZZO:
I am blind.
Silence.
ESTRAGON:
Perhaps he can see into the future.
VLADIMIR:

Since when?
POZZO:
I used to have wonderful sight— but are you friends?
ESTRAGON:
(*laughing noisily*). He wants to know if we are friends!
VLADIMIR:
No, he means friends of his.
ESTRAGON:
Well?
VLADIMIR:
We've proved we are, by helping him.
ESTRAGON:
Exactly. Would we have helped him if we weren't his friends?
VLADIMIR:
Possibly.
ESTRAGON:
True.
VLADIMIR:
Don't let's quibble about that now.
POZZO:
You are not highwaymen?
ESTRAGON:
Highwaymen! Do we look like highwaymen?
VLADIMIR:
Damn it, can't you see the man is blind!
ESTRAGON:
Damn it, so he is. (*Pause.*) So he says.
POZZO:
Don't leave me!
VLADIMIR:
No question of it.
ESTRAGON:
For the moment.
POZZO:
What time is it?
VLADIMIR:
(*inspecting the sky*). Seven o'clock... eight o'clock...

ESTRAGON:
That depends what time of year it is.
POZZO:
Is it evening?
Silence. Vladimir and Estragon scrutinize the sunset.
ESTRAGON:
It's rising.
VLADIMIR:
Impossible.
ESTRAGON:
Perhaps it's the dawn.
VLADIMIR:
Don't be a fool. It's the west over there.
ESTRAGON:
How do you know?
POZZO:
(*anguished*). Is it evening?
VLADIMIR:
Anyway, it hasn't moved.
ESTRAGON:
I tell you it's rising.
POZZO:
Why don't you answer me?
ESTRAGON:
Give us a chance.
VLADIMIR:
(*reassuring*). It's evening, Sir, it's evening, night is drawing nigh. My friend here would have me doubt it and I must confess he shook me for a moment. But it is not for nothing I have lived through this long day and I can assure you it is very near the end of its repertory. (*Pause.*) How do you feel now?
ESTRAGON:
How much longer are we to cart him around? (*They half release him, catch him again as he falls.*) We are not caryatids!
VLADIMIR:
You were saying your sight used to be good, if I heard you right.

POZZO:

Wonderful! Wonderful, wonderful sight!

Silence.

ESTRAGON:

(*irritably*). Expand! Expand!

VLADIMIR:

Let him alone. Can't you see he's thinking of the days when he was happy. (*Pause.*) *Memoria praeteritorum bonorum*—that must be unpleasant.

ESTRAGON:

We wouldn't know.

VLADIMIR:

And it came on you all of a sudden?

POZZO:

Quite wonderful!

VLADIMIR:

I'm asking you if it came on you all of a sudden.

POZZO:

I woke up one fine day as blind as Fortune. (*Pause.*) Sometimes I wonder if I'm not still asleep.

VLADIMIR:

And when was that?

POZZO:

I don't know.

VLADIMIR:

But no later than yesterday—

POZZO:

(*violently*). Don't question me! The blind have no notion of time. The things of time are hidden from them too.

VLADIMIR:

Well just fancy that! I could have sworn it was just the opposite.

ESTRAGON:

I'm going.

POZZO:

Where are we?

VLADIMIR:

I couldn't tell you.

POZZO:
It isn't by any chance the place known as the Board?
VLADIMIR:
Never heard of it.
POZZO:
What is it like?
VLADIMIR:
(*looking round*). It's indescribable. It's like nothing. There's nothing. There's a tree.
POZZO:
Then it's not the Board.
ESTRAGON:
(*sagging*). Some diversion!
POZZO:
Where is my menial?
VLADIMIR:
He's about somewhere.
POZZO:
Why doesn't he answer when I call?
VLADIMIR:
I don't know. He seems to be sleeping. Perhaps he's dead.
POZZO:
What happened, exactly?
ESTRAGON:
Exactly!
VLADIMIR:
The two of you slipped. (*Pause.*) And fell.
POZZO:
Go and see is he hurt.
VLADIMIR:
We can't leave you.
POZZO:
You needn't both go.
VLADIMIR:
(*to Estragon*). You go.
ESTRAGON:
After what he did to me? Never!
POZZO:

Yes yes, let your friend go, he stinks so. (*Silence.*) What is he waiting for?

VLADIMIR:

What are you waiting for?

ESTRAGON:

I'm waiting for Godot.

Silence.

VLADIMIR:

What exactly should he do?

POZZO:

Well to begin with he should pull on the rope, as hard as he likes so long as he doesn't strangle him. He usually responds to that. If not he should give him a taste of his boot, in the face and the privates as far as possible.

VLADIMIR:

(*to Estragon*). You see, you've nothing to be afraid of. It's even an opportunity to revenge yourself.

ESTRAGON:

And if he defends himself?

POZZO:

No no, he never defends himself.

VLADIMIR:

I'll come flying to the rescue.

ESTRAGON:

Don't take your eyes off me.

He goes towards Lucky.

VLADIMIR:

Make sure he's alive before you start. No point in exerting yourself if he's dead.

ESTRAGON:

(*bending over Lucky*). He's breathing.

VLADIMIR:

Then let him have it.

With sudden fury Estragon starts kicking Lucky, hurling abuse at him as he does so. But he hurts his foot and moves away, limping and groaning. Lucky stirs.

ESTRAGON:

Oh the brute!

He sits down on the mound and tries to take off his boot. But he soon desists and disposes himself for sleep, his arms on his knees and his head on his arms.

POZZO:
What's gone wrong now?
VLADIMIR:
My friend has hurt himself.
POZZO:
And Lucky?
VLADIMIR:
So it is he?
POZZO:
What?
VLADIMIR:
It is Lucky?
POZZO:
I don't understand.
VLADIMIR:
And you are Pozzo?
POZZO:
Certainly I am Pozzo.
VLADIMIR:
The same as yesterday?
POZZO:
Yesterday?
VLADIMIR:
We met yesterday. (*Silence.*) Do you not remember?
POZZO:
I don't remember having met anyone yesterday. But tomorrow I won't remember having met anyone today. So don't count on me to enlighten you.
VLADIMIR:
But—
POZZO:
Enough! Up pig!
VLADIMIR:
You were bringing him to the fair to sell him. You spoke to us. He danced. He thought. You had your sight.

POZZO:

As you please. Let me go! (*Vladimir moves away.*) Up!

Lucky gets up, gathers up his burdens.

VLADIMIR:

Where do you go from here?

POZZO:

On. (*Lucky, laden down, takes his place before Pozzo.*) Whip! (*Lucky puts everything down, looks for whip, finds it, puts it into Pozzo's hand, takes up everything again.*) Rope! *Lucky puts everything down, puts end of rope into Pozzo's hand, takes up everything again.*

VLADIMIR:

What is there in the bag?

POZZO:

Sand. (*He jerks the rope.*) On!

VLADIMIR:

Don't go yet.

POZZO:

I'm going.

VLADIMIR:

What do you do when you fall far from help?

POZZO:

We wait till we can get up. Then we go on. On!

VLADIMIR:

Before you go tell him to sing.

POZZO:

Who?

VLADIMIR:

Lucky.

POZZO:

To sing?

VLADIMIR:

Yes. Or to think. Or to recite.

POZZO:

But he is dumb.

VLADIMIR:

Dumb!

POZZO:

Dumb. He can't even groan.

VLADIMIR:

Dumb! Since when?

POZZO:

(*suddenly furious.*) Have you not done tormenting me with your accursed time! It's abominable! When! When! One day, is that not enough for you, one day he went dumb, one day I went blind, one day we'll go deaf, one day we were born, one day we shall die, the same day, the same second, is that not enough for you? (*Calmer.*) They give birth astride of a grave, the light gleams an instant, then it's night once more. (*He jerks the rope.*) On!

Exeunt Pozzo and Lucky. Vladimir follows them to the edge of the stage, looks after them. The noise of falling, reinforced by mimic of Vladimir, announces that they are down again. Silence. Vladimir goes towards Estragon, contemplates him a moment, then shakes him awake.

ESTRAGON:

(*wild gestures, incoherent words. Finally.*) Why will you never let me sleep?

VLADIMIR:

I felt lonely.

ESTRAGON:

I was dreaming I was happy.

VLADIMIR:

That passed the time.

ESTRAGON:

I was dreaming that—

VLADIMIR:

(*violently*). Don't tell me! (*Silence.*) I wonder is he really blind.

ESTRAGON:

Blind? Who?

VLADIMIR:

Pozzo.

ESTRAGON:

Blind?

VLADIMIR:

He told us he was blind.

ESTRAGON:

Well what about it?

VLADIMIR:

It seemed to me he saw us.

ESTRAGON:

You dreamt it. (*Pause.*) Let's go. We can't. Ah! (*Pause.*) Are you sure it wasn't him?

VLADIMIR:

Who?

ESTRAGON:

Godot.

VLADIMIR:

But who?

ESTRAGON:

Pozzo.

VLADIMIR:

Not at all! (*Less sure.*) Not at all! (*Still less sure.*) Not at all!

ESTRAGON:

I suppose I might as well get up. (*He gets up painfully.*) Ow! Didi!

VLADIMIR:

I don't know what to think any more.

ESTRAGON:

My feet! (*He sits down again and tries to take off his boots.*) Help me!

VLADIMIR:

Was I sleeping, while the others suffered? Am I sleeping now? Tomorrow, when I wake, or think I do, what shall I say of today? That with Estragon my friend, at this place, until the fall of night, I waited for Godot? That Pozzo passed, with his carrier, and that he spoke to us? Probably. But in all that what truth will there be?

(*Estragon, having struggled with his boots in vain, is dozing off again. Vladimir looks at him.*) He'll know nothing. He'll tell me about the blows he received and I'll give him a carrot. (*Pause.*) Astride of a grave and a difficult birth. Down in the hole, lingeringly, the grave digger puts on the forceps. We have time to grow old. The air is full of our cries. (*He listens.*) But habit is a great deadener. (*He looks again at Estragon.*) At me too someone is looking, of me too someone is saying, He is sleeping, he knows nothing, let him sleep on. (*Pause.*) I can't go on! (*Pause.*) What have I said?

He goes feverishly to and fro, halts finally at extreme left, broods. Enter Boy right. He halts. Silence.

BOY:

Mister... (*Vladimir turns.*) Mister Albert...

VLADIMIR:

Off we go again. (*Pause.*) Do you not recognize me?

BOY:

No Sir.

VLADIMIR:

It wasn't you came yesterday.

BOY:

No Sir.

VLADIMIR:

This is your first time.

BOY:

Yes Sir.

Silence.

VLADIMIR:

You have a message from Mr. Godot.

BOY:

Yes Sir.

VLADIMIR:

He won't come this evening.

BOY:

No Sir.

VLADIMIR:

But he'll come tomorrow.

BOY:

Yes Sir.

VLADIMIR:

Without fail.

BOY:

Yes Sir.

Silence.

VLADIMIR:
Did you meet anyone?
BOY:
No Sir.
VLADIMIR:
Two other... (*he hesitates*)... men?
BOY:
I didn't see anyone, Sir.
Silence.
VLADIMIR:
What does he do, Mr. Godot? (*Silence.*) Do you hear me?
BOY:
Yes Sir.
VLADIMIR:
Well?
BOY:
He does nothing, Sir.
Silence.
VLADIMIR:
How is your brother?
BOY:
He's sick, Sir.
VLADIMIR:
Perhaps it was he came yesterday.
BOY:
I don't know, Sir.
Silence.
VLADIMIR:
(*softly*). Has he a beard, Mr. Godot?
BOY:
Yes Sir.
VLADIMIR:
Fair or... (*he hesitates*)... or black?
BOY:
I think it's white, Sir.
Silence.
VLADIMIR:
Christ have mercy on us!

Silence.

BOY:

What am I to tell Mr. Godot, Sir?

VLADIMIR:

Tell him... (*he hesitates*)... tell him you saw me and that... (*he hesitates*)... that you saw me. (*Pause. Vladimir advances, the Boy recoils. Vladimir halts, the Boy halts. With sudden violence.*) You're sure you saw me, you won't come and tell me tomorrow that you never saw me!

Silence. Vladimir makes a sudden spring forward, the Boy avoids him and exits running. Silence. The sun sets, the moon rises. As in Act 1. Vladimir stands motionless and bowed. Estragon wakes, takes off his boots, gets up with one in each hand and goes and puts them down centre front, then goes towards Vladimir.

ESTRAGON:

What's wrong with you?

VLADIMIR:

Nothing.

ESTRAGON:

I'm going.

VLADIMIR:

So am I.

ESTRAGON:

Was I long asleep?

VLADIMIR:

I don't know.

Silence.

ESTRAGON:

Where shall we go?

VLADIMIR:

Not far.

ESTRAGON:

Oh yes, let's go far away from here.

VLADIMIR:

We can't.

ESTRAGON:

Why not?

VLADIMIR:

We have to come back tomorrow.

ESTRAGON:

What for?

VLADIMIR:

To wait for Godot.

ESTRAGON:

Ah! (*Silence.*) He didn't come?

VLADIMIR:

No.

ESTRAGON:

And now it's too late.

VLADIMIR:

Yes, now it's night.

ESTRAGON:

And if we dropped him? (*Pause.*) If we dropped him?

VLADIMIR:

He'd punish us. (*Silence. He looks at the tree.*) Everything's dead but the tree.

ESTRAGON:

(*looking at the tree*). What is it?

VLADIMIR:

It's the tree.

ESTRAGON:

Yes, but what kind?

VLADIMIR:

I don't know. A willow.

Estragon draws Vladimir towards the tree. They stand motionless before it. Silence.

ESTRAGON:

Why don't we hang ourselves?

VLADIMIR:

With what?

ESTRAGON:

You haven't got a bit of rope?

VLADIMIR:

No.

ESTRAGON:

Then we can't.

Silence.

VLADIMIR:

Let's go.

ESTRAGON:

Wait, there's my belt.

VLADIMIR:

It's too short.

ESTRAGON:

You could hang onto my legs.

VLADIMIR:

And who'd hang onto mine?

ESTRAGON:

True.

VLADIMIR:

Show me all the same. (*Estragon loosens the cord that holds up his trousers which, much too big for him, fall about his ankles. They look at the cord.*) It might do in a pinch. But is it strong enough?

ESTRAGON:

We'll soon see. Here.

They each take an end of the cord and pull. #

It breaks. They almost fall.

VLADIMIR:

Not worth a curse.

Silence.

ESTRAGON:

You say we have to come back tomorrow?

VLADIMIR:

Yes.

ESTRAGON:

Then we can bring a good bit of rope.

VLADIMIR:

Yes.

Silence.

ESTRAGON:

Didi?

VLADIMIR:

Yes.

ESTRAGON:
I can't go on like this.
VLADIMIR:
That's what you think.
ESTRAGON:
If we parted? That might be better for us.
VLADIMIR:
We'll hang ourselves tomorrow. (*Pause.*) Unless Godot comes.
ESTRAGON:
And if he comes?
VLADIMIR:
We'll be saved.
Vladimir takes off his hat (Lucky's), peers inside it, feels about inside it, shakes it, knocks on the crown, puts it on again.
ESTRAGON:
Well? Shall we go?
VLADIMIR:
Pull on your trousers.
ESTRAGON:
What?
VLADIMIR:
Pull on your trousers.
ESTRAGON:
You want me to pull off my trousers?
VLADIMIR:
Pull ON your trousers.
ESTRAGON:
(*realizing his trousers are down*). True.
He pulls up his trousers.
VLADIMIR:
Well? Shall we go?
ESTRAGON:
Yes, let's go.
They do not move.
Curtain.

Chapter 10

Summary and Analysis

Summary of Act I

The setting is in the evening on a country road with a single tree present. Estragon is trying to pull off his boot, but without success. Vladimir enters and greets Estragon, who informs him that he has spent the night in a ditch where he was beaten. With supreme effort Estragon succeeds in pulling off his boot. He then looks inside it to see if there is anything there while Vladimir does the same with his hat.

Vladimir mentions the two thieves who were crucified next to Christ. He asks Estragon if he knows the Gospels. Estragon gives a short description of the maps of the Holy Land at which point Vladimir tells him he should have been a poet. Estragon points to his tattered clothes and says he was. Vladimir continues with his narrative about the two thieves in order to pass the time.

Estragon wants to leave but Vladimir forces him to stay because they are both waiting for Godot to arrive. Neither of the two bums knows when Godot will appear, or even if they are at the right place. Later it is revealed that they do not even know what they originally asked Godot for.

Estragon gets bored of waiting and suggests that they pass the time by hanging themselves from the tree. They both like the idea but cannot decide who should go first. They are afraid that if one of them dies the other might be left alone. In the end they decide it is safer to wait until Godot arrives.

Estragon asks Vladimir whether they still have rights. Vladimir indicates that they got rid of them. He then fears that he hears something, but it turns out to be imaginary noises. Vladimir soon gives Estragon a carrot to eat.

Pozzo and Lucky arrive. Lucky has a rope tied around his neck and is carrying a stool, a basket, a bag and a greatcoat. Pozzo carries a whip which he uses to control Lucky. Estragon immediately confuses Pozzo with Godot which gets Pozzo upset.

Pozzo spends several minutes ordering Lucky around. Lucky is completely silent and obeys like a machine. Pozzo has Lucky put down the stool and open the basket of food which contains chicken. Pozzo then eats the chicken and throws away the bones. Lucky stands in a stooped posture holding the bags after each command has been completed and appears to be falling asleep.

Estragon and Vladimir go to inspect Lucky who intrigues them. They ask why he never puts his bags down. Pozzo will not tell them, so Estragon proceeds to ask if he can have the chicken bones that Pozzo has been throwing away. Pozzo tells him that they technically belong to Lucky. When they ask Lucky if he wants them, he does not reply, so Estragon is given the bones.

Pozzo eventually tells them why Lucky hold the bags the entire time. He thinks it is because Lucky is afraid of being given away. While Pozzo tells them why Lucky continues to carry his bags, Lucky starts to weep. Estragon goes to wipe away the tears but receives a terrible kick in the shin.

Pozzo then tells them that he and Lucky have been together nearly sixty years. Vladimir is appalled at the treatment of Lucky who appears to be such a faithful servant. Pozzo explains that he cannot bear it any longer because Lucky is such a burden. Later Vladimir yells at Lucky that it is appalling the way he treats such a good master.

Pozzo then gives an oratory about the night sky. He asks them how it was and they tell him it was quite a good speech. Pozzo is ecstatic at the encouragement and offers to do something for them. Estragon immediately asks for ten francs but Vladimir tells him to be silent. Pozzo offers to have Lucky dance and then think for them.

Lucky dances for them and when asked for an encore repeats the entire dance step for step. Estragon is unimpressed but almost falls trying to imitate it. They then make Lucky think. What follows is an outpouring of religious and political doctrine which always starts ideas but never brings them to completion. The three men finally wrestle Lucky to the ground and yank off his hat at which point he stops speaking. His last word is, "unfinished."

The men then spend some effort trying to get Lucky to wake up again. He finally reawakens when the bags are placed in his hand. Pozzo gets up to leave and he and Lucky depart the scene. Vladimir and Estragon return to their seats and continue waiting for Godot.

A young boy arrives having been sent by Mr. Godot. Estragon is outraged that it took him so long to arrive and scares him. Vladimir cut him off and asks the boy if he remembers him. The boy says this is his first time coming to meet them and that Mr. Godot will not be able to come today but perhaps tomorrow. The boy is sent away with the instructions to tell Mr. Godot that he has seen them. Both Estragon and Vladimir discuss past events and then decide to depart for the night. Neither of them moves from his seat.

Summary of Act II

The setting is the next day at the same time. Estragon's boots and Lucky's hat are still on the stage. Vladimir enters and starts to sing until Estragon shows up barefoot. Estragon is upset that Vladimir was singing and happy even though he was not there. Both admit that they feel better when alone but convince themselves they are happy when together. They are still waiting for Godot.

Estragon and Vladimir poetically talk about "all the dead voices" they hear. They are haunted by voices in the sounds of nature, especially of the leaves rustling. Vladimir shouts at Estragon to help him not hear the voices anymore. Estragon tries and finally decides that they should ask each other questions. They manage to talk for a short while.

Estragon has forgotten everything that took place the day

before. He has forgotten all about Pozzo and Lucky as well as the fact that he wanted to hang himself from the tree. He cannot remember his boots and thinks they must be someone else's. For some reason they fit him now when he tries them on. The tree has sprouted leaves since the night before and Estragon comments that it must be spring. But when Vladimir looks at Estragon's shin, it is still pussy and bleeding from where Lucky kicked him.

Soon they are done talking and try to find another topic for discussion. Vladimir finds Lucky's hat and tries it on. He and Estragon spend a while trading hats until Vladimir throws his own hat on the ground and asks how he looks. They then decide to play at being Pozzo and Lucky, but to no avail. Estragon leaves only to immediately return panting. He says that they are coming. Vladimir thinks that it must be Godot who is coming to save them. He then becomes afraid and tries to hide Estragon behind the tree, which is too small to hide him.

The conversation then degenerates into abusive phrases. Estragon says, "That's the idea, let's abuse each other." They continue to hurl insults at one another until Estragon calls Vladimir a critic. They embrace and continue waiting.

Pozzo and Lucky enter but this time Pozzo is blind and Lucky is mute. Lucky stops when he sees the two men. Pozzo crashes into him and they both fall helplessly in a heap on the ground. Vladimir is overjoyed that reinforcements have arrived to help with the waiting. Estragon again thinks that Godot has arrived.

Vladimir and Estragon discuss the merits of helping Pozzo get off the ground where he has fallen. When Vladimir asks how many other men spend their time in waiting, Estragon replies that it is billions. Pozzo in desperation offers to pay for help by offering a hundred francs. Estragon says that it is not enough. Vladimir does not want to pick up Pozzo because then he and Estragon would be alone again. Finally he goes over and tries to pick him up but is unable to. Estragon decides to leave but decides to stay when Vladimir convinces him to help first and then leave.

While trying to help Pozzo, both Vladimir and Estragon fall and cannot get up. When Pozzo talks again Vladimir kicks him violently to make him shut up. Vladimir and Estragon finally get up, and Pozzo resumes calling for help. They go and help him up. Pozzo asks who they are and what time it is. They cannot answer his questions.

Estragon goes to wake up Lucky. He kicks him and starts hurling abuses until he again hurts his foot. Estragon sits back down and tries to take off his boot. Vladimir tells Pozzo his friend is hurt.

Vladimir then asks Pozzo to make Lucky dance or think for them again. Pozzo tells him that Lucky is mute. When Vladimir asks since when, Pozzo gets into a rage. He tells them to stop harassing him with their time questions since he has no notion of it. He then helps Lucky up and they leave.

Vladimir reflects upon the fact that there is no truth and that by tomorrow he will know nothing of what has just passed. There is no way of confirming his memories since Estragon always forgets everything that happens to him.

The boy arrives again but does not remember meeting Estragon or Vladimir. He tells them it is his first time coming to meet them. The conversation is identical in that Mr. Godot will once again not be able to come but will be sure to arrive tomorrow. Vladimir demands that the boy be sure to remember that he saw him. Vladimir yells, "You're sure you saw me, you won't come and tell me to-morrow that you never saw me!"

The two bums decide to leave but cannot go far since they need to wait for Godot. They look at the tree and contemplate hanging themselves. Estragon takes off his belt but it breaks when they pull on it. His trousers fall down. Vladimir says that they will hang themselves tomorrow unless Godot comes to save them. He tells Estragon to put on his trousers. They decide to leave but again do not move.

Analysis of the Play

Although very existentialist in its characterizations, Waiting for Godot is primarily about hope. The play revolves around Vladimir and Estragon and their pitiful wait for hope to arrive. At various times during the play, hope is constructed as a form of salvation, in the personages of Pozzo and Lucky, or even as death. The subject of the play quickly becomes an example of how to pass the time in a situation which offers no hope. Thus the theme of the play is set by the beginning:

Estragon: Nothing to be done.

Vladimir: I'm beginning to come round to that opinion.

Although the phrase is used in connection to Estragon's boots here, it is also later used by Vladimir with respect to his hat. Essentially it describes the hopelessness of their lives.

A direct result of this hopelessness is the daily struggle to pass the time. Thus, most of the play is dedicated to devising games which will help them pass the time. This mutual desire also addresses the question of why they stay together. Both Vladimir and Estragon admit to being happier when apart. One of the main reasons that they continue their relationship is that they need one another to pass the time. After Pozzo and Lucky leave for the first time they comment:

V: That passed the time.

E: It would have passed in any case.

And later when Estragon finds his boots again:

V: What about trying them.

E: I've tried everything.

V: No, I mean the boots.

E: Would that be a good thing?

V: It'd pass the time. I assure you, it'd be an occupation.

Since passing the time is their mutual occupation, Estragon struggles to find games to help them accomplish their goal. Thus they engage in insulting one another and in asking each other questions.

The difficulty for Beckett of keeping a dialogue running for so long is overcome by making his characters forget everything. Estragon cannot remember anything past what was said immediately prior to his lines. Vladimir, although possessing a better memory, distrusts what he remembers. And since Vladimir cannot rely on Estragon to remind him of things, he too exists in a state of forgetfulness.

Another second reason for why they are together arises from the existentialism of their forgetfulness. Since Estragon cannot remember anything, he needs Vladimir to tell him his history. It is as if Vladimir is establishing Estragon's identity by remembering for him.

Estragon also serves as a reminder for Vladimir of all the things they have done together. Thus both men serve to remind the other man of his very existence. This is necessary since no one else in the play ever remembers them:

Vladimir: We met yesterday. (Silence) Do you not remember?

Pozzo: I don't remember having met anyone yesterday. But to-morrow I won't remember having met anyone to-day. So don't count on me to enlighten you.

Later on the same thing happens with the boy who claims to have never seen them before. This lack of reassurance about their very existence makes it all the more necessary that they remember each other.

Estragon and Vladimir are not only talking to pass the time, but also to avoid the voices that arise out of the silence. Beckett's heroes in other works are also constantly assailed by voices which arise out of the silence, so this is a continuation of a theme the author uses frequently:

E: In the meantime let's try and converse calmly, since we're incapable of keeping silent.
V: You're right, we're inexhaustible.
E: It's so we won't think.
V: We have that excuse.
E: It's so we won't hear.
V: We have our reasons.
E: All the dead voices.
V: They make a noise like wings.
E: Like leaves.
V: Like sand.
E: Like leaves.
Silence.
V: They all speak at once.
E: Each one to itself.

Silence.

V: Rather they whisper.

E: They rustle.

V: They murmur.

E: The rustle.

Silence.

V: What do they say?

E: They talk about their lives.

V: To have lived is not enough for them.

E: They have to talk about it.

V: To be dead is not enough for them.

E: It is not sufficient.

Silence.

V: They make a noise like feathers.

E: Like leaves.

V: Like ashes.

E: Like leaves.

Long silence.

V: Say something!

One of the questions which must be answered is why the bums are suffering in the first place. This can only be answered through the concept of original sin. To be born is to be a sinner, and thus man is condemned to suffer.

The only way to escape the suffering is to repent or to die. Thus Vladimir recalls the thieves crucified with Christ in the first act:

V: One of the thieves was saved. It's a reasonable percentage. (Pause.) Gogo.

E: What?

V: Suppose we repented.

E: Repented what?

V: Oh... (He reflects.) We wouldn't have to go into the details.

E: Our being born?

Failing to repent, they sit and wait for Godot to come and save them. In the meantime they contemplate suicide as another way of escaping their hopelessness. Estragon wants them to hang themselves from the tree, but both he and Vladimir find it would be too risky. This apathy, which is a result of their age, leads them to remember a time when Estragon almost succeeded in killing himself:

E: Do you remember the day I threw myself into the Rhone?

V: We were grape harvesting.

E: You fished me out.

V: That's all dead and buried.

E: My clothes dried in the sun.

V: There's no good harking back on that. Come on.

Beckett is believed to have said that the name Godot comes from the French "godillot" meaning a military boot. Beckett fought in the war and so spending long periods of time waiting for messages to arrive would have been commonplace for him. The more common interpretation that it might mean "God" is almost certainly wrong. Beckett apparently stated that if he had meant "God," he would have written "God".

The concept of the passage of time leads to a general irony. Each minute spent waiting brings death one step closer to the characters and makes the arrival of Godot less likely. The passage of time is evidenced by the tree which has grown leaves, possibly indicating a change of seasons. Pozzo and Lucky are also transformed by time since Pozzo goes blind and Lucky mute. There are numerous interpretation of Waiting for Godot and a few are described here:

Religious interpretations posit Vladimir and Estragon as humanity waiting for the elusive return of a savior. An extension of this makes Pozzo into the Pope and Lucky into the faithful. The faithful are then viewed as a cipher of God cut short by human intolerance. The twisted tree can alternatively represent either the tree of death, the tree of life, the tree of Judas or the tree of knowledge.

Political interpretations also abound. Some reviewers hold that the relationship between Pozzo and Lucky is that of a capitalist to his labour. This Marxist interpretation is understandable given that in the second act Pozzo is blind to what is happening around him and Lucky is mute to protest his treatment. The play has also been understood as an allegory for Franco-German relations.

An interesting interpretation argues that Lucky receives

his name because he is lucky in the context of the play. Since most of the play is spent trying to find things to do to pass the time, Lucky is lucky because his actions are determined absolutely by Pozzo. Pozzo on the other hand is unlucky because he not only needs to pass his own time but must find things for Lucky to do.

Chapter 11

Study Questions

Q. Is Waiting for Godot an Existentialist play?

Or

Q. Explain the Ironic Element of the Play ?

The play, Waiting For Godot, is centred around two men, Estragon and Vladimir, who are waiting for a Mr. Godot, of whom they know little. Estragon admits himself that he may never recognize Mr. Godot, "Personally I wouldn't know him if I ever saw him." (p.23). Estragon also remarks, "... we hardly know him." (p.23), which illustrates to an audience that the identity of Mr. Godot is irrelevant, as little information is ever given throughout the play about this indefinable Mr. X. What is an important element of the play is the act of waiting for someone or something that never arrives. Western readers may find it natural to speculate on the identity of Godot because of their inordinate need to find answers to questions. Beckett however suggests that the identity of Godot is in itself a rhetorical question. It is possible to stress the for in the waiting for ...: to see the purpose of action in two men with a mission, not to be deflected from their compulsive task.

"Estragon: ... Let's go.
Vladimir: We can't.
Estragon: Why not?
Vladimir: We're waiting for Godot."

The essence of existentialism concentrates on the concept of the individual's freedom of choice, as opposed to the belief that humans are controlled by a pre-existing omnipotent being, such as God. Estragon and Vladimir have made the choice of waiting, without instruction or guidance, as Vladimir says,

"He didn't say for sure he'd come" (p.14), but decides to "wait till we know exactly how we stand".

Albert Camus, an existentialist writer, believed that boredom or waiting, which is essentially the breakdown of routine or habit, caused people to think seriously about their identity, as Estragon and Vladimir do. In The Plague, Camus suggests that boredom or inactivity causes the individual to think. This is also similar to the idea of meditation, an almost motionless activity, allowing the individual to think with clarity. Camus, and other existential writers, suggested that attempting to answer these rhetorical questions could drive someone to the point of insanity. The tramps continually attempt to prove that they exist, in order to keep their sanity:

"We always find something, eh Didi, to give us the impression that we exist?".

Waiting in the play induces boredom as a theme. Ironically Beckett attempts to create a similar nuance of boredom within the audience by the mundane repetition of dialogue and actions. Vladimir and Estragon constantly ponder and ask questions, many of which are rhetorical or are left unanswered. During the course of the play, certain unanswered questions arise: who is Godot? Where are Gogo and Didi? Who beats Gogo? All of these unanswered questions represent the rhetorical questions that individuals ask but never get answers for within their lifetime. Vis a vis is there a God? Where do we come from? Who is responsible for our suffering? The German existentialist philosopher Martin Heidegger expressed clearly that human beings can never hope to understand why they are here. The tramps repetitive inspection of their empty hats perhaps symbolizes mankind's vain search for answers within the vacuum of a universe.

Jean Paul Sartre, the leading figure of French existentialism declared that human beings require a rational basis for their lives but are unable to achieve one, and thus human life is a futile passion. Estragon and Vladimir attempt to put order into their lives by waiting for a Godot who never arrives. They continually subside into the futility of their situation, reiterating the phrase "Nothing to be done."

Vladimir also resolves with the notion that life is futile, or nothing is to be done at the beginning, replying, "All my life I've tried to put it from me... And I resumed the struggle.".

"Estragon: (anxious). And we? ... Where do we come in?".

Estragon's question is left unanswered by Vladimir. Note that these questions seem to bring pain or anxiety to Estragon. Beckett conveys a universal message that pondering the impossible questions that arise from waiting, cause pain, anxiety, inactivity and destroy people from within. Note that both Vladimir and Estragon ponder suicide, by hanging themselves from the tree, but are unable to act through to anxiety, as Estragon states, "Don't let's do anything. It's safer."

Kierkagaard's philosophical view of 'Dread' or 'Angst' (German for anxiety) as described by the German philosopher Martin Heidegger, is a state in which the individual's freedom of choice places the individual in a state of anxiety, as the individual is surrounded by almost infinite possibilities. This could explain the inactivity of both Estragon and Vladimir. Both characters are aware of different choices they can make but are hesitant, anxious and generally inactive, as shown at the end of Act one when they decide to leave but are immobile.

" Estragon: Well, shall we go?

Vladimir: Yes, let's go.

They do not move.".

Beckett infers that humans 'pass time' by habit or routine to cope with the existentialist dilemma of the dread or anxiety of their existence. Beckett believes that humans basically alleviate the pain of living or existence (which is at the crux of Existential philosophy) by habit. The idea of habit being essential for human existence substantiates Sartre's view that humans require a rational base for their lives. Beckett feels that habit protects us from whatever can neither be predicted or controlled, as he wrote about the theme of habit in his published essay concerning Proust:

"Habit is a compromise effected between the individual and his environment, or between the individual and his own organic eccentricities, the guarantee of a dull inviolability, the lightening-conductor of his existence. Habit is the ballast that chains the dog to his vomit. Breathing is habit. Life is habit."

Estragon and Vladimir constantly 'pass the time' throughout the entire play to escape the pain of waiting and to possibly to stop themselves from thinking or contemplating too deeply. Vladimir expresses this idea at the end of the play, 'Habit is a great deadener', suggesting that habit is like an analgesic - numbing the individual. The play is mostly ritual, with Estargon and Vladimir filling the emptiness and silence. "It'll pass the time," explains Vladimir, offering to tell the story of the Crucifixion. Passing the time is their mutual obsession, as exhibited after the first departure of Pozzo and Lucky:

" Vladimir: That passed the time.
Estragon: It would have passed in any case.
Vladimir: Yes, but not so rapidly."

Estragon also joins in the game - "That's the idea, let's make a little conversation." The rituals by which Estragon and Vladimir combat silence and emptiness are elaborate, original and display Beckett's skill as a writer. In the play Beckett echoes patterns of question, answer and repetition which is his alternative to all the flaccid chat and triviality of the conventionally 'well-structured play'. Since his subject is habit and boredom, he has dispensed with plot since his characters are without much history. Even the scenery is minimal - consisting of a tree and the road. Beckett deliberately employs the repetition of themes, speech and action to highlight the futility and habit of life. Gogo and Didi frequently repeat phrases, such as, "Nothing to be done". Their actions consist of ritually inspecting their hats. Nothingness is what the two tramps are essentially fighting against and reason why they talk. Beckett suggests that activity and inactivity oppose one another: thought arising from inactivity and activity terminating thought. In the second Act they admit that habit suppresses their thoughts and keeps their minimal sanity:

" Estragon: ... we are incapable of keeping silent.
Vladimir: You're right we're inexhaustible.
Estragon: It's so we won't think."

Estragon and Vladimir symbolize the human condition as a period of waiting. Most of society spend their lives searching for goals, such as exam or jobs, in the hope of attaining a higher level or advancing. Beckett suggests that no-one advances through the inexorable passage of time. Vladimir states this, "One is what one is. ... The essential doesn't change.", (p.21). This may be a mockery of all human endeavour, as it implies that mankind achieves nothing, and is ironically contradictory to Beckett's own endeavour. The tragicomedy of the play illustrates this, as two men are waiting for a man of whom they no little about. The anti-climaxes within the play represent the disappointment of life's expectations. For example Pozzo and Lucky's first arrival is mistaken for the arrival of Godot. These points reinforce Kierkagaard's theory that all life will finish as it began in nothingness and reduce achievement to nothing.

Beckett expresses in the play that time is an illusion or a 'cancer', as he referred to it, that feeds the individual the lie that they progress, while destroying them. Estragon and Vladimir through the play end as they begin, have made no progression: waiting for Godot. The few leaves that have grown on the tree by the second act may symbolize hope but more feasibly represent the illusive passage of time. Beckett wrote in his Proust essay that time is the 'poisonous' condition we are born to, constantly changing us without our knowing, finally killing us without our assent.

A process of dying seems to take place within all four characters, mentally and physically. Estragon and Vladimir may be pictured as having a great future behind them. Estragon may have been a poet, but he is now content to quote and adapt, saying, "Hope deferred maketh the something sick" the something being the heart from a quote from the Bible. Vladimir may have been a thinker, but finds he is uncertain of his reasoning, as when questioned by Estragon about their whereabouts the day before replies angrily (not rationally), "Nothing is certain when you're about." (p.14). Time also erodes Estragon's memory, as shown here:

" *Vladimir:* What was it you wanted to know?

Estragon: I've forgotten. (Chews.) That's what annoys me.".

Time causes their energies and appetites to ebb. The fantasized prospect of an erection - a by-product of hanging - makes Estragon 'highly excited'. The dread of nightmares plague Estragon during the day ailments and fears become more agonizing. It is an example of Beckett using 'ordinary' images to depict mankind's decay. Time destroys Pozzo's sight and strips the previous master of almost everything. Beckett's bitterness towards time is illustrated by Pozzo's bleak speech:

"(suddenly furious). Have you not done tormenting me with your accursed time! ... one day I went blind ... one day we were born, one day we shall die, the same day, the same second, is that not enough for you? (Calmer.) They give birth astride of a grave, the light gleams an instant, then it's night once more."

When the structure of action is closing in through the course the play, with the past barely recognizable and the future unknown, the here and now of action, the present acting on stage becomes all-important. Existentialist theories propose that the choices of the present are important and that time causes perceptional confusion. Note how shadowy the past becomes to Estragon, as he asks questions such as, "What did we do yesterday?" Moreover, all the characters caught in the deteriorating cycle of events do not aspire to the future.

The play consists of two acts which represent two cycles of time or two mirrors reflecting endlessly. The pattern of time appears to be circular or cyclic, as opposed to linear. Linear time seems to have broken down, as events do not develop with inevitable climaxes historically. The boy returns with the same message, Godot never comes and tomorrow never seems to arrive. Vladimir mentions that "time has stopped".

Estragon and Vladimir are moving relentlessly towards a presumably unobtainable event, (the coming of Godot), within their finite existence, with a continually receding end. It could be described to the curve on a graph that mathematicians would call asymptotic: all the time drawing closer to a value, while never reaching it. Estragon portrays the horror of their uneventful repetitive existence:

"Nothing happens, nobody comes, nobody goes, it's

awful!" The fact that Estragon and Vladimir never seem to reach an event or end is the reason for them wanting to control the end themselves, as Estragon says, "Like to finish it?" The 'leaf motif' is an existentialist theory inferring that life repeats itself with a slight change (as in music - where a motif is a repetition of a structure with a minute alteration of rhythm or notes). Estragon highlights the 'leaf motif' theory, saying that a similar person with smaller feet will fill his boots: "Another will come, just as ... as ... as me, but with smaller feet". The endless eternal return theory is vividly portrayed at the beginning of the second act:

" Then all the dogs came running
And dug the dog a tomb-
He stops, broods, resumes:
Then all the dogs came running
And dug the dog a tomb".

The play is deliberately unnatural and abstract because it is intended to have universal meaning. The world of Estragon and Vladimir is fragmented of time and place and is submerged with vague recollections of culture and the past. For example Estragon remembers the Bible with uncertainty:

" I remember the maps with of the Holy Land. Coloured they were."

The lack of knowledge of the tramps' culture and past symbolize the breakdown of culture and tradition in the twentieth century. After surviving two World Wars, the tradition of the West has been shattered and culture has greatly changed. The Holocaust showed the atrocities of war and destroyed peoples' beliefs about human nature. The effects of political reforms, such as communism, marxism, and science has obliterated society's belief in the church. Nietzche declared the "death of God", as he felt that religion no longer offered a suitable framework for living. Esrtagon and Vladimir's uncertainty symbolizes the uncertainty of living in the twentieth century and more generally the uncertainty of existence. Estragon is uncertain about their location and timing inquiring, "You're sure it was here? ... You're sure it was this evening?"

Beckett infers that out of certainty arises certainty. Out of the uncertainty of waiting Vladimir becomes aware with certainty that they are waiting, thinking with clarity, "... what do we do now that we're happy ... go on waiting ... waiting ... let me think ... it's coming ... go on waiting".

Beckett displays the sheer randomness of life through the events of the play. Life is portrayed as unfair, risky and arbitrary. Estragon shows the chance involved in the health of his lungs stating, "My left lung is very weak! ... But my right lung is as sound as a bell!" Estragon and Vladimir ponder why one out of the three thieves was saved, which displays the luck or misfortune involved in life. The chaos of this world portrays the absurdity of the characters within the play.

Proust believed that an individual wakes a literally new person with their past memories intact to help them govern their actions in the present. Beckett raises questions about the past or memory governing the individual's identity. The characters identities are uncertain, as the past and their memories are uncertain. Vladimir tries to come to terms with his existence and the human condition: "It's too much for one man. ... On the other hand what's the point of losing heart now".

Bishop Berkeley proposed the philosophical hypothesis that being perceived was being or existing. Vladimir desperately asks the boy, "You did see us, didn't you?" and Estragon later questions, "Do you think God sees me?" because they are uncertain about their own senses, reality and existence. Beckett poses the theory that reality is based on the human perception. Schopenhauer devised the vision, akin to Buddhism, that the desiring self does not exist in any 'real' sense, except through the painful consequences of willful self-assertion.

Estragon asks, "We've lost our rights?", while Vladimir replies, "We got rid of them." Perhaps they are pondering the idea that they have no choice in their future and think their fate is preordained, although this would contradict the existentialist notion of free will. The tramps cannot perceive the future and therefore would be unable to know if their future is preordained. Equally, the tramps could have 'no rights' because they are devoted to the task of waiting. Heidegger said that instead of trying to comprehend one's existence each individual must choose a goal and follow it with passionate conviction.

Kierkagaard ultimately advocated a 'leap of faith' into a Christian way of life, which, although incomprehensible, was the only commitment he believed could save the individual from despair. Beckett seems to portray the incomprehensibility and irrationality of faith or hope and perhaps feels advocating 'a leap of faith' limits the individual's choice.

Despite Beckett's denial of Godot's symbolism to God, Godot does have a strong connection towards a god of some kind. Godot could be a hero, a religious symbol, a role model but most importantly a symbol of hope. Note the more Gogo and Didi converse about this supposed Mr. Godot (who may not exist) the more importance this god-like figure or symbol acquires. Vladimir illustrates the absurdity and the delusive nature of hope, as he has premonitions of Godot's arrival:

"Listen! ... Hssst! (... They listen, huddled together.) I thought it was ... Godot. ... I could have sworn I heard shouts." (p.19). Gogo replies more realistically, "Pah! The wind in the reeds." Camus talked of the Absurd in The myth of Sisyphus, meaning a life lived solely for its own sake in a universe that no longer made sense because there was no God to resolve the contradictions. Absurdity in the play is a by-product of their metaphysically absurd condition it is the best they can hope for, the worst they always expect.

Beckett distrusted language because it falsified he believed, the deepest self. His bleak vision of human ignorance, impotence and loneliness made communication an absurd endeavour. James Joyce strongly influenced Beckett and Joyce wrote Finnigan's wake, in which he practically composed his own language to add truthful meaning to his expression. Beckett is simultaneously torn between the inability to express and his need to express.

Estragon and Vladimir talk to each other and share ideas, but it is clear that both characters are self-absorbed and incapable of truly comprehending each other. Estragon and Vladimir regularly interrupt one another with their own thoughts, showing their individual self-absorption. Estragon admits, "I can't have been listening." (p.18), and Vladimir says, "I don't understand." displaying the failures of language as a means of communication.

Each character inhabits a world that has been shaped by thousands of individual experiences, accumulated through their five senses, arranging elements in their minds differently. Conversation occurs but the arrangement of words, poor starved strings do not bridge the gulf that exists between them. The silences seem to punctuate conversations that represent the void, emptiness and loneliness between people. Lucky's breakdown of speech and final collapse into silence could portray Beckett's ultimate response to the chaos, randomness and meaninglessness of the universe: silence.

Beckett portrays the human condition as a period of suffering. Heidegger theorized that humans are 'thrown into the world' and that suffering is part of existence. Proust describes this point as the, 'sin of being born', which Estragon and Vladimir refer to as Vladimir ponders about repenting being born. Estragon's references to Christ represent his sympathy towards suffering as well as symbolizing human suffering:

" Vladimir: What's Christ got to do with it? ...

Estragon: All my life I've compared myself to him. ... And they crucified quick!" Estragon feels that Christ's suffering on the crucifix was short while Beckett implies that the suffering of life is long. Estragon's suffering is shown more directly in the stage directions, when he attacks the messenger boy: " Estragon releases the Boy, moves away, covering his faces with his hands. ...Estragon drops his hands. His face convulsed."

Beckett perhaps feels that to reduce the individual's suffering one must detach oneself from one's emotions. Vladimir wishes himself and Estragon to "try and converse calmly" (p.62) for this reason and it explains Estragon's apprehension of being embraced and Vladimir's fear of laughing, "One daren't even laugh any more" (p.11). They perhaps wants to distance themselves from emotion to numb the pain of living. Early Greek philosophers believed in objectivity - distancing oneself. The Buddhist religion believes in separating oneself from the torrent of human emotions. Beckett makes it sound as though the noblest human condition is to be emotionally robotic - conditioned out of human feeling by boredom.

Beckett infers that life may not offer any alternatives to suffering - namely love or pleasure. The only consolation is that suffering is a precondition of contemplation or creativity it inspires. For example, out of Estragon's and Vladimir's suffering arise very imaginative techniques for passing time.

Beckett uses of bathos, staccato-like speech or actions and vulgarity flavoured with black or tragicomic humour to present a reductive view of human nature. Vladimir's perpetual need to urinate illustrates one of these vulgarities. Beckett's pessimism is understandable. He lived through two world wars, fighting the second World War for the French resistance against the Nazis. He would have witnessed the atrocities of human nature, chaos, the pointlessness of violence and the breakdown of communication. He would inevitably spent time during the war helplessly waiting for something to happen.

Estragon injects bathos into the serious debate about the thief who was saved by Christ by declaring with bluntness a reductive statement, "People are bloody ignorant apes." (p.13). Estragon and Vladimir often behave comically, finding interest in the banal - reducing human experiences to the mundane. The tramps comic, banal behaviour is very similar to the behaviour of another pair of comic characters - Laurel and Hardy:

" Vladimir: Pull on your trousers.
Estragon: What?
Vladimir: Pull on your trousers.
Estragon: You want me to pull off my trousers?
Vladimir: Pull ON your trousers.
Estragon: (realizing his trousers are down) True. (He pulls up his trousers.)"

Laurel and Hardy journeyed and shared a reasonably dependent relationship, tested by bouts of exasperation while seeming to not to age and none the wiser. They coped in perpetual nervous agitation, Laurel the most anxious while Hardy tended to solicit a philosophic calm. Neither characters were especially competent and Laurel was the weaker of the two often being defeated by the most trivial or trifling requirements. For example, in Way Out West (1937) (A readers Guide to Samuel Beckett - Hugh Kenner):

" Hardy: Get on the mule.

Laurel: What?

Hardy: Get on the mule."

The Seventeenth-century French philosopher Blaise Pascal viewed human life in terms of paradoxes: The human self is itself a paradox and contradiction. Estragon and Vladimir are full of contradictions, as their emotions often change erratically from violence to sympathy, from the philosophical to the banal. Pozzo's cruelty towards Lucky emphasizes the contradictions in human nature. They share a master-slave relationship in which Pozzo can be the worst of all tyrants, shouting authoritarian instructions at Lucky, such as, "Up pig!" (p.23), and yet can be equally filled with self-pity:

" I can't bear it ... any longer ... the way he goes on ... you've no idea ... it's terrible".

Beckett's devotion to and relationship with Joyce was not quite that of the master's secretary but Joyce did dictate part of Finnigan's Wake to the younger Beckett and some said that Beckett was his own model for a Pozzo-Lucky relationship. Beckett himself summed up his own contradictory situation as a writer in a 1949 dialogue with Georges Duthuit:

"The expression that there is nothing to express, no power to express, no desire to express, together with the obligation to express."

This contradictory statement is very reminiscent of the final lines of the play, which show the contradiction between words and action:

" 'Well? Shall we go?' 'Yes, let's go.' They do not move."

A sense of balance within the universe is illustrated in the play, as the silences counteract the conversation, the actions counteract the inactivity. Balance satisfies the mind which recoils from the random. Estragon represents a man of the body and Vladimir represents a man of the mind. Together they represent the divide of self: the mind and body, in Freudian terms - the id and the ego. Pascal thought it important to recognize that the self consists of the mind and body. Note the physical troubles of Estragon, concerning his boots, and the philosophical problems, such as time and existence, facing Vladimir:

" Vladimir: (gloomily). It's too much for one man. (Pause. Cheerfully.) On the other hand what's the good of losing heart now, that's what I say. We should have thought of it a million years ago, in the nineties." (p.10). Estragon: Ah stop blathering and help me off with this bloody thing." (p.10).

To summarize Waiting For Godot as a display of Beckett's bleak view of life would be a simplistic presumption, as Estragon and Vladimir epitomize all of mankind (as Estragon refers to himself as "Adam",p.37), showing the full range of human emotions. Estragon and Vladimir do suffer but equally show glimpses of happiness and excitement. They are excited by Pozzo's arrival and Estragon is "highly excited" about the prospect of an erection. Equally, as acts of random violence and anger are committed signs of affection are displayed between the characters. Gogo and Didi are the affectionate names Estragon and Vladimir call each other. Didi apologizes for his behaviour and displays affection: "Forgive me ... Come, Didi. ... Give me your hand. ... Embrace me!" (p.17). Even brief signs of happiness are portrayed, as Gogo finds Lucky amusing, "He's a scream. ... (Laughs noisily.)" (p.35). Although Gogo and Didi fear being 'tied' or dependent on each other. This can be seen as either positive or negative. The pessimistic view is that they cannot escape waiting for Godot, from each other or from their situation in general. The optimistic view of the play shows a range of human emotion and the need to share experiences alongside the suffering of finite existence governed by the past, acting in the present and uncertain of the future.

Q. Discuss the Proposition that Waiting for Godot is an Existentialist play, Within the First Act. To what Extent does the play offer a Bleak Assessment of the Human Condition ?

Or

Q. Define the Role of the two Protagonists ?

The play, Waiting for Godot, is centred around two men, Estragon and Vladimir, who are waiting for a Mr. Godot, of whom they know little. Estragon admits himself that he may never recognize Mr. Godot, "Personally I wouldn't know him if I ever saw him." (p.23). Estragon also remarks, "... we hardly know him." (p.23), which illustrates to an audience that the identity of Mr. Godot is irrelevant, as little information is ever given throughout the play about this indefinable Mr. X. What is an important element of the play is the act of waiting for someone or something that never arrives. Western readers may find it natural to speculate on the identity of Godot because of their inordinate need to find answers to questions. Beckett however suggests that the identity of Godot is in itself a rhetorical question. It is possible to stress the for in the waiting for ...: to see the purpose of action in two men with a mission, not to be deflected from their compulsive task.

" Estragon: ... Let's go.
Vladimir: We can't.
Estragon: Why not?
Vladimir: We're waiting for Godot." (p.14).

The essence of existentialism concentrates on the concept of the individual's freedom of choice, as opposed to the belief that humans are controlled by a pre-existing omnipotent being, such as God. Estragon and Vladimir have made the choice of waiting, without instruction or guidance, as Vladimir says, "He didn't say for sure he'd come" (p.14), but decides to "wait till we know exactly how we stand" (p.18).

Albert Camus, an existentialist writer, believed that boredom or waiting, which is essentially the breakdown of routine or habit, caused people to think seriously about their identity, as Estragon and Vladimir do. In The Plague, Camus suggests that boredom or inactivity causes the individual to think. This is also similar to the idea of meditation, an almost motionless activity, allowing the individual to think with clarity. Camus, and other existential writers, suggested that attempting to answer these rhetorical questions could drive someone to the point of insanity. The tramps continually attempt to prove that they exist, in order to keep their sanity:

"We always find something, eh Didi, to give us the impression that we exist?" (p.69).

Waiting in the play induces boredom as a theme. Ironically Beckett attempts to create a similar nuance of boredom within the audience by the mundane repetition of dialogue and actions. Vladimir and Estragon constantly ponder and ask questions, many of which are rhetorical or are left unanswered. During the course of the play, certain unanswered questions arise: who is Godot? Where are Gogo and Didi? Who beats Gogo? All of these unanswered questions represent the rhetorical questions that individuals ask but never get answers for within their lifetime. Vis a vis is there a God? Where do we come from? Who is responsible for our suffering? The German existentialist philosopher Martin Heidegger expressed clearly that human beings can never hope to understand why they are here. The tramps repetitive inspection of their empty hats perhaps symbolizes mankind's vain search for answers within the vacuum of a universe.

Jean Paul Sartre, the leading figure of French existentialism declared that human beings require a rational basis for their lives but are unable to achieve one, and thus human life is a futile passion. Estragon and Vladimir attempt to put order into their lives by waiting for a Godot who never arrives. They continually subside into the futility of their situation, reiterating the phrase "Nothing to be done." Vladimir also resolves with the notion that life is futile, or nothing is to be done at the beginning, replying, "All my life I've tried to put it from me... And I resumed the struggle."

"Estragon: (anxious). And we? ... Where do we come in?"

Estragon's question is left unanswered by Vladimir. Note that these questions seem to bring pain or anxiety to Estragon. Beckett conveys a universal message that pondering the impossible questions, that arise from waiting, cause pain, anxiety, inactivity and destroy people from within. Note that both Vladimir and Estragon ponder suicide, by hanging themselves from the tree, but are unable to act through to anxiety, as Estragon states, "Don't let's do anything. It's safer."

Kierkagaard's philosophical view of 'Dread' or 'Angst' (German for anxiety) as described by the German philosopher Martin Heidegger, is a state in which the individual's freedom of choice places the individual in a state of anxiety, as the individual is surrounded by almost infinite possibilities. This could explain the inactivity of both Estragon and Vladimir. Both characters are aware of different choices they can make but are hesitant, anxious and generally inactive, as shown at the end of Act one when they decide to leave but are immobile.

" Estragon: Well, shall we go?

Vladimir: Yes, let's go.

They do not move."

Beckett infers that humans 'pass time' by habit or routine to cope with the existentialist dilemma of the dread or anxiety of their existence. Beckett believes that humans basically alleviate the pain of living or existence (which is at the crux of Existential philosophy) by habit. The idea of habit being essential for human existence substantiates Sartre's view that humans require a rational base for their lives. Beckett feels that habit protects us from whatever can neither be predicted or controlled, as he wrote about the theme of habit in his published essay concerning Proust:

"Habit is a compromise effected between the individual and his environment, or between the individual and his own organic eccentricities, the guarantee of a dull inviolability, the lightening-conductor of his existence. Habit is the ballast that chains the dog to his vomit. Breathing is habit. Life is habit."

Estragon and Vladimir constantly 'pass the time' throughout the entire play to escape the pain of waiting and to possibly to stop themselves from thinking or contemplating too deeply. Vladimir expresses this idea at the end of the play, 'Habit is a great deadener', suggesting that habit is like an analgesic - numbing the individual. The play is mostly ritual, with Estargon and Vladimir filling the emptiness and silence. "It'll pass the time,", (p.12), explains Vladimir, offering to tell the story of the Crucifixion. Passing the time is their mutual obsession, as exhibited after the first departure of Pozzo and Lucky:

" Vladimir: That passed the time.

Estragon: It would have passed in any case.

Vladimir: Yes, but not so rapidly."

Estragon also joins in the game - "That's the idea, let's make a little conversation." The rituals by which Estragon and Vladimir combat silence and emptyness are elaborate, original and display Beckett's skill as a writer. In the play Beckett echoes patterns of question, answer and repetition which is his alternative to all the flaccid chat and triviality of the conventionally 'well-structured play'. Since his subject is habit and boredom, he has dispensed with plot since his characters are without much history. Even the scenery is minimal - consisting of a tree and the road. Beckett deliberately employs the repetition of themes, speech and action to highlight the futility and habit of life. Gogo and Didi frequently repeat phrases, such as, "Nothing to be done". Their actions consist of ritually inspecting their hats. Nothingness is what the two tramps are essentially fighting against and reason why they talk. Beckett suggests that activity and inactivity oppose one another: thought arising from inactivity and activity terminating thought. In the second Act they admit that habit suppresses their thoughts and keeps their minimal sanity:

"Estragon: ... we are incapable of keeping silent.

Vladimir: You're right we're inexhaustible.

Estragon: It's so we won't think."

Estragon and Vladimir symbolize the human condition as a period of waiting. Most of society spend their lives searching for goals, such as exam or jobs, in the hope of attaining a higher level or advancing. Beckett suggests that no-one advances through the inexorable passage of time. Vladimir states this, "One is what one is. ... The essential doesn't change.", (p.21). This may be a mockery of all human endeavour, as it implies that mankind achieves nothing, and is ironically contradictory to Beckett's own endeavour. The tragicomedy of the play illustrates this, as two men are waiting for a man of whom they no little about. The anti-climaxes within the play represent the disappointment of life's expectations. For example Pozzo and Lucky's first arrival is mistaken for the arrival of Godot. These points reinforce Kierkagaard's theory that all life will finish as it began in nothingness and reduce achievement to nothing.

Beckett expresses in the play that time is an illusion or a 'cancer', as he referred to it, that feeds the individual the lie that they progress, while destroying them. Estragon and Vladimir through the play end as they begin, have made no progression: waiting for Godot. The few leaves that have grown on the tree by the second act may symbolize hope but more feasibly represent the illusive passage of time. Beckett wrote in his Proust essay that time is the 'poisonous' condition we are born to, constantly changing us without our knowing, finally killing us without our assent. A process of dying seems to take place within all four characters, mentally and physically. Estragon and Vladimir may be pictured as having a great future behind them. Estragon may have been a poet, but he is now content to quote and adapt, saying, "Hope deferred maketh the something sick" (p.10) the something being the heart from a quote from the Bible. Vladimir may have been a thinker, but finds he is uncertain of his reasoning, as when questioned by Estragon about their whereabouts the day before replies angrily (not rationally), "Nothing is certain when you're about." (p.14). Time also erodes Estragon's memory, as shown here:

" Vladimir: What was it you wanted to know?

Estragon: I've forgotten. (Chews.) That's what annoys me."

Time causes their energies and appetites to ebb. The fantasized prospect of an erection - a by-product of hanging - makes Estragon 'highly excited' (p.17). The dread of nightmares plague Estragon during the day ailments and fears become more agonizing. It is an example of Beckett using 'ordinary' images to depict mankind's decay. Time destroys Pozzo's sight and strips the previous master of almost everything. Beckett's bitterness towards time is illustrated by Pozzo's bleak speech: "(suddenly furious). Have you not done tormenting me with your accursed time! ... one day I went blind ... one day we were born, one day we shall die, the same day, the same second, is that not enough for you? (Calmer.) They give birth astride of a grave, the light gleams an instant, then it's night once more." (p.89). When the structure of action is closing in through the course the play, with the past barely recognizable and the future unknown, the here and now of action, the present acting on stage becomes all-important. Existentialist theories propose that the choices of the present are important and that time causes perceptional confusion. Note how shadowy the past becomes to Estragon, as he asks questions such as, "What did we do yesterday?" (p.14). Moreover, all the characters caught in the deteriorating cycle of events do not aspire to the future.

The play consists of two acts which represent two cycles of time or two mirrors reflecting endlessly. The pattern of time appears to be circular or cyclic, as opposed to linear. Linear time seems to have broken down, as events do not develop with inevitable climaxes historically. The boy returns with the same message, Godot never comes and tomorrow never seems to arrive. Vladimir mentions that "time has stopped" (p.36).

Estragon and Vladimir are moving relentlessly towards a presumably unobtainable event, (the coming of Godot), within their finite existence, with a continually receding end. It could be described to the curve on a graph that mathematicians would call asymptotic: all the time drawing closer to a value, while never reaching it. Estragon portrays the horror of their uneventful repetitive existence: " Nothing happens, nobody comes, nobody goes, it's awful!" (p.41).

The fact that Estragon and Vladimir never seem to reach an event or end is the reason for them wanting to control the end themselves, as Estragon says, "Like to finish it?" (p.21). The 'leaf motif' is an existentialist theory inferring that life repeats itself with a slight change (as in music - where a motif is a repetition of a structure with a minute alteration of rhythm or notes). Estragon highlights the 'leaf motif' theory, saying that a similar person with smaller feet will fill his boots: "Another will come, just as ... as ... as me, but with smaller feet" (p.52). The endless eternal return theory is vividly portrayed at the beginning of the second act:

"Then all the dogs came running
And dug the dog a tomb-
He stops, broods, resumes:
Then all the dogs came running
And dug the dog a tomb".

The play is deliberately unnatural and abstract because it is intended to have universal meaning. The world of Estragon and Vladimir is fragmented of time and place and is submerged with vague recollections of culture and the past. For example Estragon remembers the Bible with uncertainty:

" I remember the maps with of the Holy Land. Coloured they were." (p.12).

The lack of knowledge of the tramps' culture and past symbolize the breakdown of culture and tradition in the twentieth century. After surviving two World Wars, the tradition of the West has been shattered and culture has greatly changed. The Holocaust showed the atrocities of war and destroyed peoples' beliefs about human nature. The effects of political reforms, such as communism, marxism, and science has obliterated society's belief in the church. Nietzche declared the "death of God", as he felt that religion no longer offered a suitable framework for living. Esrtagon and Vladimir's uncertainty symbolizes the uncertainty of living in the twentieth century and more generally the uncertainty of existence. Estragon is uncertain about their location and timing inquiring, "You're sure it was here? ... You're sure it was this evening?" (p.15). Beckett infers that out of certainty arises certainty. Out of the uncertainty of waiting Vladimir becomes aware with certainty that they are waiting, thinking with clarity, "... what do we do now that we're happy ... go on waiting ... waiting ... let me think ... it's coming ... go on waiting" (p.65).

Beckett displays the sheer randomness of life through the events of the play. Life is portrayed as unfair, risky and arbitrary. Estragon shows the chance involved in the health of his lungs stating, "My left lung is very weak! ... But my right lung is as sound as a bell!" Estragon and Vladimir ponder why one out of the three thieves was saved, which displays the luck or misfortune involved in life. The chaos of this world portrays the absurdity of the characters within the play.

Proust believed that an individual wakes a literally new person with their past memories intact to help them govern their actions in the present. Beckett raises questions about the past or memory governing the individual's identity. The characters identities are uncertain, as the past and their memories are uncertain. Vladimir tries to come to terms with his existence and the human condition: "It's too much for one man. ... On the other hand what's the point of losing heart now" (p.10).

Bishop Berkeley proposed the philosophical hypothesis that being perceived was being or existing. Vladimir desperately asks the boy, "You did see us, didn't you?" (p.52), and Estragon later questions, "Do you think God sees me?" (p.76), because they are uncertain about their own senses, reality and existence. Beckett poses the theory that reality is based on the human perception. Schopenhauer devised the vision, akin to Buddhism, that the desiring self does not exist in any 'real' sense, except through the painful consequences of wilful self-assertion.

Estragon asks, "We've lost our rights?", while Vladimir replies, "We got rid of them." (p.19). Perhaps they are pondering the idea that they have no choice in their future and think their fate is preordained, although this would contradict the existentialist notion of free will. The tramps cannot perceive the future and therefore would be unable to know if their future is preordained. Equally, the tramps could have 'no rights' because they are devoted to the task of waiting. Heidegger said that instead of trying to comprehend one's existence each individual must choose a goal and follow it with passionate conviction.

Kierkagaard ultimately advocated a 'leap of faith' into a Christian way of life, which, although incomprehensible, was the only commitment he believed could save the individual from despair. Beckett seems to portray the incomprehensibility and irrationality of faith or hope and perhaps feels advocating 'a leap of faith' limits the individual's choice. Despite Beckett's denial of Godot's symbolism to God, Godot does have a strong connection towards a god of some kind. Godot could be a hero, a religious symbol, a role model but most importantly a symbol of hope. Note the more Gogo and Didi converse about this supposed Mr. Godot (who may not exist) the more importance this god-like figure or symbol acquires. Vladimir illustrates the absurdity and the delusive nature of hope, as he has premonitions of Godot's arrival: "Listen! ... Hssst! (... They listen, huddled together.) I thought it was ... Godot. ... I could have sworn I heard shouts." (p.19). Gogo replies more realistically, "Pah! The wind in the reeds." Camus talked of the Absurd in The myth of Sisyphus, meaning a life lived solely for its own sake in a universe that no longer made sense because there was no God to resolve the contradictions. Absurdity in the play is a by-product of their metaphysically absurd condition it is the best they can hope for, the worst they always expect.

Beckett distrusted language because it falsified he believed, the deepest self. His bleak vision of human ignorance, impotence and loneliness made communication an absurd endeavour. James Joyce strongly influenced Beckett and Joyce wrote Finnigan's wake, in which he practically composed his own language to add truthful meaning to his expression. Beckett is simultaneously torn between the inability to express and his need to express. Estragon and Vladimir talk to each other and share ideas, but it is clear that both characters are self-absorbed and incapable of truly comprehending each other. Estragon and Vladimir regularly interrupt one another with their own thoughts, showing their individual self-absorption. Estragon admits, "I can't have been listening." (p.18), and Vladimir says, "I don't understand." (p.17), displaying the failures of language as a means of communication.

Each character inhabits a world that has been shaped by

thousands of individual experiences, accumulated through their five senses, arranging elements in their minds differently. Conversation occurs but the arrangement of words, poor starved strings do not bridge the gulf that exists between them. The silences seem to punctuate conversations that represent the void, emptiness and loneliness between people. Lucky's breakdown of speech and final collapse into silence could portray Beckett's ultimate response to the chaos, randomness and meaninglessness of the universe: silence.

Beckett portrays the human condition as a period of suffering. Heidegger theorized that humans are 'thrown into the world' and that suffering is part of existence. Proust describes this point as the, 'sin of being born', which Estragon and Vladimir refer to as Vladimir ponders about repenting being born. Estragon's references to Christ represent his sympathy towards suffering as well as symbolizing human suffering:

" Vladimir: What's Christ got to do with it? ...

Estragon: All my life I've compared myself to him. ... And they crucified quick!" (p.52).

Estragon feels that Christ's suffering on the crucifix was short while Beckett implies that the suffering of life is long. Estragon's suffering is shown more directly in the stage directions, when he attacks the messenger boy:

" Estragon releases the Boy, moves away, covering his faces with his hands. ...Estragon drops his hands. His face convulsed." (p.50).

Beckett perhaps feels that to reduce the individual's suffering one must detach oneself from one's emotions. Vladimir wishes himself and Estragon to "try and converse calmly" (p.62) for this reason and it explains Estragon's apprehension of being embraced and Vladimir's fear of laughing, "One daren't even laugh any more" (p.11). They perhaps wants to distance themselves from emotion to numb the pain of living. Early Greek philosophers believed in objectivity - distancing oneself. The Buddhist religion believes in separating oneself from the torrent of human emotions. Beckett makes it sound as though the noblest human condition is to be emotionally robotic - conditioned out of human feeling by boredom.

Beckett infers that life may not offer any alternatives to suffering - namely love or pleasure. The only consolation is that suffering is a precondition of contemplation or creativity it inspires. For example, out of Estragon's and Vladimir's suffering arise very imaginative techniques for passing time.

Beckett uses of bathos, staccato-like speech or actions and vulgarity flavoured with black or tragicomic humour to present a reductive view of human nature. Vladimir's perpetual need to urinate illustrates one of these vulgarities. Beckett's pessimism is understandable. He lived through two world wars, fighting the second World War for the French resistance against the Nazis. He would have witnessed the atrocities of human nature, chaos, the pointlessness of violence and the breakdown of communication. He would inevitably spent time during the war helplessly waiting for something to happen.

Estragon injects bathos into the serious debate about the thief who was saved by Christ by declaring with bluntness a reductive statement, "People are bloody ignorant apes." (p.13). Estragon and Vladimir often behave comically, finding interest in the banal - reducing human experiences to the mundane. The tramps comic, banal behaviour is very similar to the behaviour of another pair of comic characters - Laurel and Hardy:

" Vladimir: Pull on your trousers.

Estragon: What?

Vladimir: Pull on your trousers.

Estragon: You want me to pull off my trousers?

Vladimir: Pull ON your trousers.

Estragon: (realizing his trousers are down) True. (He pulls up his trousers.)"

Laurel and Hardy journeyed and shared a reasonably dependent relationship, tested by bouts of exasperation while seeming to not to age and none the wiser. They coped in perpetual nervous agitation, Laurel the most anxious while Hardy tended to solicit a philosophic calm. Neither characters were especially competent and Laurel was the weaker of the two often being defeated by the most trivial or trifling requirements. For example, in Way Out West (1937) (A readers Guide to Samuel Beckett - Hugh Kenner):

" Hardy: Get on the mule.
Laurel: What?
Hardy: Get on the mule."

The Seventeenth-century French philosopher Blaise Pascal viewed human life in terms of paradoxes: The human self is itself a paradox and contradiction. Estragon and Vladimir are full of contradictions, as their emotions often change erratically from violence to sympathy, from the philosophical to the banal. Pozzo's cruelty towards Lucky emphasizes the contradictions in human nature. They share a master-slave relationship in which Pozzo can be the worst of all tyrants, shouting authoritarian instructions at Lucky, such as, "Up pig!" (p.23), and yet can be equally filled with self-pity: " I can't bear it ... any longer ... the way he goes on ... you've no idea ... it's terrible" (p.34). Beckett's devotion to and relationship with Joyce was not quite that of the master's secretary but Joyce did dictate part of Finnigan's Wake to the younger Beckett and some said that Beckett was his own model for a Pozzo-Lucky relationship. Beckett himself summed up his own contradictory situation as a writer in a 1949 dialogue with Georges Duthuit: "The expression that there is nothing to express, no power to express, no desire to express, together with the obligation to express." This contradictory statement is very reminiscent of the final lines of the play, which show the contradiction between words and action:

" 'Well? Shall we go?' 'Yes, let's go.' They do not move."

A sense of balance within the universe is illustrated in the play, as the silences counteract the conversation, the actions counteract the inactivity. Balance satisfies the mind which recoils from the random. Estragon represents a man of the body and Vladimir represents a man of the mind. Together they represent the divide of self: the mind and body, in Freudian terms - the id and the ego. Pascal thought it important to recognize that the self consists of the mind and body. Note the physical troubles of Estragon, concerning his boots, and the philosophical problems, such as time and existence; facing Vladimir:

" Vladimir: (gloomily). It's too much for one man. (Pause. Cheerfully.) On the other hand what's the good of losing heart now, that's what I say. We should have thought of it a million years ago, in the nineties." (p.10).

Estragon: Ah stop blathering and help me off with this bloody thing." (p.10).

To summarize Waiting For Godot as a display of Beckett's bleak view of life would be a simplistic presumption, as Estragon and Vladimir epitomize all of mankind (as Estragon refers to himself as "Adam",p.37), showing the full range of human emotions. Estragon and Vladimir do suffer but equally show glimpses of happiness and excitement. They are excited by Pozzo's arrival and Estragon is "highly excited" about the prospect of an erection. Equally, as acts of random violence and anger are committed signs of affection are displayed between the characters. Gogo and Didi are the affectionate names Estragon and Vladimir call each other. Didi apologizes for his behaviour and displays affection: "Forgive me ... Come, Didi. ... Give me your hand. ... Embrace me!" (p.17). Even brief signs of happiness are portrayed, as Gogo finds Lucky amusing, "He's a scream. ... (Laughs noisily.)" (p.35). Although Gogo and Didi fear being 'tied' or dependent on each other. This can be seen as either positive or negative. The pessimistic view is that they cannot escape waiting for Godot, from each other or from their situation in general. The optimistic view of the play shows a range of human emotion and the need to share experiences alongside the suffering of finite existence governed by the past, acting in the present and uncertain of the future.

Q. Define the various themes of "Waiting for Godot" ?

Or

Q. Describe Anarchy as major theme of the play ?

"We're headed for collapse, if you want my opinion, Missy. I can see it in the fallin' off of the quality of vagrants. There was a time you could find real good company in almost any jungle you'd pick, men who could talk, men who'd read a book now and then and now, what do you find, a lot of dirty little guttersnipes no decent tramp would want to associate with.

Well, it's been that way all through history."

In Kosovska Mitrovica during February 2001, the city library, after 130 years of work no longer exists. More than 11 thousand books in Serbian language were destroyed, recycled as old paper at the Factory of Waste Paper in Vladicin Han. Any books regardless of language with topics related to Serbian culture were not spared. Luckily by pure chance, the last bundle to be thrown into the melting pot fell apart saving around a thousand books. It is alleged that the present director Mr. Harjrullah Mustafa, who is an ethnic Albanian is responsible for the destruction of the books in an attempt to eradicate the Serbian culture. This is evidence supporting that the destruction of cultures continues today. We have seen the effects of civilization's deterioration in the West. With the collapse of values, what remains is a mass of hollow men falling away from articulation into the abyss of uncertainty. Christian traditions of 1900 years has dissolved into nothing. Values that once determined behaviour, motivated the weak to be strong, and encouraged right from wrong have become nonexistent. Men lack activity conversations are bleak time stands still. Without a centre to provide a strong foundation, things fall apart. Without a God and pronounced values, cultures collapse. Total collapse into meaninglessness would never be conceived as a possibility of a creature made in His image. Values that once flowed from the heaven's now flow barren with no chance of revival. Heaven will not direct no more. With the collapse of values mere anarchy is loosed upon the world. The truth of this predicament is clearly illustrated in Samuel Beckett's Waiting for Godot. The author presents this collapse by his characters lack of activity, absurd and meaningless conversations, and their treatment of time.

The collapse of values is expressed by the inactivity of the characters in Waiting for Godot. His central characters, Estragon and Vladimir are waiting for Godot, of whom they know little. Estragon himself admits that he may never recognize Godot saying, "Personally I wouldn't know him if I ever saw him." The rest of the story follows with the two main characters waiting, without instruction or guidance just to "wait til we know exactly how we stand," says Vladimir. Albert Camus believed that boredom or waiting, which is essentially the breakdown of routine or habit, causes the individual to think. He believed that attempting to answer these rhetorical questions of identity could drive someone to the point of insanity."

We always find something, eh Didi, to give us the impression that we exist?" Waiting in the play induces boredom that is illustrated by the mundane repetition of actions. The two tramps repetitively inspect their empty hats and attempt to pass the time playing games and entertaining themselves. Baseless optimism positive pretending false hope they wait. The opening of the play reveals a poor homeless tramp struggling desperately to pull his boots off. One foot is apparently swollen and sore, and he struggles in vain. That activity took a while to carry out, and after finally removing the boot, his partner plays with his hat and notes there's "Nothing to be done."

These scenes collaborate to pursue the drift toward confusion. Man has no purpose, existence seems to be something imposed upon us by some unknown force. The world seems utterly chaotic, and though there is no apparent meaning to it, the characters suffer as a result of it. As time passes, Vladimir and Estragon quarrel, make up, contemplate suicide, try to sleep, entertain each other with stories, eat a carrot and gnaw on some chicken bones. Their pathetic attempts to fabricate a purpose all aim to distract themselves from the fact their situation is hopelessly unfathomable. It is unquestionable that the characters in Beckett's play are simply low in every aspect of human activity.

The individual has no place, modern man has no voice and is lacking in substance and will. Both characters are aware of different choices they can make but are hesitant, anxious, and generally inactive, as shown at the end of Act I when they decide to leave but are immobile. Throughout the play, Vladimir and Estragon remain stupidly cheerful, they act rather comical and their pointless activities make their hollowness apparent. T.S. Eliot's "The Hollow Men," describes a world distant and terrifying.

No man can withstand the immense pressure of a mass society, and the timidity puts him into a paralyzed trance. The two tramps do nothing their lives are futile their work is barren. The setting of the play mirrors the barren wasteland of modern men. It is home to a herd of sheep in search of nothing, with nowhere to go. Values drive behaviour, without a strong sense of duty, actions are bleak and the fall from virtuous conduct is inevitable. This is the collapse of values, two tramps returning to the same place, every day to wait for Godot, who never comes. They merely deflate.

Without values, the centre cannot hold without meaning, conversations become dull. The low caliber of dialogue in the play shows empty men amidst a paralyzing sea of fear. There is utter confusion and it is seen in the characters inability to complete sentences, repetition of phrases and words, rhetorical or unanswered questions and their absurd vocabulary. Estragon and Vladamir continually subside into the futility of their situation, reiterating the phrase, "Nothing to be done." Vladimir also resolves with the notion that life is futile, or nothing is to be done. They back out from suicide saying, "Don't let's do anything. It's safer."

Together the decide to fill the emptiness and silence with cheap entertainment. "It'll pass the time," explains Vladimir when he offers to tell the story of the Crucifixion. "That passed the time," he says after the first departure of Pozzo and Lucky. Life becomes a game to them, passing back ideas in order to stop themselves from thinking or contemplating too deeply and escaping the pain of waiting. "That's the idea, let's make a little conversation," suggests Estragon. Beckett deliberately employs the repetition of themes, speech and action to highlight the futility and habit of life. In the second act, they admit "we are unable of keeping silent." Throughout the play the characters all seem to not recognize the past, as they constantly ask questions such as, "What did we do yesterday?" Their world is fragmented, submerged with vague recollections of culture and the past. For example, Estragon remembers the Bible with uncertainly. "I remember the maps with of the Holy Land. Colored they were." The lack of knowledge and dull conversation shows the breakdown of culture and tradition in the twentieth century. The tradition of the West has been shattered and the culture destroyed. The effects of political reforms, such as communism, Marxism, and science has obliterated society's belief in the church. Nietzsche declared the "death of God," as he felt that religion no longer offered a suitable framework of living. Either God does not exist, or he does not care.

Whichever is the case, chance and luck determines human life in the absence of divine involvement. Estragon and Vladimir's uncertainty mirrors the uncertainty of living in the modern world. Estragon's constant inquiring of, "You're sure it was here?... You're sure it was this evening?" Out of the uncertainty of waiting, Vladimir becomes aware with certainty that they are waiting, thinking with clarity, "...what do we do now that we're happy...go on waiting...waiting...let me think...it's coming....go on waiting. "Estragon and Vladimir talk to each other and share ideas, but its they regularly interrupt one another wit their own thoughts. Estragon admits, "I can't have been listening," and Vladimir says, "I don't' understand," this displays the failures of communication. Conversations do exists but the arrangement of words, and the silences seem to punctuate conversations that represent the void, emptiness between people. Lucky's breakdown speech and final collapse into silence represents the ultimate response to the chaos, randomness and meaningless of the universe: silence.

Time is meaningless in Waiting for Godot, there is a cyclic, albeit indefinite pattern where the past, present and future mean nothing. Time, essentially is a mess. Estragon may have been a poet before, but he is not content to quote scripture in his own rendition saying, "Hope deferred maketh the something sick", the something being the heart. Time erodes the memory, and deteriorates into a cycle of events that do not aspire but simply stand still. The pattern of time appears to be this way as opposed to linear.

Linear time seems to have broken down, as events do not develop with inevitable climaxes historically. The boy returns with the same message, Godot never comes and tomorrow never seems to arrive. Vladimir mentions that, "Time has stopped." Estragon and Vladimir ad moving relentlessly towards a presumably unobtainable event, withing their finite existence, with a continually receding end. Estragon sums it up saying, "Nothing happens, nobody comes, nobody goes, it's awful!" Time is equivalent to what is announced in the title: the act of waiting. Yet, it mysteriously starts up again each day as it returns to the beginning. Nothing is completed because nothing can be completed.

The inherent meaninglessness of a world based on chance degenerates human life into something that is worthless and can be toyed by fortune. Pozzo becomes blind and has no recollection of the day before, and even claims that Lucky has always been mute, even though Lucky at the previous meeting, gave a long philosophical discourse when commanded to "think." The disregard for human life is a result of not having any values. One who does not sanctify the lives of others cannot possibly make something of their own. We sink down to the low, and become slaves to ourselves. Human life is treated arbitrarily and in an almost ruthless manner, meaningless. Jean Paul Sartre declared that human beings require a rational basis for their lives but are unable to achieve one, and thus human life is a futile passion. Vladimir rests with the notion that life is futile, or nothing to be done. All human endeavor is futile due to the collapse of values. Mankind achieves nothing, life will finish as it began in nothingness and reduce achievement to nothing. Vladimir states, "One is what one is..the essential doesn't change." The best lack all conviction. The worse are full of passionate intensity. Time feeds the individual of today with the lie that they progress while destroying them. To the end, they have made no progression: they are still waiting for Godot.

When Waiting for Godot opened in Londn in 1955,

Kenneth Tynan remarked, "It has no plot, no climax, no denouement no beginning, no middle and no end."In essence, this is the description of the modern world. Time has no meaning, life has no climax, no beginning and no end. Sophocles spoke of "No greater evil than anarchy."

Innocense in the world no longer exists, it is drowned in a sea of the masses, held down by the blood-dimmed tide. Things fall apart the centre cannot hold. Beckett illustrated the terrible predicament of the modern world. A world without values, and without a God. We are left with characters who are paralyzed in motion, meaningless in conversation, and who slave away as time stands still. Wait. That is all to be done in a world with destroyed values, the eyes of this generation is like "sunlight on a broken column." And this is the way the world ends, "not with a bang, but a whimper."

Q. Discuss the role of Godot ?

Or

Q. Discuss how Godot makes feel his presence by being absent from the play ?

In some works of literature, a character who appears briefly, or does not appear at all, is a significant presence. An example of this can be found in the play Waiting for Godot, by Samuel Beckett.

The play deals with a hope for a change and a chance to be saved of two old frineds. One of the character is Godot, someone who never shows up. The reader finds out about him only through the conversations in the play. Although Godot is never physically present on stage, his presence is everywhere. The whole play, including all the actions and the theme itself, is affected by the mention of Godot. No one in the play ever really saw him, or ever will. His appearance is not as important as a belief in him.

The two friends, Estragon and Vladimir spend their lives waiting for this one person to show up, this one miracle to happen. It never does, but as Vladimir says, "It passes the time." It might appear surprising that the lives of two people can be based on the life of a third one, whom they never actually met. But in reality, they do not need him as a person.

All they need is something to believe in, something to wait for. Most people spend their lives witing for something, but they are not sure of what exactly. Vladimir and Estragon can consider themselves lucky.

They know specifically what, or rather whom, they are waiting for: Godot. This faceless character affects their lives. He is a reason they are still alive. Every day, Estragon wants to kill himelf, but not only is there not enough rope, but there is also a hope that maybe, just maybe, Godot will appear the next day and everything will be different. Interestingly enough, Godot is also the one who keeps two friends coming back to the same spot, instead of wandering off and looking for a better place to live. Because of the endless promise that this one person will actually come, they do not leave the place.

Whether or not Godot exists does not make any difference. The belief in him keeps two people from killing themselves, yet living in a ditch. It keeps them away from the places where they want to go and at the same time, it keeps them together. This belief serves the most important function: it gives purpose to their lives. Estragon and Vladimir are homeless, old and weary, and maybe they are right in thinking that they'd be better off being dead. Certainly Godot can be looked at as death itself, and that's what the two friends are waiting for. Still, death is considered to be a change and that's what Vladimir and Estragon want. And Godot, no matter what/who he is, is the one who can give them this change that they so desperately need. Waiting for Godot is Not an Absurdist Play

Samuel Beckett's stage plays are gray both in colour and in subject matter. Likewise, the answer to the question of whether or not Beckett's work is Absurdist also belongs to that realm of gray in which Beckett often works. The Absurdist label becomes problematic when applied to Beckett because his dramatic works tend to overflow the boundaries, which scholars attempt to assign. When discussing Beckett, the critic inevitably becomes entangled in contradiction. The playwright's own denial "that there is a philosophical system behind the plays" and his explicit refusal "to reduce them to codified interpretations" suggests, one could argue, that to search for such systems or interpretations in Beckett's work is, at best, a fruitless endeavor (Beckett quoted. in McMillan 13). Let me suggest, however, that Beckett's own statements and criticisms not be taken as a deterrent to the study of his work. His objections threaten only those interpretations which "reduce" his work. The challenge for the critic, then, is to evaluate.

Q. Compare and contrast the play with Virginia Woolf's Mrs. Dalloway ?

Or

Q. What are the unique features of the play Waiting for Godot ?

Virginia Woolf's Mrs. Dalloway and Samuel Beckett's Waiting for Godot are representative works of two separate movements in literature: Modernism and Post-Modernism. Defining both movements in their entirety, or arguing whether either work is truly representative of the classifications of Modernism and Post-Modernism, is not the purpose of this paper rather, the purpose is to carefully evaluate how both works, in the context of both works being representative of their respective traditions, employ the use of symbolism and allusion. Beckett's play uses "semantic association" in order to convey meaning in its use of symbolism Woolf's novel employs a more traditional mode of conveying meaning in its own use: that is, the meaning of symbols in Mrs. Dalloway is found within the text itself. Woolf's novel exists as its own entity, with the reader using the text as the only tool in uncovering any symbolic meaning, while Beckett's play stimulates the audience in such a way that the audie.

Q. What is the underlying truth of the play?

Or

Q. How this play is a shock for Catholicism?

Samuel Beckett's Waiting for Godot has been said by many people to be a long book about nothing. The two main characters, Vladimir and Estragon, spend all their time sitting by a tree waiting for someone named Godot, whose identity is never revealed to the audience. It may sound pretty dull at first but by looking closely at the book, it becomes apparent that there is more than originally meets the eye. Waiting for

Godot was written to be a critical allegory of religious faith, relaying that it is a natural necessity for people to have faith, but faiths such as Catholicism are misleading and corrupt.

Vladimir and Estragon spend all their time through out the book waiting for "Godot." It is unclear to the audience if either of them have ever seen Godot or even talked to him.

"Pozzo: Who is Godot?

...Vladimir: Oh he's a... he's a kind of acquaintance.

Estragon: Nothing of the kind, we hardly know him.

Vladimir: True...we don't know him very well...but all the same... Estragon: Personally I wouldn't even know him if I saw him".

Waiting for Godot - God Isn't Coming

Waiting for Godot, Samuel Beckett's existential masterpiece, for some odd reason has captured the minds of millions of readers, artists, and critics worldwide, joining them all in an attempt to interpret the play. Beckett has told them not to read anything into his work, yet he does not stop them. Perhaps he recognizes the human quality of bringing personal experiences and such to the piece of art, and interpreting it through such colored lenses. Hundreds of theories are expounded, all of them right and none of them wrong. A play is only what you bring to it, in a subconscious connection between you and the playwright.

One popular interpretation of Waiting for Godot relates it to the Second Coming of Jesus Christ, as related in the New Testament. There are significant "clues" and "evidence" to make this connection, and as the main tenant of the Existentialist movement, which grew out and of WWII experiences of not only Beckett, but all the other great Existentialists, Camus, Sartre, and Ianesco.

Seeing Myself in Waiting for Godot

Some people wondered why in high school my favorite book was Waiting for Godot, a drama described on the title page as "a two-act play in which nothing happens twice." In fact, my liking a play that does not portray a series of connected incidents telling a story but instead presents a pattern of images showing bewildered people in an incomprehensible universe initially baffled me too, as my partiality was more felt than thought. But then I read a piece by the critic Martin Esslin, who articulated my feelings. He wrote in "The Search for the Self" that throughout our lives we always wait for something, and Godot simply represents the objective of our waiting—an event, a thing, a person, death. It is in the act of waiting that we experience the flow of time in its purest most evident form.

I realized that I was seventeen in high school passively waiting for something amazing to happen to me just like Vladimir and Estragon. I also realized that experiencing time flowing by unproductively was not for me regardless of how "pure".

Q. What is the Meaninglessness of Samuel Beckett's Waiting for Godot?

Or

Q. Why the character of Godot has been kept so Mysterious by the author?

In Waiting for Godot, Samuel Beckett produces a truly cryptic work. On first analyzing the play, one is not sure of what, if anything, happens or of the title character's significance. In attempting to unravel the themes of the play, interpreters have extracted a wide variety symbolism from the Godot's name. Some, taking an obvious hint, have proposed that Godot represents God and that the play is centered on religious symbolism. Others have taken the name as deriving from the French word for a boot, godillot. Still, others have suggested a connection between Godot and Godeau, a character who never appears in Honore de Balzac's Mercadet Ou, le faiseur. Through all these efforts, there is still no definitive answer as to whom or what Godot represents, and the writer has denied that Godot represents a specific thing, despite a certain ambiguity in the name. Upon study, however, one realizes that this ambiguity in meaning is the exact meaning of Godot. Though he seems to create greater symbolism and significance in the name Godot, Beckett actually rejects the notion of truth in language through the insignificance of the title character's name. By creating a false impression of religious symbolism in the name Godot Beckett leads the interpreter to a dead end.

For one to make an association between God and the title character's name is completely logical. In fact, in producing the completely obvious allusion, Beckett beckons the interpreter to follow a path of religious symbolism. Throughout the play, references to Christianity are so often mentioned that one can scarcely identify a religious undercurrent the presence of religion is not really below the surface. In the opening moments of the play, Vladimir asks "Hope deferred make something sick, who said that?" (8A). The real quotation, "Hope deferred maketh the heart sick," comes from Proverbs 13:12 of the Bible. Shortly after, Vladimir asks if Estragon has ever read the Bible and continues on a discussion of the Gospels, the "Saviour," and the two thieves surrounding Christ during the crucifixion (8B-9B).

By inserting religious discussions in the first few moments play, the playwright encourages the interpreter to assume the play's themes are greatly connected with religion. Then, when the discussion turns to Godot, Estragon associates their request from Godot with "A kind of prayer" (13A). The connection between God and Godot is seemingly firmly established, leaving room for a variety of interpretations. Vladimir and Estragon are the faithful adherents to God, and wait for Him, or a messianic figure, to come. Perhaps Vladimir and Estragon are representatives of hope by demonstrating unwavering faith to a God who does not present himself or, on the other hand, are showing the folly of blind faith as espoused by Beckett. Considering Lucky's burdens and suffering and his alteration on Jesus' last words in his speech, "unfinished," he could be a Christ figure (29B). Pozzo could represent the earthly form of a God that treats his adherents like he treats Lucky. The range of possible religious interpretations is virtually endless.

In truth, the proponents of these interpretations have fallen victim to a ruse, for Godot does not represent God. Considering that the work becomes nearly incomprehensible at times, one finds the religious explanation too simple. If Beckett provides such clear references to religion, it seems he would simply call his title character God. Furthermore, Beckett, himself, has denied the existence of a key or myth to the play. The playwright did not produce religious ambiguities because Godot represents God the ambiguities themselves hold the true significance. The word Godot is meaningless in itself, and those who associate the word with religious themes are fooled by Beckett's language. The play leads some along a long and tedious path of interpretation ultimately, the path hits a dead-end. Language is not synonymous with truth, and the interpreter emerges with nothing.

The meaninglessness of Godot is further explained through its connection to godillot or Estragon's boots. The play begins as "Estragon, sitting on a low mound, is trying to take off his boot. He pulls at it with both hands, panting. He gives up, exhausted, rests, tries again. As before " When Godot is substituted for the boot, the meaning becomes obvious. The interpreter struggles with the significance of the word, exhausts himself, and begins again. Moments later, Estragon increases the level of intensity, tearing at the boot. Finally, Gogo "with a supreme effort succeeds in pulling off his boot. He peers inside it, feels about inside it, turns it upside down, shakes it, looks on the ground to see if anything has fallen out, finds nothing, feels inside it again, staring sightlessly before him". After much work, one can find the significance of Godot, and, just as Estragon announces, "There's nothing to show". The meaning of Godot is nonexistent, and the effort to find one is futile and exhausting. No matter how many times one searches, one will not find significance in the word. The action continues in the second act, when the two discover that Estragon's boots have been changed. The two discuss the situation: "Estragon: Mine were black. These are brown. Vladimir: You're sure yours were black? Estragon: Well they were a kind of gray. Vladimir: And these are brown. Show. Estragon: Well they're kind of green. 43B"

The conversation shows the utter meaninglessness of Godot. Gogo cannot even decide the true colour of either pair of boots. Every thought or action to discover the meaning of Godot is ridiculous. The interpretations of the name vary, but, just as in the boots, there is nothing inside. Whereas the boots in the first act were too tight, Estragon decides that these are "too big" and concludes the discussion frustrated, saying, "That's enough about these boots" (45A). The search for meaning in Beckett's language is frustrating and futile, and, because there is no real meaning to Godot, the interpreter can never get all the significance to come together. An exact fit is impossible.

As the insignificance of Godot is established the lack of meaning expands to other names in episodes with Pozzo. Pozzo, himself, affirms the lack of meaning in a name as he periodically refers to "Godin... Godet... Godot... anyhow you see who I mean". He confuses the name with other words and seemingly feels no real need to learn the right one. Regardless of the language he uses, Vladimir and Estragon understand what he means. By correctly naming Godot, Pozzo would give too much significance to the name. In refusing to even regard the name as important, Pozzo communicates the misleading nature of Beckett's language and acts appropriately. In addition, Vladimir and Estragon expand the scope of meaninglessness to other names when Pozzo first meets the pair. Introducing himself, Pozzo exclaims, "I am Pozzo!" and asks "I say does that name mean nothing to you?". The name does, in fact, mean absolutely nothing. Just as Godot is meaningless, so are the play's other names. Vladimir and Estragon continue to repeat the name Pozzo, while interchanging it with Bozzo, and Vladimir concludes, "I once knew a family called Gozzo". The insignificance of all the words comes to the fore. Pozzo, Bozzo, Gozzo, and Godot are indistinguishable nonsense. When Vladimir and Estragon are referred to with their nicknames, all five names of the play have two syllables and end in a vowel sound. Furthermore, if the silent, final letter is removed from Godot, it appears as a mere variation of Gogo and Didi as Godo. In this way, characters' names are reduced to incomprehensible utterances that an infant might make. Beckett's language is totally separate from knowledge or truth. His names cannot be distinguished from one another and are completely devoid of any real meaning.

Godot, a meaningless word or mere sound, reveals the insignificance of all Beckett's language. While the play contains obvious ambiguities intc the word's meaning, they are all for show. There is no real meaning. The interpretation of Godot's religious significance, while this significance is clearly alluded to, leads to interpreter into a long, blind alley of meaninglessness. Just as Estragon's boots contain nothing inside them, there is no central meaning to the word Godot. Furthermore, this meaninglessness can be expanded to all of Beckett's language full of hints of a greater significance, language hides the triviality of all things described. Only after this revelation can one finally get towards the central meaning of Beckett's play there is no meaning. His characters engage in ridiculous language to pass the time and to "give [them] the impression [they] exist". Illusions of significance continue throughout the play, but, in truth, the play comes from nothing and ultimately ends in nothing. Beckett exposes the pitfalls of a language that attempts to create meaning when none exists. Waiting for Godot is not a commentary on religion or really anything for that matter. Its meaning comes in its meaninglessness. That is the play's greater truth.

Q. How the Christian Philosophy Explains Waiting for Godot?

Or

Q. Give the Religious Significance of the play ?

"The human predicament described in Beckett's first play is that of man living on the Saturday after the Friday of the crucifixion, and not really knowing if all hope is dead or if the next day will bring the life which has been promised." — William R. Mueller

In the five decades since Waiting for Godot's publication, many of the countless attempts to explain the play have relied on some variation of this religious motif proposed by William Mueller. Though Beckett's open text invites the reader to hunt for an interpretation, statements as decisive as this one overstep the search and leave little room for any other possibility. His idea has a compelling textual basis, but its finality violates the spirit of the play. Kenneth Tynan suggests that "Beckett's Waiting for Godot is a dramatic vacuum...It has no plot, no climax, no denouement no beginning, no middle, and no end." Such an idea forces any analyst of this enigmatic masterpiece to tread lightly and makes definite criticism nearly impossible. Before examining an explanation as conclusive as Mueller's we must acknowledge that we cannot hope to determine "the meaning" of this play. Neither the text nor its author makes a claim to any intrinsic meaning, yet a new meaning is born each time a reader or viewer partakes of the play.

With such cautions in mind, we can now approach Mueller's religious hypothesis with a safe detachment. The first utterance of Godot phonetically brings God to mind, and evidence throughout the play assures the reader that this path is a valid one to follow. On the most mundane level, Vladimir supports Mueller's premise with his guess at the timeframe of the play: "He said it was Saturday. I think" We discover, however, that even this statement hides beneath the uncertainty as Estragon challenges, "But what Saturday? And is it Saturday? Is it not rather Sunday? Or Monday? Or Friday?". His questioning reasserts that this work defies explanation and reminds us that we are following only one possible solution to an unsolvable problem.

If we read this drama with the intention of fitting Mueller's theory to the play (or perhaps the play to his theory), a vast number of previously unnoticed interpretive opportunities arise. Though the nondescript tree can be universally symbolic, when viewed from a religious standpoint it conjures an image of Christ's cross. The setting places this tree alongside an unspecified country road of which time, location and destination all are irrelevant. Metaphorically, the undefined beginning could easily be Christ's crucifixion and the end his resurrection, but the road also could represent the journey from his birth to his death or from the beginning of the human struggle to its salvation. Before the first word of dialogue ever is spoken, a key paradox explodes open:

crucifixion, a seemingly fatal end, instead marks the beginning of Christian faith and possibly the metaphysical beginning of this play. Of course these suppositions may border on the absurd, but still they show just how easily this play can take on a life of its own.

The opening conversation between Vladimir and Estragon provides the reader with initial proof that the "Godot=God" hypothesis can be an accurate one. Beckett later will tempt the reader to make such an assumption with the unmistakable correlation between Lucky's conception of God as "with white beard" and the child messenger's identical description of Godot. In the first few pages Vladimir immediately steers the conversation towards religion, ambiguously reminding Estragon, "One of the thieves was saved".

As he attempts to enlighten his friend on the message of the Bible, Vladimir provides initial evidence of Beckett's views on religion. He explains that only one of the four Gospels portrays the thief as being saved, and yet "everybody" believes this version. Could this be the author's subtle exposition of the religious logic gap? Estragon explicitly states the thought when he says, "People are bloody ignorant apes". Though we must make our judgements carefully, the early pages of the text suggest a cynicism that seems to parallel the religious metaphor throughout the rest of the work.

Despite Beckett's apparent wariness of religion (or perhaps because he wishes to make folly of it), the question of faith appears frequently in Waiting for Godot. Most obviously, the metaphor stems from the eternal waiting that the Christian faces in his belief that Christ will return but at an unknown time. The play first addresses this central tenet of faith in an early dialogue between Vladimir and Estragon:

Estragon: And if he doesn't come?
Vladimir: We'll come back to-morrow.
Estragon: And then the day after that.

This "coming back and waiting" is the identifying image of Vladimir and Estragon and is one of the points that Beckett parodies most heavily. The satire continues with the exchange, "[Estragon] Don't let's do anything. It's safer. [Vladimir] Let's wait and see what he says". Through these two characters Beckett portrays an entire race frozen by inaction. Over and over religion's immobilizing effect appears: "To Godot? Tied to Godot? What an idea! No question of it (he pauses) For the moment".

Alongside this theme of waiting, other religious institutions enter the debate, as when Estragon describes his supplication to Godot as "a kind of prayer". Vladimir asks, "And what did he reply?", to which Estragon must answer, "That he'd see.". Again we see the indeterminacy of faith, the endless waiting, the unanswered appeals and "the normal thing". On a less philosophical level there is commentary on two of the Church's most central practices, those of confession and absolution. Early in the play Estragon attempts to share a dream Vladimir and thus gain relief from it, but his partner adamantly refuses to hear him. The opening pages even parody the idea of holy solemnity and sanctity when Vladimir says, "You'd make me laugh if it wasn't prohibited".

Examples of the play's mockeries of religion abound, but some of the less satirical religious allusions also deserve notice. The scene in which Vladimir feeds Estragon on only scraps of food and tells him, "Make it last, that's the end of them" is strikingly reminiscent of the moment in each of the four Gospels when Jesus feeds a crowd of five thousand on just five loafs and two fishes. In the debate over the appearance of the tree, Estragon insists, "Looks to me more like a bush", thus invoking Exodus' picture of Moses on Mount Sinai. Several religious references also appear during the first encounter with Pozzo, including the words "crucify", "angel" and "Adam". Though most of these ideas are unrelated, the overall tone that they create compels the reader to apply the rest of the story to a religious mold.

Turning the consideration towards Pozzo next brings light to the significance of messengers in this play. In his first appearance Pozzo enters with all the embellishments of a false prophet and initially Estragon and Vladimir even believe that it is Godot who has come. With prophetic confidence Pozzo deems himself "made in God's image" and has the company of an ardent follower—more accurately, though, this follower is somewhat of a subjugee. In Lucky's domination by Pozzo we get the idea of entrapment, suggested by Pozzo himself when he says, "The Net. He thinks he's entangled in a net".

In one respect this puns on the message in Matthew 4 of "becoming fishers of men," but it also provides a critique of the oppressiveness of religion. Pozzo whips Lucky, burdens him with sandbags, leads him by a rope and tells him when to act. At the extreme, Lucky can speak only when Pozzo gives him his hat and allows him to. When pretending to "play Lucky" Vladimir and Estragon bring this enslavement to greater light, saying, "Curse me!...Tell me to think...Tell me to dance". If Pozzo can be linked with some religious element, could we be looking at Beckett's view of the controlling nature of the church? We must admit that Lucky seems to want or even need the domination, but couldn't this in itself add more strength to such an argument?

The importance of messengers does not simply end with Pozzo and Lucky. Godot sends the Boy much as Christ arrives as his father's messenger, and both meet similar mistreatment at the hands of the people they come to address. The Boy strengthens the allusion by describing the way his master loves him but treats his brother poorly, a relationship reminiscent of that between Cain, Abel and their Lord. (Ironically, the names Cain and Abel both make explicit appearances later in the text). Furthermore, the messenger bolsters the resolve of Vladimir and Estragon with the promise that Godot will one day just as the promise of Christ's coming gives strength to his followers. Several Christ-like images accompany the religious symbols and references scattered throughout the play. When Estragon and Vladimir must lift Lucky, one on each side, we see an image much like that of Christ in his dying moments. The same representation appears again when Pozzo suffers in blindness and must be supported by Vladimir and Estragon. Unbelievably enough, Estragon himself makes appearances that seem to mirror Christ's final earthly days. He talks of spending the night in a ditch, an analogy to the cave that housed the Lord after his death.

(Perhaps, this thought makes Vladimir's song and its five references to the word "tomb" more significant that it otherwise seems) After discussing the ditch and learning that Estragon has been beaten, Vladimir takes the persona of Veronica and tenderly reaches out to embrace him. He then plays the unpious Peter and claims to have never left his side. In a moment of tenuous friendship, Estragon shortly after suggests that "the best thing would be to kill me, like the other" the name of this "other" should by now rest firmly in our minds. The final expression of the image comes when Estragon rises from sleep and Pozzo examines the cut on his leg, thus recalling the Apostle's examination of Christ's wounds after his rising.

If we are correct in constructing this godly metaphor for Godot, we must also include Beckett's apparent attitude of incredulous disbelief towards the absurd attendees. Shortly after he appears for the first time, Pozzo assures Vladimir and Estragon that their wait is well spent: "If I had an appointment with a Godin...Godet...Godot...I'd wait till it was black night before I gave up". As we see at the end of each act, they do exactly this and intend to do the same at the play's close. Yet though they wait so devotedly, neither has an idea of what they are waiting for. Estragon admits, "Personally I wouldn't even know him if I saw him" and later asks, "Are you sure it wasn't him?". Through this comic pair Beckett seems to be mocking the rationality of humans who dedicate themselves towards such an unknown end.

The author does not portray the act of waiting as ludicrous in itself, but draws attention to the endless irritation and talks of suicide that fill Vladimir's and Estragon's waiting. We see the author's comment on such frustrations in Pozzo's aphorism, "The tears of the world are a constant quantity". Estragon speaks the pain of such interminable waiting in describing, "Nothing happens, nobody comes, nobody goes, it's awful!". Beckett then makes clear note of their aimlessness with comments like, "This is becoming really insignificant" and "We always find something, eh Didi, to give us the impression that we exist?".

As the true existentialist would agree, Beckett portrays Estragon and Vladimir as passing their time with useless trifles and senseless hope. He comments on the despair caused by such empty longing in the exchange began by Vladimir, "He's thinking of the days when he was happy" and ended by Estragon, "We wouldn't know". Beckett offers endless opinion on this existence, allowing Vladimir to describe it as "indescribable. It's like nothing. There's nothing".

With this elaborate religious framework now conceived, we must examine the cynicism with which Beckett paints such a picture. If Mueller's likening of this book to the interim between crucifixion and resurrection really is accurately, perhaps Beckett's most biting statement is that Sunday closes without any coming. Vladimir probably offers the best summary of the author's views when he utters, "Hope deferred maketh something sick".

Throughout the play Beckett gives a glimpse of the interminable waiting that faith demands, shaded by the view that it is unnatural and unwise. He also makes clear notice of the unnatural significances shown to religion. Perhaps this examination itself demonstrates the extremes to which people will go to extract religious significance. Very early in the play Vladimir first introduces the notion of religion as he asks, "Did you ever read the Bible?". Estragon, with all possible profanation, responds, "the Bible...I must have taken a look at it...I remember the maps of the Holy Land. Coloured they were. Very pretty".

In the end, is there sufficient evidence to draw so heavily on a religious motif in this play? Though Beckett surely intended some degree of meaning to the religious undertones, in making our case we have fallen into one of Beckett's most wily traps. In a play to which there can simultaneously be assigned no meaning and infinite meaning, we have obstinately found an explanation. As Kenneth Tynan suggests, "Waiting for Godot frankly jettisons everything by which we recognize theater." We have tried to apply our methods of dealing with all other drama and in doing so have violated this masterpiece.

Tynan continues, "A play, it asserts and proves, is basically a means of spending two hours in the dark without getting bored." Dark in this case is much more than a physical condition. Though we can tell ourselves that this explanation is correct, we still wander through this text as blindly as ever, probably having provided the soul of Samuel Beckett with a hearty laugh for even attempting to define the undefinable. Though in this analysis we concur with the majority of literary interpretations, we dare not consider ourselves fulfilled-most of this play's vast psychological landscape has yet to be traversed. We must not assume ourselves masters of this work, for in the game of insults played between Vladimir and Estragon, the most defaming title of all is that of "Crritic!"

Q. Discuss Waiting for Godot as a clear Criticism of Christianity ?

Samuel Beckett may have denied the use of Christian mythology in Waiting for Godot, but the character of Lucky proves otherwise. We can read Lucky as a symbolic figure of Christ, and, as such, his actions in the play carry a criticism of Christianity, suggesting that the merits of Christianity have decreased to the point where they no longer help man at all.

The parallels between Christ and Lucky are strong. Lucky, chained with a rope, is the humiliated prisoner, much like Jesus was the prisoner of the Romans after Judas turned him in. Estragon beats, curses, and spits on Lucky exactly as the Roman treated Jesus when preparing him for crucifixion. Lucky carries the burden of Pozzo's bags like a perpetual cross, and he is being led to a public fair where he will be mocked and sold the Romans paraded Jesus on the hill where for public scorn. As Jesus fell three times under the weight of his burden, Lucky falls many times with the weight of the luggage, stool, coat, and picnic basket.

Furthermore, Estragon wipes Lucky's eyes-like Veronica wiped Jesus' face-so he will "feel less forsaken" (p. 21b), which alludes directly to Jesus' cry from the cross: "Eloi, Eloi, lama sabachthani?" [My God, My God, why have you forsaken me?] (Mark 15:34). Lucky slowly chokes as the rope cuts into his neck crucifixion suffocated Jesus.Pozzo, paraphrasing

Estragon's question, then asks a rhetorical question concerning Lucky: "Why he doesn't make himself comfortable?". This question refers specifically to the taunt spectators hurled at Jesus, "Save yourself, why don't you? Come down off the cross if you are God's son," and refers generally to Christ's mission of suffering on earth.

Pozzo replies that Lucky doesn't want to drop the luggage because "he wants to mollify me, so that I will give up the idea of parting with him," and Lucky "imagines that when I see how well he carries I'll be tempted to keep him on in that capacity".

Likewise, Jesus believed that he had to carry out his burden-crucifixion-to awaken man's faith in God for time to come. Jesus commissioned his apostles to "make disciples of all nations...teach them to carry out everything I have commanded you. And always know that I am with you". Jesus wanted humanity to act in his own memory, or to keep himself on in that capacity, which was that of teacher, comforter, and ultimately deliverer of salvation.

In that vein, Pozzo says he took on Lucky explicitly, and Christianity by extension, to "understand beauty, grace, truth of the first water". But he soon feels both have outlived their usefulness:

Vladimir: After having sucked all the good out of him you chuck him away like... a banana skin. Really...

Pozzo: (groaning, clutching his head) I can't bear it...any longer...the way he goes on...you've no idea...it's terrible...he must go...(he waves his arms)...I'm going mad...(he collapses, his head in his hands)...I can't bear it... any longer... Pozzo: (sobbing) He used to be so kind...so helpful...and entertaining...my good angel...and now...he's killing me.

This exchange establishes a time frame with two windows, then and now. In the past, Pozzo had benefitted from Lucky now, the benefits are gone. Something, therefore, has occurred in the time between the two windows that has reduced Lucky's capabilities and overall effect (this change will be further explored later). Furthermore, it is an abstract effectiveness, rather than a material effectiveness, that has deteriorated because Lucky remains an adequate luggage carrier. Lucky can no longer offer what soothed and satisfied Pozzo's spirit instead, he torments it. When Pozzo says that Lucky is killing him, he is not referring to any violent acts by Lucky, but rather to what constitutes spiritual abuse. While he was once a benefit, Lucky now becomes a liability to Pozzo, prompting his plans to discard the slave. Describing the disposal of a faithful human in terms of the comic symbol of a banana peel further reduces the worth of Lucky: a banana peel is trash.

If we consider Lucky as a symbol for a dying Christ, this exchange shows two things. First, Jesus' redemptive sacrifice is no longer worth what it once was. Second, this failure translates into the spiritual failure, or even the liability, of Christianity.

Just as the worth of Jesus' sacrifice has changed, the actions and words of Lucky have also degenerated: "He used to dance the farandole, the fling, the brawl, the jig, the fandango, the hornpipe. He capered. For joy. Now that's the best he can do". Lucky's broad range of mirthful dances has now been reduced to a single sequence of stiff movements performed on command to cheer up two thieves. The reduction and sacrifice of an articulate Christ to a suffering man is now a mechanized action for amusing bored men. Further, the sacrifice eventually will be tossed like the banana peel.

The allusion to Christianity suggests that, like the dance, the religion has changed as the actual foundations of its faith-Jesus' actions and words-have deteriorated from graceful fluidity to rusty creaking. Christ's eloquent surface stories, which underneath held true meaning, have become Lucky's words, and though Lucky "used to think prettily once," he now speaks in a running babble that borders on unintelligibility. Lucky's speech is like a runaway parable his verbal "tirade" almost conceals all meaning. Upon close examination, however, it furthers the idea of the dwindling value of the Christian faith:

Given the existence as uttered forth in the public works of Puncher and Wattmann of a personal God quaquaquaqua with a white beard...who from the heights of divine apathia divine athambia divine aphasia loves us dearly. Lucky talks in complexity, mimicking scientific style. He states givens and cites texts, but his speech lacks the coherence and organization of a science. The quaquaquaqua loosely translates into series of stuttered "which's" and shows a roughness far from the "beauty" and "grace" once shown Pozzo. Underneath this scientific incoherence, though, Lucky states the subject of his discourse: Christ, the "personal God." The opposition of the scientific tone and the topic of faith hints at the constant struggle for one to find its place within the other. In this speech, faith and science actually detract from each other, diminishing both of their values. This duel between ideas and language will come up again in the future exploration of Bishop Berkeley, a scientific theologian.

As Christians believe, Christ was God as well as a human, with all of humanity's accompanying strengths and weaknesses. He was literally God as a person ("personal God"), and he lived among heights of humanity's shortcomings, which Lucky paraphrases in three cryptic "A" words. "Apathia" is a lack of caring "aphasia" is an inability to speak and "athambia's" meaning is unknown to me, but I would point out its proximity to atheism, or the belief in no God. Christ was introduced into the "A's" of a spiritually empty world, which lacked interest, expression, and belief in God. With his simple, yet powerful words and his miracles, Christ had the tools and the opportunity to fill man's hollow. Yet the emptiness is still present-it is even the stimulus for Lucky to mention the three "A's" in his present discourse. Christ failed to fulfill his purpose. Lucky continues his tirade in the same manner, speaking of the antipodal places in Christ's teachings, heaven and hell: that is to say blast hell to heaven so blue still and calm so calm so calm with a calm which even though is intermittent is better than nothing.

Lucky's stilted rhetoric generally restates what Christ preached, but it also shows how Christ's teachings can be confusing and contradictory. One way to interpret the punctuation-less passage is to separate "blast hell" from "to heaven" and treat them as two separate commands. The command then becomes an instruction to turn away from the temptations of hell and look toward the peace of heaven. This is, of course, the central theme of many of Christ's teachings. Why then would Lucky express it in such a way that allows one to read the phrases together?

Connected, the passage tells us to "blast hell to heaven," or place sin and temptation together in the middle of heaven. This would not only disrupt heaven's peace, but also flatten the entire structure and hierarchy of Christianity, placing God and the Devil, Good and Evil, on a level plane. Furthermore, why would Lucky point out the weaknesses of the faith, that heaven's calm is "intermittent" and merely "better than nothing?" Because the creation of a faith immediately creates the shortcomings of the faith as a corollary. Christ's words, as retold by Lucky, establish the spatial hierarchy of the Christian faith and simultaneously flatten that same space, as well as the same faith.

Lucky is not finished he persists, exploring a similar idea: that man in short that man in brief in spite of the strides of alimentation and defecation wastes and pines wastes and pines and concurrently simultaneously.

The body's excretory system parallels Christianity. The act of eating necessitates the removal of what was eaten likewise, the act of believing necessitates the questioning and ultimate removal of the same belief. Constant eating yields constant defecation, with no net satiation. Similarly, ingesting the faith removes the same faith immediately after the body processes it and finds only enough value to sustain, never to satisfy. And sustenance is not enough. Just as the value of $100 today will be worth much less in just ten years, as man progresses though time with no net improvement, his value actually decreases, or "wastes." And man pines for more. Christianity, therefore, has only a limited sustaining effect in the short-term (just as it touches man's lips), and as a long-term, advancing faith, it is a waste. It flows out of man's bowels the very next moment.

Lucky then begins to explore how the faith is reduced, placing his argument in the context of his pseudo-scientific talk: "no matter what matter the facts are there". Berkeley was an Irish Bishop who attempted in his writings to reconcile science and the Christian doctrine. He said that matter exists if it is perceived by some mind, and that matter, therefore, exists because God is always thinking of everything.

In effect Berkeley was able to harmonize God and science. Science exists because God thinks about it thinking about science constitutes God. Now the Bishop is dead, literally and metaphorically. Lucky's tirade makes a weak attempt to revive the Bishop's ideas by putting the language of science and faith together. But instead of harmonizing, they clash. In the context of this dissonance, in a desperate attempt to save faith in the face of questioning, the quote is a command just to accept the evidences of faith even if science disagrees- "no matter what matter." Faith now disregards science, and because of this, it is in a much weaker position to defend questions without scientific support to back it up. Christianity's strength has been reduced.

Lucky also shows the devaluation of the Christian faith with the constant oblique references to "Cunard." Sir Samuel Cunard founded the line of Cunard steamships in the mid-nineteenth century. His ships played a pivotal role in the Crimean War (1853-1856), which was caused by a dispute between Russia, France, and Turkey over Holy Places in Jerusalem. This reference is particularly apt because in early 1948, the year Beckett wrote this play, Israel became a nation containing many of the same Holy Places.

The very next day the Arabs, composed partially of Christians, attacked the Israelis and stormed East Jerusalem and the Holy Places. Men, at the very time Beckett conceived Godot, were murdering each other to possess the city where one religion of peace and sharing began. Christianity, in part, made the city of Jerusalem special, and that act, in turn, destroys what is most special: life. Lucky finally brings to a close his discourse with an encyclopedia of unheeded evidence of Christianity: in spite of the tennis on on the the beard the flames the tears the stones so blue so calm alas alas on on the skull the skull the skull in Connemara in spite of the tennis the labors abandoned left unfinished. This portion of the text points in many directions toward one underlying purpose. Some creative research seems in order. Tennis was originally named jeu de paume, which translates "a game of the palm." This could allude to Christ's stigmata, which he showed to Thomas as evidence of his identity and resurrection. The flames allude to the Pentecostal flames that descended upon the apostles as tongues of fire, filling them with the Holy Spirit and allowing them to speak in foreign tongues so as to communicate the word of God to foreigners.

The tears, I think, refer to Mary Magdalene's tears upon finding Jesus' tomb empty. She then saw a man who asked her why she was weeping, to which she replied because Jesus' body had been removed from the tomb. That man then revealed himself to be Jesus, and Mary became the first witness of Jesus' resurrection and ascension. Likewise, the stone refers to the giant stone which was sealed over the opening of Jesus' tomb. According to Matthew, an angel appeared to the tomb's guards, moved the stone as if it were a pebble, and made the guards believers. Lastly, the skull refers to Golgotha, or Skull Place, where Jesus was crucified. At this place, according to the New Testament, the earth shook as God eclipsed the sun at the moment Jesus died, fulfilling Christ's own prophecy of the events of his death. The passage lists evidence of evidence, but its fragmentation and sheer eclecticism work to undermine the value of the evidence, and by extension, devalue the faith.

Still, each allusion is an allusion to evidence, which makes the final words of the quote even more significant: "labors abandoned left unfinished." Despite all of the witnesses and miracles, words and actions, the Christian faith is abandoned and left unfinished. The Christian campaign, even with Christ's revelations, can't outshadow its empirical shortcomings and truly mollify man. Thus it fails.

People at one time experienced and believed the evidences when they happened. People at one time gained help, or at least comfort or entertainment, from Christ and Christianity. But just as Christ then abandoned his life on the cross, leaving his future unfinished, man has now abandoned the Christian faith, never translating its teachings into reality. One could say man only followed Christ's example.

The tirade finally ends when Pozzo, Estragon, and Vladimir triumphantly tackle Lucky, like the mob which turns upon Jesus, silencing him, shouting "Crucify him! Crucify him!" Lucky serves Pozzo well, insisting on carrying his burden. But his burden is an empty symbol: bags filled with sand. In the same way, Christ, by his example, taught humanity to shoulder burden, but, according to Waiting for Godot, the burden is not worth carrying. Christ was both the beginning and the end of Christianity, just as Lucky began his service with high intentions, but ends as a slave who speaks only gibberish, on his way to the auction block. In the end, they both destroy what they hoped to create.

Q. Does the Mystery of Godot Seem to be Awful at Some Times?

Or

Q. Is the wait of both the Persons for Godot worth Getting Meaning?

When the play first opened, it was criticized for lacking meaning, structure, and common sense. These critics, however, failed to see that Beckett chose to have his play, Waiting for Godot, capture the feeling that the world has no apparent meaning. In this misunderstood masterpiece, Beckett asserts numerous existentialist themes. Beckett believed that existence is determined by chance. This basic existentialist tenet is first asserted in Vladimir's discussion of a parable from the Bible. Of the two thieves crucified at the same time as Christ, one was saved and one was damned. Given this knowledge, Vladimir ponders: "...how is it...that of the four Evangelists only one speaks of a thief being saved. The four of them were there - or thereabouts - and only one speaks of a thief being saved....Of the other three, two don't mention any thieves at all and the third says that both of them abused [Christ]....But all four were there." The reports of the Evangelists shows that probability determines human life. That each Evangelist speaks of a different fate for the thieves prove the role of chance in our existence.

It is generally accepted that one thief was saved and another one damned, which further illustrates the probability of life. In addition, Beckett expands on this paradox by stating, "Do not despair one of the thieves was saved. Do not presume one of the thieves was damned." Because fate is determined by chance, there is nothing anyone can do to insure their savior. In the play, it is stated that Godot himself beats the minder of sheep but cherishes the minder of goats. The arbitrariness of Godot's decisions elude to the arbitrariness of life itself, raising questions over who will be saved and who will be damned. In the play, Pozzo remarks about his fate in comparison to Lucky's: "Remark that I might easily have been in his shoes and he in mine. If chance had not willed it otherwise." In Stoppard's play Rosencrantz and Guildenstern are Dead, Rosencrantz and Guildenstern flip a coin that escapes the natural laws of reason. Here, the existentialist viewpoint focuses on refuting probability in favour of chance.

To many people, Godot symbolizes God. The name Godot even reflects an attenuated version of the word God. Godot's silence but ubiquitous presence resembles that of God's, and Vladimir and Estragon's helplessness mirrors our own frailty. Vladimir and Estragon wait for Godot, hoping that he will give them meaning, help them find answers to their questions, and that he will save them from their situation. Many critics have argued that Godot does not necessarily symbolize God, merely "the objective of our waiting - an event, a thing, a person, a death."

Another basic existentialist tenet on which Beckett reflects is the meaninglessness of time. Because past, present, and future mean nothing, the play follows a cyclic pattern. Vladimir and Estragon return to the same place each day to wait for Godot and encounter the same basic people each day. Pozzo and Lucky pass by Vladimir and Estragon one day, both in healthy states, and return the next day, one blind and the other mute. Pozzo cannot recollect the previous meeting, and even claims that Lucky has always been mute.

In changing Pozzo and Lucky's situation, Beckett shows that time's meaninglessness degrades human life to the point of being equally unpurposed. Likewise, Godot's messenger does not recognize Vladimir and Estragon from day to day. This suggests that the people we meet today are not the same as they were yesterday and will not be the same tomorrow. Stoppard investigated this concept by confusing the identities of Rosencrantz and Guildenstern. They often could not tell the difference between themselves, offering further evidence on the uncertainty of life.

Beckett also examines Sartre's description of "bad faith" self-deceptive attempts to dodge reality by making excuses for one's actions. Vladimir and Estragon fool themselves by engaging in petty discourse that reflects the absurdity of life. They even contemplate suicide numerous times for numerous reasons, but ultimately persist in the futility of life. They choose to wait, just as Rosencrantz and Guildenstern submit to the futility of their own lives and merely await death.

Q. What is the technology and ethics depicted in Beckett's Waiting for Godot?

After a cursory examination of present day world politics, it seems there exist no sterling examples of society's progression towards utopia, or even a higher state of tolerance or knowledge. It is not that humanity does not seek knowledge or improvement. It is not a fault that curiosity drives society's scientists to explain and improve the world beyond the realm of the philosophers. The fault lies in how easily this motive can be manipulated by the vices of greed, the propaganda of the mass media, the centuries-old, unwavering human thirst for power. It is this desire for power and profit, not the journey in creating new technologies and deducing the mechanisms of life and the universe, which becomes convoluted and thus halts the growth process, just as a biologist can halt or suspend the process of life, of dividing cells, by a simple chemical treatment of colchicine.

Though the treatment of cells with a solution of colchicine is meant to preserve the cells in a state that can be studied, after this treatment they are no longer viable. They cannot continue their mitotic or meiotic divisions they cannot continue to reproduce, to be continually studied. Theirs is a one-time-only offer. Even with this simple example some say that moral questions arise. Is it really right for humans to kill other living things, no matter how small, to further their own "understanding"? Or is this simply the price, or penance, humanity pays to be able to explain, in somewhat greater detail than was previously possible, the processes, functions, and malfunctions of life?

This example, being defined only in terms of dividing cells, their origin undisclosed, seems fairly straightforward in its ability to answer this conflicting question. If the research is being done to improve the quality of life for humanity in general, then there can be no quarrel with it. But then where can humanity draw the line, for there are always those fanatics with whom every country has had at least one ghastly experience, who have argued that their use of technology, perhaps in extermination of another race, was really for the good of humanity, that the people they extinguished were the scourge of the earth and of God, whoever God might be.

Thus the battleground between the two opposing sides, science and technology on one side and morality and humanitarianism on the other, is established, and a peaceful resolution is seemingly nowhere in sight. Unless, that is, humanity can learn to view the two sides not as separate opposing forces, but as two dependent variables in the equation to create a combination of their components. As such, greater emphasis on one side can only create a hazardous effect. Samuel Beckett and Kurt Vonnegut are authors who demonstrate the necessity of a careful balance between technology and ethical principles, highlighting the need for humanity to turn its focus on the intuitive core and values or risk despair and utimately, destruction.

Beckett's play, Waiting for Godot, is a melancholy, depressing work which underscores the demise of those who, in no relation to their possession or lack of technology, refuse to take charge of their own well-being. His two characters, Estragon and Vladmir, can find nothing constructive to do with themselves. They wait in the filth and squalor of a ravaged landscape for someone to save them from their agonizingly boring and meaningless lives - the only problem is that he never comes. They suffer from boots that don't fit and therefore cause terrible sores, they have no tasty food to eat, no fire to recline by. But this does not mean that Vladimir and Estragon have absolutely no power to alter the course of their lives. They have the tools to incite change, the tools of reasoning and bodies that are still in working order, but they lack the willpower to follow through.

Didi and Gogo, as they call each other, contemplate several courses of action to modify their situation, one of which is that they leave each other and go their separate ways to seek what fortune they may, realizing that they might actually do something without their counterpart there to hold them back and argue the pros and cons. They also consider the more morbid option of suicide by hanging, but stall because they can't come up with a suitable method to ensure they both die and neither is left alone. Also convenient in perpetuating this cycle is the fact that they are waiting for their savior, a man by the name of Godot, a man who can tell them what best to do. Instead of making the best of their somewhat limited opportunities, Vladimir and Estragon revel in diversions, little changes in emotional scenery which for their duration lend the illusion that life is bearable after all.

The largest and most significant diversion of this type is their encounter with Pozzo and Lucky, a strange little man and his slave. During their conversation with Pozzo and Lucky, instead of seeing how much better off they are than the slave of this odd couple, Didi and Gogo merely remark that it passed the time more swiftly than usual. It is not technology which they must rely upon to rectify their woes and wrongs, but their own inner core of strength to believe that change can actually be achieved. Therefore, Beckett's work does not cry out against the evils of technology, but rather against the undeniable importance of being in touch with one's own self-will and motivation. The problem lies not in the fact that they are poor loathsome buggers without food, antibiotics, transportation, etc., the so-called "comforts of modern life," but that they will not retrieve their inner initiative to find something better for themselves - they'd rather sit by a tree and wait for Godot.

Although Billy Pilgrim, the main character of Kurt Vonnegut's Slaughterhouse Five, also displays this passivism toward life, the reasons for it are directly related to technology and its failures in the hands of humanity. Billy was a chaplain's assistant during World War II, the bloodiest war anyone had witnessed up to that date. During the course of the war Billy witnessed many atrocities, most notably the bombing of Dresden. The bombing of Dresden was accomplished with traditional tactics, but the death toll of 135,000 was significantly greater than that of Hiroshima where 71,379 were killed with the dropping of the atomic bomb.

His reaction to these events, rather than try to fight them, was to go back in time, relive old, happy memories. At one point, Vonnegut gives a detailed description of what Billy really thought would be the best use of the wonderful technology which the Allies employed to win the war: "the steel cylinders were taken from the rack and shipped back to the United States of America, where factories were operating night and day, dismantling the cylinders, separating the dangerous contents into minerals...The minerals were then shipped to specialists in remote areas. It was their business to put them into the ground, to hide them cleverly, so they would never hurt anybody again". The dismantling of weapons and reversion of war proving impossible, Billy focused on other things.

Billy came to believe in an imaginary planet called Tralfamadore, where the people were green and got around in flying saucers. But the cool scenery and amazing technology weren't what made Billy most excited, it was his discovery that time was continuous, that the good times in his memories were still happening and could be visited over and over again. The doctrine of Tralfamadore was simple "'Ignore the awful times and concentrate on the good ones'". So Billy did just that he tried to educate those around him to this wonderful new concept to which he had been introduced, not unlike "prescribing corrective lenses for Earthling souls". But alas,

Billy was judged crazy, and no one would believe him. Thus, life for Billy appeared fruitless, because "Among the things which Billy Pilgrim could not change were the past, the present, and the future".

Billy's seemingly worthless life does not imply that life is actually meaningless because humans have even greater capacities for annihilation. Instead, once again the approach to finding meaning and making improvement was too passive. Billy correctly identified that technology was part of the world's nasty predicament, but he failed to notice that his tactic of shutting out reality allowed absolutely no chance for improvement, just as Gogo and Didi's refusal to move from their spot was exactly contrary to their mutual wish for something better. The solution for these people, and humanity in general, is not to blame technology or the lack of it, but to improve life through clearly defining the uses of technology and realizing that humans are not just machines, but emotional beings. This can only be achieved if the human side of technology, what future consequences it will have not only on people's physical lives, but their emotional lives as well, is first taken into careful consideration.

What does "careful consideration" entail? Prioritizing. If humanity waited for the perfect methods to come up as it went about making technological and scientific advancements, then nothing would ever happen: i.e. if early physicians hadn't had the gall to go out and dig up corpses from the graveyard, the intricacies of human anatomy might have remained a mystery indefinitely. But although perfection can't be expected, high standards are a different thing and can be anticipated. Instead of devoting all time and energy to developing viable treatments for cancer and AIDS, we have scientists who are at the mercy of huge biotech and pharmaceutical companies. We've got scientists developing "The New Pill That Can End Aging" (Reader's Digest, November 2003) along with Viagra and Propecia, pills for impotent and balding men. Do we see a little misdirection of effort? Yes. Aging, impotence, and hair loss are not threatening an entire population with imminent death, like the AIDS epidemic in Africa. Aging and impotence have not stricken the child population like leukemia. We must start to care about what's really important, we must consider all of the body and mind as we improve technology, and we must think about its implications for future generations. At that time, technology will have been put to its fullest use and will easily go hand in hand with human values.

Albert Camus' The Stranger and Samuel Beckett's Waiting for Godot

Many differences and similarities are found between Albert Camus' novel, The Stranger, and Samuel Beckett's play, Waiting for Godot. The characters in each story is very different from their society and at the same time, thy are very similar to each other. To understand in what ways they are similar, there must be and understanding of how they are different from the society in which they live in. First of all, the major difference from the novel and the play is their desire for God's salvation. Recall when Meursault was in jail, he did not want the magistrate to pray for God to save his soul unlike Vladimir and Estagon, who waits many years for their god. They both live their life for one reason: to wait for Godot. However, to wait for someone who is not going to come is just as pointless as not doing anything at all, just like Meursault who lives his life at the spur of the moment. Neither of them makes important goals in their lives. Meursault can care less about his promotion and Vladimir and Estragon could have done something worth while with the last fifty years of their lives. Because of this, they found ways of passing time. Vladimir and Estragon tries hanging themselves and call each other names while Meursault goes smoking, drinking with Raymond, listen to Salamando and have casual sex all because they do not have anything else to do. They all feel their very existence is insignificant. Whether they live or died would not change anything. One life is as good as another. Vladimir and Estragon's expression of their emotions contrast to Meursault's lack of emotions. After Vladimir and Estragon fight, they resolve their disputes by embracing each other. Meursault's honesty prevents him from showing any emotions that he does not have. These ways of expressing their emotions reveals their views of life. Meursault knows who he is in life but is just indifferent to it. He did not care if everybody thought he was strange or his associates is a pimp.

However, Vladimir and Estragon does not know who they are in life. To wait for someone who is not coming is pointless. They assume a role that their "Godot" would give to them without living their own life. Although Vladimir and Estragon seems lifeless, they do possess some emotion that are a sign of life. Their abuse of one another shows their impotence and dependency to each other just like any human being is dependent on someone else such as their parents. They would not hang themselves unless they both are able to do so. Meursault does not have any close relationship in which he is dependent on someone else.

They all have desires such as death, meeting Godot, sex, and swimming in the beach but Meursault do not show much emotions to someone else. Even when ask about marriage, he still does not reply with any enthusiasm or dismay, just the answer. This independence is an example of how he is disconnected to others. It reveals his pessimistic views of life compared to Vladimirs' and Estragons'. Vladimir's thought of Pozzo at first was that he was inhumane because of the way he treats Lucky but later sways and thinks of him as a great man. This demonstrates how weakly he validates his opinions and how foolish he is to be easily persuaded. In contrast, Meursault was the total opposite. He did not cry during his mother's funeral because that was expected of him nor did he change his lifestyle because society wants him to, and because he validates his beliefs strongly, he had to pay it with his life. Near the end in which Meursault is abut to die, he states that he is ready to live. This freedom from condemnation by society through death contrasts Vladimir's and Estragon's freedom to break free from their cycle.

They can very easily break free from the cycle just by walking away but yet do not. This suggest an impotence in human beings. Vladimir realize that he is part of an ongoing cycle. He say "let's go" but instead they sit and do nothing.

The quotation "nothing to be done" can apply to both the novel and the play because neither of them did anything apart from their routines. They all are very subtle to change. There are many existential themes incorporated into the novel and play. The question of how these people live their meaningless life is still being ask today, but who determines how they should live their lives? To better answer the question, there must be a better understanding of their views and compare them other views.

Q. What are the aspects that hover around the characterization in Godot?

Or

Q. Compare these characters with other Plays.

Characterization is an important aspect of Waiting for Godot and The Plague. In both works, the authors use characters to express their own views and enable the reader to understand themes and messages.

In The Plague, Camus discloses a small part of himself in each of the primary characters. The main character, Dr. Bernard Rieux, represents Camus' own rejection of needless suffering and his overwhelming compassion and respect for people searching for meaning in life (Lebesque 80). He silently accepts all that happens in the course of the epidemic, waiting patiently for the pestilence to die away. His role in the book can be summed up when he tells Father Panaloux that "Salvation's much too big a word for me. I don't aim so high. I'm concerned with man's health and for me his health comes first" (219). Rieux rejects any form of heroism, focusing all of his energy on his duties as a doctor. Dr. Tarrou, the other protagonist in the work, shares a smaller portion of the narrative duties. Unlike Rieux, Tarrou often gives a personal, more moral account of the events happening around town. He often gives his own opinions on something, rather than a simple impartial explication. Tarrou expresses a desire for simplicity and directness while also wishing to rid himself of all evil. He identifies the plague with the death penalty and launches into an elaborate story about how his father was a lawyer and regularly fought for the death penalty. His emotional reactions against capital punishment express Camus' own views of a world in which the murder of people is legal and human existence becomes worthless (Rhein 44).

Characterization is key in establishing the theme of Waiting for Godot. Vladimir and Estragon seem to have two modes of existence: together and by themselves. One critic observes, "As members of a cross-talk act, Vladimir and Estragon have complementary personalities" (Esslin 29).

Vladimir seems to be the more stable of the two, while Estragon is more of a dreamer. Vladimir pretty much makes all of the decisions, and he is the only one to remember significant events from the past. He is always the one to remind Estragon that they must wait for Godot, and he seems to be the only one who cares about the consequences of not waiting. Being the more religious of the two, he is more concerned about the fate of the two thieves and wonders why one was saved while the other was damned, whereas Estragon simply accepts the story.

Vladimir is also more compassionate toward humanity and recognizes that he does not contribute to society. Estragon focuses more on himself than anything else. He is much less concerned with meeting Godot, and he is devoid of religion. When Pozzo and Lucky fall down and cry for help, it is Vladimir who realizes that this is a unique chance to help them. Vladimir: It is not everyday that we are needed... To all mankind they were addressed, those cries for help still ringing in our ears!... But at this place, at this moment in time, all mankind is us, whether we like it or not... Let us represent worthily for once the foul brood to which a cruel fate consigned us! (51) For one shining moment, Vladimir recognizes that he is stuck, and that this is his chance to actually exist by contributing to society. Soon though, he realizes that he must wait for Godot to come before he can do anything, and he slumps into his normal self. Vladimir and Estragon illustrate man's struggle in that they both must wait for Godot even though they are different people with different values. Neither Vladimir nor Estragon is able to contribute to society, even though Vladimir would like to. Thus, neither man exists. This is a central theme in Waiting for Godot.

If a person serves no purpose and effects nothing, then how can one prove that the person exists?

Q. What were the different Moods in the play?

Or

Q. Does fate play an important role in the life of a person?

Reading a work of literature often makes a reader experience certain feelings. These feeling differ with the content of the work, and are usually needed to perceive the author's ideas in the work. For example, Samuel Beckett augments a reader's understanding of Waiting For Godot by conveying a mood, (one which the characters in the play experience), to the reader. Similarly, a dominant mood is thrust upon a reader in Beowulf. These moods which are conveyed aid the author in conveying ideas to a reader.

In Waiting for Godot, Beckett uses many pauses, silences, and ellipses (three dots (...) used to create a break in speech) to express a feeling of waiting and unsureness. There is a twofold purpose behind this technique. For one, it shows that Vladimir and Estragon, the two main characters who are waiting for Godot, are unsure of why they are waiting for him. This also foreshadows that they will be waiting a very long time. In some cases in literature, an idea can only be conveyed properly if those on the receiving end of the idea are able to experience the feelings that a character is experiencing in the work. For example, in order for a reader to feel how and understand why Vladimir and Estragon feel as though they do while they wait, it is essential for that reader to either understand or experience the same feelings that Vladimir and Estragon are experiencing. Vladimir and Estragon are waiting waiting for Godot, to be exact and Beckett wants the reader to feel as if he or she were waiting also. Along with the feeling of waiting that a reader may experience, he or she might also understand how Vladimir and Estragon feel at times:

Unsure, not very anxious to move on, and constantly having to wait. A feeling of timelessness is even evoked, allowing almost anyone from nearly any time to understand Vladimir and Estragon's predicament. Many times people may feel overwhelmed by a higher force unalterable to them. This force may control something such as their fate. In the Anglo-Saxon culture, a popular belief was that of fate. The writers of Beowulf may have known that not all people believe in the power of fate. Therefore, to properly convey such an idea as the inevitability of fate in the epic, the writers included events which, when read, are also "experienced" by the reader. For example, the narrator of Beowulf states how fate is not on Beowulf's side. After many years of winning countless battles, Beowulf was killed by a dragon in a fierce fight. While he was fighting, and because the narrator had stated that fate was not on his side, the reader could identify with Beowulf and feel how he may have at the time: Overwhelmed, overpowered, and as if a force greater than he was controlling him (his fate).

Moods that are created, such as that of longing or waiting, and fear or inevitability, in Waiting for Godot and Beowulf, respectively, hold a distinct purpose. The moods presented usually serve the purpose of helping the author express more fully an the idea or ideas that he or she wishes to convey. Also, by conveying a universal mood, or one that nearly everyone is able to comprehend and interpret, the work of literature's longevity is augmented. This will further help the reader to interpret the work and understand more fully the moods presented.

Comparing the Human Condition in Rosencrantz and Guildenstern are Dead and Waiting for Godot

Inspired by Beckett's literary style, particularly in 'Waiting for Godot', Stoppard wrote 'Rosencrantz and Guildenstern are Dead'. As a result of this, many comparisons can be drawn between these two plays. Stoppard's writing was also influenced by Shakespeare's 'Hamlet'. Rosencrantz and Guildenstern as minor characters exist within Shakespeare's world providing Stoppard with his protagonists. However, the play is not an attempt to rewrite 'Waiting for Godot' in a framework of Shakespeare's drama.

In studying these texts, the reader is provoked into analysing, comparing and contrasting them. In particular the characters in 'Rosencrantz and Guildenstern are Dead' provide intriguing material to consider the human condition. The characters, their personality traits and responses to stimuli, as well as what directs and motivates them, is worthy of discussion.

Stoppard gives Rosencrantz and Guildenstern an existence outside 'Hamlet', although it is one of little significance and they idle away their time only having a purpose to their lives when the play rejoins the 'Hamlet' plot, after they have been called by the King's messenger: "There was a messenger...that's right. We were sent for." Their lives end tragically due to this connection with 'Hamlet', predetermined by the title, but the role provided them with a purpose to their otherwise futile lives, making them bearable. Their deaths evoke sadness and sympathy leaving the reader grieving for them.

In contrast to Stoppard's play 'Waiting for Godot' is much bleaker in the respect that Vladimir and Estragon seem to have no purpose or direction in their lives. Their only hope rests on the mysterious Godot who never comes, however they do remain alive at the end. This leads the reader to question which pair of characters are the most unfortunate. Rosencrantz and Guildensten may not have been saved from death but they have been saved from the futility of life which Vladimir and Estragon exclaim: "We can't go on like this" yet ironically they are left to do so.

In 'Waiting for Godot', we know little concerning the protagonists, indeed from their comments they appear to know little about themselves and seem bewildered and confused as to the extent of their existence.

Their situation is obscure and Vladimir and Estragon spend the day (representative of their lives) waiting for the mysterious Godot, interacting with each other with quick and short speech. Although Beckett's characters seem to expect so little from life, Vivian Mercier observes that they are never the less frustrated. "They expect so little from life, and yet their minimal expectations are frustrated." We laugh at the character's because the scenes are humorous, yet it is human unhappiness that we are laughing at.

Beckett creates this humour in such a way that there is no discernible purpose behind it. Rosencrantz and Guildenstern are two Elizabethans not easily told apart who play games to idle away the time, relying on others for amusement and impetus. They resemble Vladimir and Estragon in their interdependent relationship with one another, however characteristically they are very different. Rosencrantz and Guildenstern are incompetent and unfortunate. They continually appear to be bemused and lost, unaware of what they are doing and why they are doing it, yet still feel omnipotent and able to escape. Martin Esslin comments on their situation "Beckett's characters are no antique heroes and they are mostly unaware of the depth of their predicament."

At one point Guildenstern says "We are entitled to some direction...I would have thought". Guildenstern begins to accept this feeling that his life is out of his control and says "We move idly towards eternity, without possibility of reprieve or hope of explanation" "We'll know better next time". Rosencrantz and Guildenstern's deaths shows how effectively Stoppard created these characters by the audience's emotional reaction to their vulnerability and predicament.

Rosencrantz and Guildenstern are unable to get their own names correct and similarly other characters in the play confuse them, highlighting their insignificance: "My name is Guildenstern, and this is Rosencrantz. I'm sorry - his name's Guildenstern and I'm Rosencrantz". They obviously cannot register their own identities or value. This strange lack of identity and individuality is odd as they are actually quite different. Human nature is such that we believe we are the centre of our world and yet we are merely insignificant in someone else's. Stoppard exemplifies this in 'Rosencrantz and Guildenstern are Dead' by the unique connection the play has with Shakespeare's "Hamlet' on which it is based.

Stoppard integrates the two plays by drawing out two minor characters from 'Hamlet' turning them into the protagonists, bringing them to the forefront of the stage in his play. He creates an identity for them separate to that in 'Hamlet'. Likewise the protagonists in 'Hamlet' are reduced to minor characters in Stoppard's production. Stoppard is known for grafting much of his best works onto plays that are already well established, such as his play 'On the Razzle' (1981) which is an adaptation of an Austrian play 'Einen Jux will er sich machen' by Johann Nestroy.

The first reference to 'Hamlet' shows Rosencrantz and Guildernstern's role in Shakespeare's play. They are sent for by Claudius although they don't know for what purpose. Claudius greets them "The need we have to use you did provoke our hasty sending."

Rosencrantz "We were sent for"

Guildenstern "Yes"

Rosencrantz "Thats why were here" He looks around, seems doubtful

Despite their confusion and hesitation, they seem to regain their identity and purpose when they re-enter the 'Hamlet' plot. Hamlet greets them "My excellent good friends! How dost thou Guildenstern?"

The other story they become a part of is that of the Player and the Tragedians. From their speeches it becomes clear how important it is for them to have an audience. The Player illustrates their dependence on others, because good performers are nothing without an audience and in this quest for an audience they "look on every exit being an entrance somewhere else."

Central to both plays is the theme of futile waiting and nothing happening which the audience can relate to the feelings of frustration and ineffectiveness. In 'Waiting for Godot', Vladimir and Estragon live their lives in paralysed anticipation in case Godot comes but they may not even recognise him if he does. This shows the resilience of humans to retain hope, often until the end. Their whole lives are resting on 'Godot' which is never defined. Whether it is supposed to be God or death or something else is unclear. Every evening they wait for this 'Godot' who they have probably never met "He's a kind of acquaintance", "We hardly know him". They seek to pass the time, representative of human fear that the end will come but also afraid that it will not. Stoppard suggests the outcome to this will be as a result of fate or chance and tries to show how chance can be a key part of human life.

The possibility of chance is discussed in the first few pages where the two protagonists are tossing coins and the outcome is left to fate and probability. All the possible meanings of the word 'chance' are shown in the following quotes illustrating its importance.

Player "It was chance, then?" (coincidental)

Guildenstern "You found us."

Player "Oh yes."

Guildenstern "You were looking?" (deliberate)

Player "Oh no"

Guildenstern "Chance then" (Luck)

Player "Or fate." (Predestination, fixed destiny idea)

Guildenstern "Yours or ours?" (subtle irony hinting at the ending of the play)

Player "It could hardly be one without the other"

Guildenstern "Fate then"

Player "Oh yes. We have no control." The Player readily accepts destiny and the unknown future, unlike Rosencrantz and Guildenstern who like to feel that they do have control in their lives.

In 'Waiting for Godot' the subject of chance and probability is also considered:

Estragon "I don't know, there's an even chance, or nearly."

Vladimir "Well, what'll we do?"

Estragon "Well, don't lets do anything, its safer."

Q. How Technological Advances vs. Human Values in the play?

Technological advances occur all around, whizzing by, while human values change little and at a much slower pace.

Commercially bottled water stands as just one of a sundry of items that human technology has conjured up over the years. It seems as though the average person can not go through a day without seeing a symbol of this phenomenon, whether it is a vending machine, an empty container lying in the gutter, or a person clutching a plastic bottle in their hand. Also an ever-present technological advance is the cellular phone, "can you here me now?" It is almost a guarantee that during the course of a class period, a ringtone or the buzzing of the vibrating mode will shake the air. Human nature exists right along side its technology. Kurt Vonnegut and Samuel Beckett use their writings to illustrate what needs to be a part of human existence besides human values and technology. For all of the newfangled contributions to the modernization of human civilization, the values that humans live by have not progressed quite as swiftly. Technological advances occur all around, whizzing by, while human values change little and at a much slower pace.

Billy Pilgrim, Kurt Vonnegut's main Slaughterhouse-Five character, rode through life on one of those moving sidewalk, conveyer belt contraptions. He did not make any special efforts to enhance his situation. If one were to cut and paste the novel so that the story of Billy Pilgrim's life went in chronological order, it would become apparent that he merely lived his life. The world still moved around him, war, fire-bombing, the progression of the television set, but Billy took a passive role in his own existence. Billy Pilgrim stays the same humdrum being his entire life. Vonnegut used the repetition of Billy's life and phrases such as "Somewhere a big dig barked" to exhibit how some things just do not change (168). He points out that the people in the novel "are so sick and so much the listless playthings of enormous forces" (164). Billy knows that he is going to die anyway, regardless of what he does or does not do, and he plainly wants to remain unscathed during his journey. Vonnegut used this publication as a vehicle to show that it is not enough to live a life to its end, the approach that Billy employed. Billy Pilgrim's stance, as told by Kurt Vonnegut, tells people that they need to actively participate in their lives in order to legitimately embrace living.

Samuel Beckett spent two acts divulging a couple of days in the lives of Vladimir and Estragon in Waiting for Godot. The setting, "A country road. A tree," is such that the events in the play could happen in any century, anywhere there is a country road and a tree. Vladimir and Estragon occupy space along a roadside talking about and waiting for life to happen.

They discuss hanging themselves, "Let's hang ourselves immediately!" but put it off and never get around to it (12). The most prominent display of their lack of action is at the end of each act when one of them asks, "Well? Shall we go?" and the other responds,

"Yes, let's go," and neither move (59, 109). Beckett created a couple of spectators who did things to pass the time. They anticipate the coming of a man who never shows up. Godot will never come today, but he will tomorrow. The two travelers who come across them on the road, Pozzo and Lucky, do not recognize Vladimir and Estragon the second time around. Vladimir and Estragon are nobodies who do not impact anyone else's lives but their own. Beckett's piece demonstrates what people's lives would be like if they existed but did little of anything else. The main characters wait for their ship to come in when they should really be paving their own way. They, and everyone outside of that fictional setting, should construct their own meaning and apply it to their lives instead of waiting for live to happen.

The world of today can be likened to The Beatles' song "Revolution 9." In the midst of all of the verbal and musical sound clips coming forth in stereo, the one staple of the song is the spoken phrase, "Number nine." It recurs in the same voice every now and then throughout. All of those sound clips can be compared to the advancing technology that encompasses civilization, and the repeating phrase can be looked at as human values. The surrounding noise goes by and changes while that phrase does not. Civilization has witnessed the evolution of the phonograph to the iPod, the typewriter to the laptop, the polio vaccine to the mapping of the human genome, working hours in the kitchen to the introduction of t.v. dinners. With all of those developments, humans still have to confront discrimination of all kinds, and values hold strong. Take a look at today's movies. There are only so many plots to attach a story to, and many movies look alike. Some of the teen movies and romantic comedies are interchangeable, seen one and you've seen them all.

People like to think that society has come for from what

it was in the past, and, yes, there are some changes with time, but there is still so much to overcome. On average, women do not recieve as much pay as their male counterparts in the same occupational fields. Human euthanasia pulls at the strings of human values as well. Recently, a case made national news about an incapacitated Florida woman and her husband's fight to disconnect her feeding tube, because of a conversation she had with her husband, and her parents' wish to keep her alive.

A doctor sits in a Michigan jail because of his participation in assisted suicides when the situation can be viewed as a person with the means to help another person following through on their last desire. Humans bold enough to chose their own paths and not hang around or wait for something to be handed to them should be able to lead their lives to where they want to go. Present human values need an update because they are holding back those who recognize the need for change. Technology will keep progressing. Now, if only human values could catch up.

Chapter 12

Critical Essays

From Beckett to Stoppard: Existentialism, Death, and Absurdity

Absurdism, one of the most exciting and creative movements in the modern theater, is a term applied to a particular type of realistic drama which has absorbed theater audiences and critics for the past three decades. One specific area, appropriately labeled "Theatre of the Absurd" by the American critic Martin Esslin in the 1960's, offers its audience an existentialist point of view of the outside world and forces them to consider the meaning of their existence in a world where there appears to be no true order or meaning. Inching ever closer to a realistic representation of life, the evolution of absurdist drama from Samuel Beckett to Tom Stoppard brings a new focus to absurdism and expands the role of philosophy and metaphor in theatrical drama.

Before discussing the ways in which the Theatre of the Absurd has evolved, it is beneficial to understand where and how it developed. Many theater historians and critics label Alfred Jarry's French play, Ubu Roi as the earliest example of Theatre of the Absurd. Absurdism also has origins in Shakespearean drama, particularly through the influence of the Commedia dell'Arte. The current movement of absurdism, however, emerged in France after World War II, as a rebellion against the traditional values and beliefs of Western culture and literature. It began with the existentialist writers like Jean-Paul Sartre and Albert Camus and eventually included other writers such as Eugene Ionesco, James Joyce, Samuel Beckett,

Jean Genet, Edward Albee, and Harold Pinter, to name a few. Its rules are fairly simple: 1.) There is often no real story line instead there is a series of "free floating images" which influence the way in which an audience interprets a play. 2.) There is a focus on the incomprehensibility of the world, or an attempt to rationalize an irrational, disorderly world. 3.) Language acts as a barrier to communication, which in turn isolates the individual even more, thus making speech almost futile. In other words, absurdist drama creates an environment where people are isolated, clown-like characters blundering their way through life because they don't know what else to do. Oftentimes, characters stay together simply because they are afraid to be alone in such an incomprehensible world.

Despite this negativity, however, absurdism is not completely nihilistic. Martin Esslin explains: the recognition that there is no simple explanation for all the mysteries of the world, that all previous systems have been oversimplified and therefore bound to fail, will appear to be a source of despair only to those who still feel that such a simplified system can provide an answer.

The moment we realize that we may have to live without any final truths the situation changes we may have to readjust ourselves to living with less exulted aims and by doing so become more humble, more receptive, less exposed to violent disappointments and crises of conscious - and therefore in the last resort happier and better adjusted people, simply because we then live in closer accord with reality.

Therefore, the goal of absurdist drama is not solely to depress audiences with negativity, but an attempt to bring them closer to reality and help them understand their own "meaning" in life, whatever that may be. Samuel Beckett's understanding of this philosophy best characterizes how we should perceive our existence as he says, "Nothing is more real than Nothing."

Building on these components of absurdism, we can now proceed to analyze the way in which absurdist drama has evolved. The two dramatists who best reveal this process of evolution are Samuel Beckett and Tom Stoppard. Using

Beckett as a starting point and Stoppard as an ending point, one gets a small sense of the ways in which absurdist theater has changed and keeps changing. In comparing and contrasting these two dramatists' works, specifically changes in structure and metaphorical intent, the evolution of absurdism ventures beyond its original borders into a new and distinct realistic theater.

Of the three plays which clearly reveal this evolution, Samuel Beckett's Waiting For Godot will be addressed first, followed by another one of his plays, Endgame, and finally a discussion of Tom Stoppard's play Rosencrantz and Guildenstern Are Dead. All of these plays metaphorically address the issue of "ending" or "dying" and through such a focus offer us a clear example of one way in which absurdism has evolved.

Beckett's most popular absurdist play, Waiting For Godot, is one of the first examples critics point to when talking about the Theatre of the Absurd. Written and first performed in French in 1954, Godot had an enormous impact on theatergoers due to its strange and new conventions. Consisting of an essentially barren set, with the exception of a virtually leafless tree in the background, clown-like tramps, and highly symbolic language, Godot challenges its audience to question all of the old rules and to try to make sense of a world that is incomprehensible. At the heart of the play is the theme of "coping" and "getting through the day" so that when tomorrow comes we can have the strength to continue.

Structurally, Godot is a two-act play which is primarily cyclical. It begins with two lonely tramps on a roadside who are awaiting the arrival of a figure referred to as Godot and ends with the same premise. Many critics have concluded that Act Two is simply a repeat of Act One. In other words, Vladimir and Estragon may forever be "waiting for Godot." We are never given an answer to their predicament. As an audience, we can only watch them do the same things, listen to them say the same things, and accept the fact that Godot may or may not come. Much like them, we are stuck in a world where our actions dictate our survival. We may search for an answer or a meaning to our existence, but we most likely will never find it. Anthony Jenkins writes, "there can be no answers Godot may or may not exist and may or may not arrive we know no more about him than do Vladimir and Estragon". Thus, this play is structurally arranged in such a way as to make us believe that Godot will probably never come, and that we must accept the uncertainty of life.

The two main characters, Vladimir and Estragon, spend their days reliving their past trying to make sense of their existence, and even contemplate suicide as a form of escape. As characters, however, they are the prototypical absurdist figures who remain detached from the audience. They essentially lack identities and their vaudeville mannerisms, particularly when it comes to contemplating their suicides, has a more comic effect on the audience than a tragic one. This is perhaps best observed in the beginning scene of the play when they contemplate hanging themselves:

VLADIMIR: What do we do now?
ESTRAGON: Wait.
VLADIMIR: Yes, but while waiting.
ESTRAGON: What about hanging ourselves?
VLADIMIR: Hmm. It'd give us an erection.
ESTRAGON: (highly excited). An erection!

What follows is a discussion of who should hang themselves first. Vladimir suggests Estragon go first since he is lighter and therefore won't break the bough and leave the other one alone and alive. The conversation continues:

ESTRAGON: (with effort). Gogo light- bough not break- Gogo dead. Didi heavy- bough break- Didi alone. Whereas
VLADIMIR: I hadn't thought of that.
ESTRAGON: If it hangs you it'll hang anything.
VLADIMIR: But am I heavier than you?
ESTRAGON: So you tell me. I don't know. There's an even chance. Or nearly.
VLADIMIR: Well? What do we do?
ESTRAGON: Don't let's do anything. It's safer.
VLADIMIR: Let's wait and see what he says.
ESTRAGON: Who?

VLADIMIR: Godot.

ESTRAGON: Good idea.

This comical scene, replete with the image of death, ends up making the audience laugh rather than take the two tramps seriously. And, the fact that Estragon and Vladimir choose to not hang themselves suggests a much more existentialist, absurdist view of death and a less tragic one.

What remains archetypal in Godot concerning the absurdist metaphor is the way in which each character relies on the other for comfort, support, and most of all, meaning. Vladimir and Estragon desperately need one another in order to avoid living a lonely and meaningless life. The two together function as a metaphor for survival. Like the characters who proceed and follow them, they feel compelled to leave one another, but at the same time compelled to stay together.

At the end of Act One, Vladimir and Estragon discuss their partnership, saying:

ESTRAGON: Wait! (He moves away from Vladimir.) I sometimes wonder if we wouldn't have been better off alone, each one for himself. (He crosses the stage and sits down on the mound.) We weren't made for the same road.

VLADIMIR: (without anger). It's not certain.

ESTRAGON: No, nothing is certain.

Vladimir slowly crosses the stage and sits down beside Estragon.

VLADIMIR: We can still part if you think it would be better.

Silence.

ESTRAGON: No, it's not worth while now.

Silence. (35-36)

The same conversation takes place again at the end of Act Two:

ESTRAGON: Didi.

VLADIMIR: Yes.

ESTRAGON: I can't go on like this.

VLADIMIR: That's what you think.

ESTRAGON: If we parted that might be better for us.

VLADIMIR: We'll hang ourselves to-morrow. (Pause).

Unless Godot comes.

ESTRAGON: And if he comes?

VLADIMIR: We'll be saved.

They consider parting, but, in the end, never actually part. Andrew Kennedy explains these rituals of parting saying, "each is like a rehearsed ceremony, acted out to lessen the distance between time present and the ending of the relationship, which is both dreaded and desired"(57). Therefore, Vladimir and Estragon's inability to leave each other is just another example of the uncertainty and frustration they feel as they wait for an explanation of their existence. For them and for us, death seems forever on the horizon, and therefore ending becomes "an endless process"(Kennedy 48).

Samuel Beckett's other absurdist play, Endgame, carries on this same kind of thinking but is much more tragic and serious in its metaphor for death than Godot. Like Godot, there is no apparent action in the play. Hamm and Clov, the two main figures, are even more isolated than Vladimir and Estragon. Confined to a small, bare room, the blind and disabled Hamm postulates on the subjects of life and death, while interacting with and depending on his servant/son Clov to fill in meaning where there appears to be a void.

Resembling Estragon and Vladimir are Hamm's parents Nagg and Nell, who are confined to trash bins at the front left of the stage. They, like the two tramps, exchange memories of a once coherent world and spend their time eating pap and biscuits. However, unlike Godot, Endgame is not absolutely cyclical. Instead, it emphasizes only one cycle and works its way toward some kind of ending, or in other words, has the vague feeling of a finale. Even though death does not come at the end of Endgame, there is a strong sense that it is nearby and the waiting will not be as long, as suggested by the chess-like title.

Like Godot, Endgame's comic quality keeps it from being too tragic in its metaphoric message. Sarah Lawall writes, "The characters popping out of ashcans, the jerky, repetitive motions with which Clov carries out his master's commands, and the often obscene vaudeville patter accompanied by appropriate gestures, all provide a comic perspective that keeps Endgame from sinking into tragic despair". However, the seriousness with which Hamm talks about death and ending in his soliloquies is not entirely undercut by the comedy. References to death are abundantly scattered throughout the play.

While Godot emphasizes survival no matter what the cost, Endgame is doing virtually the same, but with a much more serious, empathetic tone. The audience is still somewhat detached from the characters on stage, but at the same time there is more of a feeling of sorrow for the characters in Endgame than Godot. As Lawall suggests, this may have something to do with the fact that Endgame "describes what it is like to be alive, declining toward death in a world without meaning". Jacques Lemarchand describes it another way, "this may be the very game we play all the time, without ever believing it to be as close as it is to its end".

The metaphor for death or coming to the "end" of something is apparent in the very first lines of the play as Clov states, "Finished, it's finished, nearly finished, it must be nearly finished". Hamm's response to Clov's ramblings as he awakens is "Me to play." Hamm's reluctance to die, however, follows shortly after as he says, "And yet, I hesitate to end. Yes, there it is, it's time it ended and yet I hesitate to- to end". This beginning scene suggests something that is quite common in most absurdist plays, the unwillingness to end or to die. Yet, there remains a struggling to understand death, to give it some meaning so that life has meaning. So as not to completely depress his audience, Beckett begins the play with a fairly comical musing on death. For example, two scenes in the first four pages concerning death are actually quite funny. Clov and Hamm discuss the connection between food and death saying:

HAMM: I'll give you nothing more to eat.

CLOV: Then we'll die.

HAMM: I'll give you just enough to keep you from dying. You'll be hungry all the time.

CLOV: Then we won't die. (458)

A few lines later Hamm implores, "Why don't you kill

me?" to which Clov replies, "I don't know the combination of the cupboard"(458). Both of these are meant to make the audience chuckle just a bit. On the other hand, Beckett juxtaposes a conversation between Nagg and Nell shortly after, which takes a more serious view of unhappiness and longing for death. It involves more introspection and a clearer understanding of the situation. After listening to Nagg's joke, Nell responds:

NELL(without lowering her voice): Nothing is funnier than unhappiness, I grant you that. But-

NAGG(shocked): Oh!

NELL: Yes, yes, it's the most comical thing in the world. And we laugh, with a will, in the beginning. But it's always the same thing. Yes, it's like the funny story we have heard too often, we still find it funny, but we don't laugh anymore. (461) Certainly, the theme of the play resides in Nell's concluding words about life and meaninglessness. Nevertheless, the comedic aspects of the play help the actors and the audience deal with the potentially negative issue about death in a more positive, cathartic way.

Another absurdist element that is present in Godot and is also reiterated in Endgame is the love/hate, dependent relationship of Hamm and Clov. Like their predecessors Vladimir and Estragon, Hamm and Clov need each other emotionally, and more so, physically. Hamm's disabled state makes him need Clov more than Clov needs Hamm, but Clov needs Hamm simply because Hamm's home is the only home he has, and even if he did leave there is no place for him to go in the void which exists outside. Kennedy's rituals of parting exist in this play, as well, and perhaps mean more than they do in Godot. Whereas in Godot, Vladimir and Estragon may have the luxury of meeting others should they choose to leave one another, Hamm and Clov do not appear to have that option in Endgame. An early conversation establishes this:

HAMM: Why do you stay with me?

CLOV: Why do you keep me?

HAMM: There's no one else.

CLOV: There's nowhere else. (458)

Midway though the play, a similar reference to leaving is brought up again:

CLOV: So, you all want me to leave you.

HAMM: Naturally.

CLOV: Then I'll leave you.

HAMM: You can't leave us.

CLOV: Then I won't leave you. (466)

Thus, by the end of the play, we know that Clov will not leave Hamm. He has had plenty of chances to do so, just as Vladimir and Estragon have, but in the end he never does. Clov even says he will never leave in one of his more contemplative speeches about life with Hamm. Standing at the door he says:

CLOV: I say to myself- sometimes, Clov, you must learn to suffer better than that if you want them to weary of punishing you- one day, I say to myself- sometimes, Clov, you must be there better than that if you want them to let you go- one day. But I feel too old, and too far, to form new habits. Good it'll never end, I'll never go.

And, just as we know that Clov will not leave Hamm, Hamm also realizes Clov will not leave him. The closing lines of the play echo this acceptance as Hamm states, "Old stancher! You...remain". So, while Godot and Endgame are alike in the absurdist methods they use, they differ in their level of metaphorical importance. Clearly, Endgame is a beginning to move beyond absurdism, in that, where Beckett only hints at the inevitability of death in Godot, it becomes more obvious in Endgame that death is inching ever closer and is within our sights. This realization, in turn, harkens back to Esslin's comment on the function of absurdity to help us "live in closer accord with reality." Tom Stoppard will complete this eventual evolution, or process toward death, in his absurd play, Rosencrantz and Guildenstern Are Dead.

Obviously influenced by Beckett, Stoppard's play certainly imitates Godot and Endgame. Like the two previous plays, Stoppard's main characters, Rosencrantz and Guildenstern, are two individuals who find themselves in the centre of an incomprehensible world. While Godot is "about the uncertainty and frustration felt by Didi and Gogo in their interminable waiting in limitless time, Stoppard's is about the uncertainty felt by Rosencrantz and Guildenstern in trying to understand the origin and meaning of events which they come to realize are carrying them to their deaths". What essentially makes them different is while the characters in Godot wait, but never change, the characters in Rosencrantz have to change.

As Michael Hinden suggests, Stoppard's play is an example of his ability "to absorb and to work through Beckett, not to get around him". So, it follows that Stoppard uses the absurdist template to build on and go beyond. In Rosencrantz, Stoppard introduces us to an absurd world, but a world nevertheless which possesses some type of order. Unlike the previous plays, there are rules that must be followed. Godot and Endgame subscribe to the belief that man has no role to play, and thus can only make up reasons for existence. Rosencrantz, however, postulates that man plays a defined role, but it is a role that is unfathomable. Victor Cahn supports this difference, explaining that Stoppard "brings his characters into a new world, one where elements of absurdity are disguised under a mask of order and reason worn by a society which Stoppard has made us come to see as perhaps absurd itself". So, Stoppard uses Beckett's absurdist tendencies as a model, but goes beyond the traditional absurdist play in several ways.

The first thing that Stoppard does that differs from Beckett is he provides his characters with a stronger sense of identity. Vladimir and Estragon are nobodies in Godot. We don't know much about them, as a whole. Rosencrantz and Guildenstern, on the other hand, become more real to us. In including the Hamlet sub-play, Stoppard gives them an identity, a meaning in their incomprehensible existence. They are Elizabethan courtiers who have been summoned to Elsinore to glean what afflicts Prince Hamlet. Here, Stoppard is playing with the audience's pre-knowledge of the tragedy of Hamlet. Therefore, when they view this play, they already know the outcome of the play based on their knowledge of Hamlet or their understanding of the play's title. This, in turn, makes the characters of Rosencrantz and Guildenstern more realistic and more subject to the audience's pity, thereby breaking the distance between audience and actor. In this manner, Rosencrantz also differs by having a structure which is linear, not cyclical. Stoppard's play has a definite end, a movement toward death which does come and is certain. Joseph Duncan explains, "the courtiers become part of a pattern of events- whose cause or purpose they do not understand- which they cannot or will not escape and which both gives them their only identity and carries them to their deaths".

Like Hamm in Endgame, Rosencrantz and Guildenstern are extremely preoccupied with contemplating their deaths. What is unique about Rosencrantz and signifies the final evolution of the absurdist view is Stoppard's abrupt answering of the absurdist question: What is the meaning of life or death in an irrational world? The answer is simply the realization that death comes to all living things and is something that can never be understood or explained, but something that simply is. And, unlike Godot and Endgame, death does come at the end of the play. The end result remains a metaphorical treatise on the way in which we perceive death and how we condition ourselves to believe in its existence.

In his essay, "Theatre at the Limit," John Perlette rightly points out that Stoppard "knows that direct and immediate access to the reality of death is simply beyond the capacity of his audience" and that the only solution is to present that "illusory spectacles of death are the only kinds in which we are prepared to believe". This philosophy is best represented through the character of The Player, and it is The Player's job to convince Rosencrantz and Guildenstern that this is the case. Ideally, Rosencrantz and Guildenstern represent the concept of Everyman, or put more simply, they are no different from us. When their own deaths are presented to them two different times, they blindly do not see what they are headed for because the reality of what must be is too close to realism for them. The same is true for modern man. We accept only what we can believe in, and to believe in death is to believe in our own absence of presence. In more realistic terms, we see death as a tragic end which metaphorically symbolizes "an abrupt exit from one's own drama into a place incomprehensibly other". Stoppard's ultimate conclusion on this subject is that we as human beings will be better off if we learn to accept that death is just as incomprehensible as life, and the only way to psychological happiness must come from dismissing social conventions and beliefs of death and reconciling it with the ultimate view that we live in a world which defies reason and meaning. Unlike Vladimir and Estragon, Rosencrantz and Guildenstern do much more than wait for something to happen to them. In fact, they are constantly being bombarded with attention, which tends to irritate them on several occasions. They have come to realize that their actions are somehow connected to a larger force, which may or may not have control of their actions.

Consistently throughout the play, Rosencrantz and Guildenstern test this theory of control. When they first arrive in Elsinore (or in the Hamlet play) they contemplate what they should do:

ROS: Shouldn't we do something something-constructive?

GUIL: What did you have in mind?... A short, blunt human pyramid...?

ROS: We could go.

GUIL: Where?

ROS: After him.

GUIL: Why? They've got us placed now- if we start moving around, we'll all be chasing each other all night.

ROS (at footlights): How very intriguing! (Turns.) I feel like a spectator- an appalling business. The only thing that makes it bearable is the irrational belief that somebody interesting will come on in a minute...

GUIL: See anyone?

ROS: No. You?

GUIL: No. (At footlights.) What a fine persecution- to be kept intrigued without ever quite being enlightened...(Pause.) We've had no practice.

As the Hamlet play continues, they begin to feel themselves being "caught up" in the action. People are coming at them from all sides, and they feel they are being pulled in all different directions. In Godot and Endgame, this is certainly not the case. Stoppard hints that they do have the luxury of "choice" and that there are a few moments where they can escape from their predicament.

Guildenstern recognizes this when they are on the boat taking Hamlet to England saying, "Free to move, speak, extemporize, and yet. We have not been cut loose... we may seize the moment, toss it around while the moments pass, a short dash here, an explanation there, but we are brought full circle"(101). Eventually this theorizing continues until the end of the play when they realize their situation as Guildenstern's last lines question the validity of choice: "There must have been a moment, at the beginning, where we could have said- no. But somehow we missed it". And the absurdity of the situation is heightened even more when he continues, "Well, we'll know better next time".

Getting back to the issue of death, and the certain uncertainty of it, Stoppard sets up an argument between The Player and Guildenstern to show that just as there are two levels of life there are two levels of death: stage death and real death. As The Player is narrating the dumb-show to Rosencrantz and Guildenstern, Guildenstern asks the Player what the actors know about death. The Player tells him that it is "what they do best". The conversation continues:

GUIL(fear, derision): Actors! The mechanics of cheap melodrama! That isn't death! (More quickly). You scream and choke and sink to your knees, but it doesn't bring death home to anyone- it doesn't catch them unawares and start the whisper in their skulls that says- "One day you are going to die." (He straightens up.) You die so many times how can you expect them to believe in your death?

PLAYER: On the contrary, it's the only kind they do believe. They're conditioned to it... Audiences know what to expect, and that is all they are prepared to believe in.

GUIL: No, no, no...you've got it all wrong...you can't act death. The fact of it is nothing to do with seeing it happen- it's not gasps and blood and falling about- that isn't what makes death. It's just a man failing to reappear; that's all- now you see him, now you don't, that's the only thing that's real.

At the end of the play, still unconvinced by The Player's definition of death, Guildenstern loses his patience with The Player and pulls his dagger on him, in an attempt to show him what "real" death is all about:

GUIL: I'm talking about death- and you've never experienced that. And you cannot act it. You die a thousand casual deaths- with none of that intensity which squeezes out life...and no blood runs cold anywhere. Because even as you die you know that you will come back in a different hat. But no one gets up after death- there is no applause- there is only silence and some second-hand clothes, and that's- death.

Guildenstern then proceeds to stab The Player who falls to the ground and dies. Thinking he has really killed The Player, Guildenstern is satisfied with his argument that real death and stage death are not congruent. However, he is denied this satisfaction because The Player gets up and is applauded by the Tragedians for his very believable "act" of dying. The Player reemphasizes, "What did you think? (Pause.) You see, it is the kind they do believe in- it's what is expected". Like Rosencrantz and Guildenstern, we as the audience are also convinced of The Player's death. As Perlette suggests, "we 'believe' because we do not believe". So, as a result, we can "'believe' by suspending our disbelief only if that disbelief is there to be suspended in the first place". This illusion is what The Player has been trying to explain all along, and what Stoppard wants us to understand most about his play. Therefore, as Cahn has suggested, Rosencrantz and Guildenstern are at the end of their play "the ultimate victims of absurdity".

When we compare and contrast the plays Godot, Endgame, and Rosencrantz, we can list many ways in which they are alike in their absurdist tendencies and many ways in which they are different. What remains essentially important is not so much that they are different, but the degree to which they are different. Beckett's treatment of death as something to come, something always on the horizon out of reach, is probably more happily acceptable to the viewer than Stoppard's view. But despite the negative connotations death holds, both Beckett and Stoppard use the metaphor of death to help us understand how our lives are absurd and how, once we accept this, we can be happier, healthier individuals. The evolution of absurdism is most clearly represented by the degree to which Stoppard uses the linear metaphor of death to bring us closer to his characters and closer to ourselves. He goes beyond absurdism by breaking the distance between the audience and the actors. We feel more for his characters and we sympathize with their inability to completely change their fates, as we ourselves struggle with the same problem. Again, the words of Martin Esslin come to mind, and the Theatre of the Absurd in all of its intellectual complexities and intricacies helps us to see our role in life. Esslin writes:

The human condition being what it is, with man small, helpless, insecure, and unable ever to fathom the world in all its hopelessness, death, and absurdity, the theatre has to confront him with the bitter truth that most human endeavor is irrational and senseless, that communication between human beings is well-nigh impossible, and that the world will forever remain an impenetrable mystery. At the same time, the recognition of all these bitter truths will have a liberating effect: if we realize the basic absurdity of most of our objectives we are freed from being obsessed with them and this release expresses itself in laughter.

Essay on Waiting for Godot

The purpose of human life is an unanswerable question. It seems impossible to find an answer because we don't know where to begin looking or whom to ask. Existence, to us, seems to be something imposed upon us by an unknown force. There is no apparent meaning to it, and yet we suffer as a result of it. The world seems utterly chaotic. We therefore try to impose meaning on it through pattern and fabricated purposes to distract ourselves from the fact that our situation is hopelessly unfathomable. "Waiting for Godot" is a play that captures this feeling and view of the world, and characterizes it with archetypes that symbolize humanity and its behaviour when faced with this knowledge. According to the play, a human being's life is totally dependant on chance, and, by extension, time is meaningless therefore, a human's life is also meaningless, and the realization of this drives humans to rely on nebulous, outside forces, which may be real or not, for order and direction.

The basic premise of the play is that chance is the underlying factor behind existence. Therefore human life is determined by chance. This is established very early on, when Vladimir mentions the parable of the two thieves from the Bible. "One of the thieves was saved. It's a reasonable percentage" (Beckett, 8). The idea of "percentage" is important because this represents how the fate of humanity is determined it is random, and there is a percentage chance that a person will be saved or damned. Vladimir continues by citing the disconcordance of the Gospels on the story of the two thieves. "And yet...how is it - this is not boring you I hope - how is it that of the four Evangelists only one speaks of a thief being saved. The four of them were there - or thereabouts - and only one speaks of a thief being saved" (Beckett, 9). Beckett makes an important point with this example of how chance is woven into even the most sacred of texts that is supposed to hold ultimate truth for humanity.

All four disciples of Chirst are supposed to have been present during his crucifixion and witnessed the two thieves, crucified with Jesus, being saved or damned depending on their treatment of him in these final hours. Of the four, only two report anything peculiar happening with the thieves. Of the two that report it, only one says that a thief was saved while the other says that both were damned. Thus, the percentages go from 100%, to 50%, to a 25% chance for salvation. This whole matter of percentages symbolizes how chance is the determining factor of existence, and Beckett used the Bible to prove this because that is the text that humanity has looked to for meaning for millenia. Even the Bible reduces human life to a matter of chance. On any given day there is a certain percent chance that one will be saved as opposed to damned, and that person is powerless to affect the decision. "The fate of the thieves, one of whom was saved and the other damned according to the one of the four accounts that everybody believes, becomes as the play progresses a symbol of the condition of man in an unpredictable and arbitrary universe".

God, if he exists, contributes to the chaos by his silence. The very fact that God allows such an arbitrary system to continue makes him an accomplice. The French philosopher Pascal noted the arbitrariness of life and that the universe worked on the basis of percentages. He advocated using such arbitrariness to one's advantage, including believing in God because, if he doesn't exist, nobody would care in the end, but if he does, one was on the safe side all along, so one can't lose. It is the same reasoning that

Vladimir uses in his remark quoted above, "It's a reasonable percentage." But it is God's silence throughout all this that causes the real hopelessness, and this is what makes "Waiting for Godot" a tragedy amidst all the comical actions of its characters: the silent plea to God for meaning, for answers, which symbolizes the plea of all humanity, and God's silence in response. "The recourse to bookkeeping by the philosopher [Pascal] no less than the clownish tramp shows how helpless we are with respect to God's silence". Either God does not exist, or he does not care. Whichever is the case, chance and arbitrariness determine human life in the absence of divine involvement.

The world of "Waiting for Godot" is one without any meaningful pattern, which symbolizes chaos as the dominating force in the world. There is no orderly sequence of events. A tree which was barren one day is covered with leaves the next. The two tramps return to the same place every day to wait for Godot. No one can remember exactly what happened the day before. Night falls instantly, and Godot never comes. The entire setting of the play is meant to demonstrate that time is based on chance, and therefore human life is based on chance.

Time is meaningless as a direct result of chance being the

underlying factor of existence. Hence there is a cyclic, albeit indefinite, pattern to events in "Waiting for Godot." Vladimir and Estragon return to the same place each day to wait for Godot and experience the same general events with variations each time. It is not known for how long in the past they have been doing this, or for how long they will continue to do it, but since time is meaningless in this play, it is assumed that past, present, and future mean nothing. Time, essentially is a mess. "One of the seemingly most stable of the patterns that give shape to experience, and one of the most disturbing to see crumble, is that of time".

The ramifications of this on human existence are symbolized by the difference between Pozzo and Lucky in Act I and in Act II. Because time is based on chance and is therefore meaningless, human life is treated arbitrarily and in an almost ruthless manner, and is also meaningless. In Act I Pozzo is travelling to the market to sell Lucky, his slave. Pozzo is healthy as can be, and there seems to be nothing wrong. Lucky used to be such a pleasant slave to have around, but he has become quite annoying, and so Pozzo is going to get rid of him. This is their situation the first time they meet Vladimir and Estragon. The next day, everything has changed. Pozzo is now blind, and Lucky is mute. Pozzo has absolutely no recollection of the previous meeting, and even claims that Lucky has always been mute even though just the day before he gave a long philosophical discourse when commanded to "think." When asked by Vladimir when he became blind, Pozzo responds "I woke up one fine day as blind as Fortune".

Vladimir, incredulous, continues asking him for details. Pozzo responds to this (violently), "Don't question me! The blind have no notion of time. The things of time are hidden from them too". Pozzo's situation symbolizes the effects of time on humans. The inherent meaninglessness of a world based on chance degenerates human life into something that is worthless and can be toyed with by Fortune. Beckett uses this change in the situation of Pozzo and Lucky to show that human life is meaningless because time is meaningless. "Although a 'stream of time' doesn't exist any longer, the 'time material' is not petrified yet,...instead of a moving stream, time here has become something like a stagnant mush". Humans try to remain oblivious of their condition. Throughout the play, Vladimir and Estragon remain stupidly cheerful, and seek distraction in pointless activities. In doing so, they act rather comical, which gives the play its humorous element.

"The positive attitude of the two tramps thus amounts to a double negation: their inability to recognize the senselessness of their position". Vladimir and Estragon try to distract themselves from the endless wait by arguing over mundane topics, sleeping, chatting with Pozzo and Lucky (again over mundane topics), and even contemplating suicide. All of this is an attempt to remain oblivious of the fact that they are waiting for a vague figure, partly of their own invention, that will never come. They do not want to realize that their lives are meaningless. This behaviour symbolizes humanity's petty distractions. Humans have nothing else to do but try to distract themselves from their situation. "...while, in the case of Vladimir and Estragon, it is just the incessant attempt to make time pass which is so characteristic, and which reflects the specific misery and absurdity of their life".

Vladimir and Estragon's attempts at distraction are attempts to make time pass, to draw them closer to the time when Godot will arrive and solve all their problems. This is pure wishful thinking, but this is all that they have to look forward to, even if the action is meaningless. The only alternative to this is death, which the two contemplate but lack the courage and initiative to carry through. In the end, the only recourse left to humans is to persist in meaningless action or perish. "Pozzo, after his vision of the emptiness and futility of human life, revives his Lucky and cries, 'On!' though they have nowhere to go and nothing to carry but sand".

To impose pattern and meaning on their world, humans will rely on nebulous outside forces for relief and distraction from their predicament. This is the only thing that can keep them going. Thus, in the play, Godot is symbolic of such an outside force, which seems to be silent and uncaring. Even so, he is still a pattern, and he infuses the two desperate tramps with a purpose to their absurd lives. By imposing pattern on chaos, Vladimir and Estragon achieve some degree of meaning. In this case, the pattern is waiting. Vladimir, in his philosophical soliloquy while contemplating whether or not to help Pozzo in Act II, declares, "What are we doing here, that is the question. And we are blessed in this, that we happen to know the answer. Yes, in this immense confusion one thing alone is clear. We are waiting for Godot to come-". An illusion of salvation is needed to cope with a meaningless life. Godot is that illusion. Therefore we see that because of all the aforementioned factors, that life is based on chance, that time is meaningless, that human life is meaningless, humans are driven to invent or rely on such "Godots," otherwise they would perish. In essence, "'Waiting for Godot' is the story of two vagabonds who impose on their slovenly wilderness an illusory, but desperately defended, pattern: waiting".

It is never clear whether Godot is real or not, which is why he is referred to as an example of a "nebulous force". In both acts, Vladimir and Estragon mistake or suspect Pozzo of being Godot. They have never actually seen Godot, and would not be able to tell him apart from a street passerby. Their only contact with him is his messenger boy that comes at the end of each day to inform them that Godot will again not be coming, but will surely come tomorrow. The boy never remembers one day from the next, another indication of the absence of a meaningful time sequence.

At the end of the second act, Vladimir, the more philosophical of the two, gets a glimpse of the truth: that they will forever be waiting for Godot, that he is merely a distraction from their useless lives, and that he can even predict, ironically, when the boy comes again, everything that the boy will say. It is at this point that a great depression overcomes Vladimir at the realisation of the truth. It is the climax of the play and its most tragic part. But Vladimir realizes that he is trapped, that he must persist in the illusion, that he has no choice. This is the definition of "going on" for humanity. There is no point. But it is the only option. "All of these characters go on, but in the old ruts, and only by retreating into patterns of thought that have already been thoroughly discredited. In the universe of this play, 'on' leads nowhere". "Waiting for Godot" is all about how the world is based on chance. A world based on chance can have no orderly time sequence, and thus time has no meaning. The extension, then, is that human life has no meaning. Realizing this, humans will create distractions and diversions, in the form of patterns and reliance on nebulous forces, to provide the purpose and meaning that is inherently lacking in their lives. "Waiting for Godot" is the classical, archetypical presentation of this facet of human existence.

Bibliography

Alvarez, A. (1973). Samuel Beckett. New York: Viking Press.

Anouilh, Jean Review in Arts Spectacles, February 27-March 5, 1953, p. 1.

Atkinson, B. (1956, April 20). Theatre: Beckett's Waiting for Godot. The New York Times, p. 21.

Bair, D. (1978). Samuel Beckett: A Biography. United States: Harcourt Brace Jovanovich.

Beckett, Samuel. (1954). The Collected Works of Samuel Beckett: Waiting for Godot. (3rd printing, 1978). New York: Grove Press.

Beckett, Samuel. (1953). Watt. New York: Grove Press.

ONE LINE: Edited with Complete Introduction, Biography, Author's Background, Complete Text, Study Questions, Select Criticism and Bibliography